In Pursuit of the Good Life

The publisher gratefully acknowledges the generous support of the Asian Studies Endowment Fund of the University of California Press Foundation.

# In Pursuit of the Good Life

Aspiration and Suicide in Globalizing South India

Jocelyn Lim Chua

**UNIVERSITY OF CALIFORNIA PRESS**
Berkeley · Los Angeles · London

University of California Press, one of the most distinguished university presses in the United States, enriches
lives around the world by advancing scholarship in the
humanities, social sciences, and natural sciences. Its
activities are supported by the UC Press Foundation and
by philanthropic contributions from individuals and
institutions. For more information, visit www.ucpress.
edu.

University of California Press
Berkeley and Los Angeles, California

University of California Press, Ltd.
London, England

Library of Congress Cataloging-in-Publication Data

A catalog record for this book is available from the
Library of Congress.

ISBN 978-0-520-28115-8 (cloth : alk. paper)
ISBN 978-0-520-28116-5 (pbk. : alk. paper)

Manufactured in the United States of America

23  22  21  20  19  18  17  16  15  14

10  9  8  7  6  5  4  3  2  1

In keeping with a commitment to support environmentally
responsible and sustainable printing practices, UC Press
has printed this book on Natures Natural, a fiber that
contains 30% post-consumer waste and meets the
minimum requirements of ANSI/NISO Z39.48-1992
(R 1997) (Permanence of Paper)

*To my parents, Chin-Huy and Albina Lim Chua*

# Contents

# Acknowledgments

This book asks what makes for a livable life. In its long path to fruition, it has been an exercise in its own question, one born of the community, inspiration, and support of others that I have enjoyed in the years of its research and writing. Over the last decade, I have accrued debts beyond measure to the generosity and patience of those who helped grow this project from its kernel to its present life.

This project took root in the Department of Anthropology at Stanford University. Purnima Mankekar and Akhil Gupta first welcomed me into the field of anthropology and nurtured both a project and an anthropologist with their acute and generous attention. Matthew Kohrman inspired with his imagination and conviction and has provided unflagging encouragement through my graduate years and beyond. Sylvia Yanagisako guided me through the complexities of fieldwork and dissertation writing and asked the questions that have never left me. Fellow graduate students provided friendship and conversation, among them Tania Ahmad, Lalaie Ameeriar, Nikhil Anand, Fernando Armstrong-Fumero, Elif Babul, Aisha Beliso-De Jesús, Ana Bezic, Munyoung Cho, Chiara de Cesari, Louise Elinoff, Nina Hazelton, Dolly Kikon, Oded Korczyn, Tomas Matza, Ramah McKay, Zhanara Nauruzbayeva, Kristin Monroe, Angel Roque, Sima Shakhsari, Mukta Sharangpani, and Rania Kassab Sweis. A writing fellowship with Stanford's Center for the Studies of Race and Ethnicity drew me into the convivial company and friendship of Matthew Daube, Jolene Hubbs, and Doris Madrigal.

This book came to fruition at the University of North Carolina at Chapel Hill, where colleagues in the Anthropology Department provided a collegial and supportive environment to think, share, and write. Special thanks to Michele Rivkin-Fish, Silvia Tomášková, and Christopher Nelson, who served as my mentors when I first arrived as a postdoctoral fellow, and to Michele Rivkin-Fish for since continuing in that role with grace and meticulous care. I have been fortunate to find inspiration and intellectual community among the members of the Moral Economies of Medicine Working Group and of the medical anthropology community between UNC and Duke; they include Lydia Boyd, Mara Buchbinder, Kia Caldwell, Nadia El-Shaarawi, Sue Estroff, Lauren Fordyce, Bill Lachicotte, Tomas Matza, Raúl Necochea, Peter Redfield, Michele Rivkin-Fish, Barry Saunders, Debra Skinner, Harris Solomon, Saiba Varma, and Rebecca Walker. Through conversation in and out of the classroom, a number of students contributed inspiration to this work while pursuing their own, including Laurel Bradley, Diana Gomez, Rachel Haase, Cassandra Hartblay, Helen Orr, Benjamin Rosado, Paul Schissel, Allison Schlobohm, and Laura Wagner.

Several individuals, at UNC and beyond, have commented on portions of the manuscript at different points in its development. I am grateful for their feedback and insights. Neel Ahuja, Anne Allison, Fernando Armstrong-Fumero, Ludek Broz, Mara Buchbinder, Tapoja Chaudhuri, Dolly Kikon, Natalia Linos, Daniel Münster, Peter Redfield, Michele Rivkin-Fish, Deen Sharp, Sara Smith, James Staples, Saiba Varma, and Tom Widger all merit special mention. I would also like to thank our writing group in the Anthropology Department at UNC, where I received the valuable feedback and support of Anna Agbe-Davies, Jean Dennison, Townsend Middleton, Amanda Thompson, and Silvia Tomášková. This book was completed during a faculty fellowship with the Institute for the Arts and Humanities at UNC. With Michele Berger at the helm, my cohort of cofellows—Daniel Cobb, Renee Alexander Craft, Mark Crescenzi, Kathleen DuVal, Tessa Joseph-Nicholas, Michele Rivkin-Fish, Jane Thraikill, and Jeff Whetstone—created a space for the vibrant exchange of ideas.

Over the past decade I have shared developing arguments with different communities. Warm thanks go to Daniel Münster and Ludek Broz for organizing a workshop on suicide and agency at the Max Planck Institute in Halle, Germany, in November 2011 and for gathering together a dynamic group of scholars who continue to inspire. I am grateful to James Staples and Tom Widger for inviting me to participate in an edited volume with *Culture, Medicine, and Psychiatry* and for bringing me further into dialogue with a community of international scholars. I also thank Deborah Durham, Johanne Eliacin, Chaise LaDousa, Kevin O'Neill, Jacqueline Solway, and Austin Zeiderman for organizing panels at the American Association of Anthropology meetings, and Elizabeth Falconi and Mikaela Rogozen-Soltar for organizing a panel at the Society for Medical Anthropology meetings, where some of this material was presented and benefited from the insights of copanelists, discussants, and audience members. I had the lucky privilege to have Sarah Pinto serve as a discussant on two of these panels and have benefited more than doubly from her careful reflections. Portions of this book were improved by the comments of numerous audiences at UNC, including the Departments of Anthropology, Social Medicine, and Women's Studies. This research has also enjoyed the support of the American Institute of Indian Studies, which funded the primary fieldwork in Kerala, from 2005 to 2007, upon which this book is based. Grants from Stanford's Department of Anthropology, the Clayman Institute for Gender Research, the Center for the Studies of Race and Ethnicity, and the UNC Carolina Asia Center, as well as a postdoctoral fellowship with the Carolina Postdoctoral Program for Faculty Diversity at UNC provided support for supplementary research and the time and space for writing.

In Thiruvananthapuram, life and research were enriched by the friendship, observations, and assistance of numerous individuals, to whom I have incurred a tremendous debt. I wish to thank K.S. and Rageedha Prasannan Kumar and their children Balu and Anu, who embraced me as family during my long and short stays in Thiruvananthapuram. Rageedha in particular was a pillar of support, and I think often and fondly of our conversations and many late afternoons spent together. Ajith, Asha, and Revathy Thampi welcomed me into their home for meals, laughter, and conversation on countless evenings. The company of friends in Thiruvananthapuram revived me in times of doubt, and for this I thank Sabitha Ajith, Augustine Sebastian, Geetha Balakrishnan, Tapoja Chaudhuri, Rays Koshy, Reeja P.S., Nagy Thomas, Grace Verssen, Caroline Wilson, and Matthew Wolfgram. Doctoral students and faculty in the Sociology Department at the University of Kerala at Kariavottam and faculty at the Center for Development Studies provided intellectual welcome and conversation. I thank my Malayalam teachers, scattered across the corners of the globe, for many years of forbearance and support: Aniladevi Kunjamma K.P., Dhanya

Menon, V. K. Bindhu, Ranjini Krishnan, and Abraham Thomas. B. Priyaranjanlal, whose work I have long admired, has transported this book to another world with his brilliant cover image.

Most important, I thank the individuals and families in Thiruvananthapuram who entrusted their stories to me. I am also grateful for the generosity of spirit and time of those mental health professionals in Kerala who, already pressed by so many obligations, gave boundlessly nonetheless. While I cannot thank each by name, my humble hope is that there may be something in this book to reflect my appreciation and gratitude.

At the University of California Press I thank Reed Malcolm for his trust in this project. I am especially grateful to the four reviewers and a member of the press's editorial review board whose comments have proved invaluable in the shaping of this book. Rachel Berchten was an adept project editor from start to finish, and Stacy Eisenstark provided steady guidance through the production process. Robin Whitaker and Michael Ritter edited with a keen eye and careful pen.

As always, I am deeply grateful to my family. My parents, Chin-Huy and Albina Lim Chua, have supported me in this journey of research and writing, even when it was not clear where it would take me. Melissa and Chris Chua have been stalwart and loyal siblings through a process that has brought me far from them both but always back again. Finally, this book grew in the warm light of the intellectual companionship and grounding love of my husband, Luther Bartelt, with whom each day is a reminder of the full expanse of living.

## ADDITIONAL ACKNOWLEDGMENTS

Portions of chapter 6 were published in "Making Time for the Children: Self-Temporalization and the Production of the Anti-Suicidal Subject in South India," *Cultural Anthropology* 26, no. 1 (2011). An earlier version of chapter 3 was published as "Tales of Decline: Reading Social Pathology into Individual Suicide in South India," *Culture, Medicine, and Psychiatry* 36, no. 2 (2012).

# Note

Names and other personal details concerning the individuals described in this book have been altered to protect their identity, most especially in the case of sensitive subjects of discussion. In some instances, patients and mental health professionals described in the clinical setting represent an amalgam of individuals to protect anonymity. Similarly, identifying attributes of institutions have been modified.

Translations from Malayalam to English are my own. Borrowings from English in spoken discourse and in writing are italicized when their usage conveys something slightly different from their customary meaning in English or where their usage is significant to the context (for instance, to signal the use of idioms of popular psychology).

I utilize the term *Malayali* to refer to the people of the state of Kerala, a term that identifies speakers of Malayalam, the official state language.

# Introduction

Rain began to fall, rising back up as steam from the hot dry pavement. Amita and I quickened our pace to a brisk walk. We were winding our way through the churning sea of late afternoon pedestrian traffic outside Chalai market in downtown Thiruvananthapuram, the capital city of the southern Indian state of Kerala. As I forged a tenuous clearing for us through the sidewalk congestion, Amita followed closely behind, commenting with amusement on my inadvertent collisions with shopping bags, schoolchildren, and half-opened umbrellas.

Turning onto the quiet lane leading to Amita's house, I found myself alone. I rounded back to retrieve my friend, likely caught up, I thought, in some last-minute bargaining with a street vendor. I didn't have to go far. Amita was just off to the side of the road, staring fixedly into the palm of a child begging for change, a girl no older than five or six. It was a strange moment of suspended animation. With one hand on her jutted hip, her face twisted into a scornful pout, Amita was viciously mimicking the child, returning the girl's plea with her own empty palm. Twisting around in her oversized dress, the girl looked up into Amita's face, ready to cut her losses and move on, yet transfixed just the same. Disturbed, I grabbed my friend's arm. Unhinged by my gesture, Amita unleashed her anger upon the child. "Why should I give you anything when I, too, am in the same condition?" Her voice quivering, Amita spoke in English while listing her problems to this accidental and uncomprehending witness: her inability to find a job adequate to her expectations, the futility of her college degree, and her family's refusal to support the marriage of her choosing to a lower-caste man. "Don't you know I also have problems? You look at me as if I have something to give you," Amita scolded the child, "but you don't understand that I have nothing."[1]

## PRECARIOUS LIVES

This book explores the ethical management of life and death at the cusp of soaring aspiration and drowning disappointment in a time of deep uncertainty. It examines these concerns in light of fears of an unfolding crisis in the state of Kerala. Since the 1990s, Kerala's reported suicide rates have ranked among India's highest, reaching double to triple the national average.[2] Family suicides in the state have also been on the rise.[3] In the capital city of Thiruvananthapuram, suicide provokes difficult questions about what makes life livable today for striving subjects like Amita, who yearns for dignified employment, companionate love, and middle-class stability but has been desperately disappointed to the point of threatening her life.

Like others in this book, Amita unsettles dominant assumptions about how life and death "should" go in the so-called developing world. The path to development in post-Independence India was built on the premise that promoting the biological survival of those like the street child would make for brighter futures. This trajectory has been confounded in the Kerala present as those brimming with hope end their own "developed" lives. Life for those like Amita has become a "precarious enterprise," not because of the famine, war, or disease that inform Paul Farmer's usage of that term, but rather because the disappointed, frustrated, and demoralized refuse to live.[4]

Once celebrated as India's developmental miracle for its progressive social indicators, in recent decades Kerala has earned the new distinction as the nation's so-called suicide capital. In Thiruvananthapuram District, home of the capital city, the suicide rate has jumped dramatically from 17.2 in 1995 to as high as 41.4 per 100,000 in 2001.[5] Of Kerala's fourteen districts, Thiruvananthapuram continues to report some of the highest rates in the state.[6] Despite the lived complexities of suicide, certain explanations for these developments dominate the popular imaginary.[7] Drawing on three years of ethnographic fieldwork in Thiruvananthapuram spanning from 2002 to 2009, I focus my attention on one key explanatory framework for contemporary suicide that prevailed in the capital city.[8] Specifically, I explore how city residents and mental health experts have widely attributed the suicide crisis to a "problem" of aspiration among Malayalis today.

Aspirational horizons in Kerala have broadened in recent decades. The liberalization of the Indian economy in the 1990s, expanded access to education under the local developmental state, and transnational migration to the Persian Gulf states and other regions of the world have widened the circulation of money, goods, people, and ideas.[9] Visions of the good life in Thiruvananthapuram are now strongly linked to consumption and other public displays of wealth, new forms of white-collar employment, higher education, and practices of cosmopolitanism. These are the projects of worth in the everyday lives of many city residents who bring to their pursuit unequal resources and different histories of personal and community struggle. But this shift in aspirational horizons has also generated deep anxiety in Thiruvananthapuram. At a time when gains and losses are steep, many city residents construe suicide to be the fallout of false or failed aspiration, a social pathology symptomatic of the lofty dreams and blighted hopes of those like Amita. This book focuses on the struggles for visions of the good life among Thiruvananthapuram's widening middle class and how those struggles sometimes desperately fail.[10]

In attending to aspiration and loss, I argue that suicide offers a powerful lens onto the experiential and affective dimensions of development and global change in the postcolonial world.[11] Suicide prompts us to ask not only how aspirant individuals like Amita strive for aspects of a livable life but also how they do so in ways structured at the intersection of historical trajectories that hold both promises and exclusions. Among Thiruvananthapuram residents, suicide registers deep contradictions and ambivalences that have emerged at the crossroads of development, economic liberalization, and global change. In the case of young people in particular, suicide can signal the ways those like Amita are at once enabled and hindered in their pursuit of visions of the good life, shaped by development and globalization's structures of aspiration while denied their full realization. In this sense, suicide is not an aberration on the path to progress, development, and modernity. Rather, it is the bitter fruit born of these historical struggles and the aspirational dilemmas they have produced in the everyday lives of city residents.

In popular imaginaries and in the media, suicide appears to cling to certain communities and social groups more than others. Local newspapers report rising suicide-murder pacts among indebted families when consumer loans become untenable. Psychologists worry for young people like Amita who strive for a first-class life at the cutting edge of disappointment, and they blame middle-class parents for raising emotionally frail and suicide-prone children spoiled by consumer indulgence and immediate gratification. Desires for economic opportunity and upward mobility have led many male migrants to the Gulf, where their failures may lead to suicide, and their absences at home are feared to precipitate mental illness and suicide among the wives and children they leave behind. Parents worry that a new generation of youth, flush with cinematic visions of romance and encouraged by the easy availability of communication technologies, is falling in love in ways that court broken hearts and suicide. By these accounts, deciphering the "right" pursuits from wayward striving is far more than a moral dilemma: it is a matter of life and death.

At a time when state welfare provisions are retracting and losses are increasingly one's own to manage, suicide serves as a critical site for debates about how people should or should not invest in relationships and futures in new landscapes of risk, desire, and possibility.[12] Indeed, while the ostensible aim of medical, legal, and social responses to suicide is to prevent willful death, these responses have been equally if not more focused on defining the terms by which life ought to be lived in contemporary Kerala. One of my principal claims in this book is that the prevention and management of suicide have often had far more to do with anxieties and contested ideas about proper objects of desire, aspiration, and progress than with any demographic "reality" of suicide per se. Suicide must therefore be examined not only or even primarily as empirical fact—one to be confirmed or debunked on the strength of numbers—but also notably as a social and moral reality that inflects political, social, and familial life in the region.

Toward this effort, I tread a path opened up by recent works in anthropology that move beyond the presupposition that life and death are diametrically opposed, to recognize how death imbues the everyday.[13] Drawing inspiration from their insights, I examine suicide not only as event or memory but also as ever-present possibility. In the long shadow of fear and uncertainty that suicide casts in Kerala, living acquires new hues and contours. Consider, for instance, how, when viewed as a social problem, suicide shapes diverse realms of meaning and practice in daily life. Social problems, the French philosopher and social theorist Michel Foucault suggested, are neither static nor self-evident. How and why certain things—whether they are behaviors, phenomena, or processes—become problems and what we understand to be the particular nature of their threat shift with time and place. Foucault used the concept of problematization to highlight the organization of meaning, discourse, practice, and institutions for defining and acting upon an issue of social concern.[14] In Thiruvananthapuram, the problematization of suicide as a pathology of aspiration not only shapes understandings and experiences of suicide; it also authorizes forms of subjectivity, management, and intervention as life-and-death necessity among the living. As we shall see in these chapters, parents in the capital city, for instance, are reforming themselves and their parenting practices in the home to prevent child suicide; patients are recalibrating investments in work, education, and love under the supervision of clinicians concerned for the psychic fallout of aspiration; and middle-class youth are turning to a growing consumer market of products and services promising personality development *(vyakthithwa vikasanam)* as the path to a suicide-free future. Rather than simply terminating life, suicide, I argue, generates new ways of living.

At the heart of this book, then, is my concern for how people come to live differently and to live differently with one another in a time of suicide. This move fundamentally reconceptualizes the clinical and sociological object of suicide, broadening our field of vision beyond the singularity of suicide as "event," to consider how suicide as hovering possibility alters commitments, meanings, and ways of living. What we find is that suicide is not only a rupture in the fabric of life but is in fact also woven into its very warp and weft. Although I shift the focus of this book to how people live with and in response to suicide, this move offers no release from the difficulties of talking and writing about a subject that demands tremendous care. Grappling, moreover, with suicide among "developed" lives in the developing world is arguably fraught with its own difficulties. At no other moment have I recognized this more clearly than in the encounter between Amita and the child on that afternoon in the street.

In the moment that the child's poverty appeared to me to be more legitimate than Amita's disappointment, I was forced to face my own liberal assumptions about what defines human suffering. Amita's devalued place in this hierarchy is mirrored in left-affiliated discourses in Kerala and in anthropological frameworks that apprehend suffering among "short, violent, and hungry lives."[15] Like many of the aspirant individuals in this book, Amita does not fit neatly among the figures that traditionally populate anthropological work on suffering, much of which has focused on the human consequences of war, famine, and disease.[16] Amita, too, has no easy place in development discourse. If the child is readily recognizable as the biological life targeted by development's quality-of-life concerns, in India's liberalizing present Amita's "qualified life" appears as embodied value in the form of educational capacities acquired, parental investments accumulated, and latent potentialities to be realized.[17] If the developmental state promotes the biological survival of the child for the sake of the population, Amita decides if hers is a livable life.

I begin with this encounter between Amita and the child and my own muddied feelings of indignation and grief in their unfolding, for several reasons. They raise from the start some of the difficulties in acknowledging suicide in the developing world, where human suffering, death, and "life in crisis" have been otherwise defined and managed as problems of survival in development and humanitarian agendas.[18] Viewed against the backdrop of the "underdeveloped" nation, threats that Amita makes against her own life—threats she has made over the years I have known her—do not simply matter more than or differently from the quiet wasting away of a street child. Rather, each suffering figure in that afternoon encounter matters in relationship to the other. It is indigent life, symbolized with the child, that is so often evoked by social critics in Kerala as the moral foil to the aspirations and frustrations of striving subjects like Amita.[19] When read against the struggle for survival, Amita's disappointments and the threats she has made against her life are too easily dismissed as wasteful extravagance and the failed obligation to stay alive. In the view of dominant assumptions about what life, death, and suffering look like in the developing world, many in this book appear troubling subjects. It is at this knotted place where we must begin to untangle some of the difficulties of grappling with suicide among developed lives in the developing world.

## REFUSING LIFE IN A NEEDY NATION

When I first began to develop this research project over a decade ago, many were puzzled. Citing high literacy rates and women's empowerment—aspects of Kerala's well-circulated reputation as India's miracle of development—friends and colleagues were unable to square the state's progressive status with the idea of suicide. Suicide, they seemed to say, makes little sense in a place that has so successfully achieved "development."

In the period after Word War II, the apparatus of development was institutionalized as a new mode of global governance. While newly independent nation-states saw the formal end of colonial rule, development discourse and institutions reinscribed new, yet familiar, hierarchies that were not simply economic in nature. More critical, Akhil Gupta observes, is how development has operated as a "form of identity in the postcolonial world," where "to be 'underdeveloped' or 'developing' is to be backward, deficient, inadequate, behind." Thus, as Gupta observes, a critical part of what constitutes the experience of modernity as "postcolonial" in India is an acute self-awareness of "backwardness."[20]

In the regional case of Kerala, this experience has been one of progress away from backwardness. In a nation positioned as development's heart of darkness, Kerala came to light within scholarly and popular imagining as India's developed outlier in the post-Independence period. Located this way, Kerala proved not the progress of the nation but rather the exceptionalism of the state.[21] In the 1970s, development scholars and economists in the West began to look upon the state, in the words of the Kerala scholar Robin Jeffrey, as an "object of fascination."[22] They marveled at falling birth and infant mortality rates, rising life expectancies, and high literacy among both men and women, all of which had been achieved in spite of relatively low levels of economic development. With respect to these and other social indicators, Kerala has not only stood far ahead of every other Indian state, but has also rivaled the profiles of some middle-income European countries.[23] Key to these claims of Kerala exceptionalism has been the high status attributed to women, an achievement linked to factors including access to health care and education, and a heavy missionary presence in the region beginning in the nineteenth century.[24] In 1957, Kerala became the first state in the world to democratically elect a communist government to power. Scholars have suggested that Kerala's development experience has been shaped by a long history of political mobilization and social reform, left-affiliated ideologies, and the state's historical emphasis on redistributive development.[25] For prominent figures in the field of international development, particularly those from the political left, Kerala offered a hopeful alternative to market-driven development to be replicated elsewhere around the world. They named this alternative the "Kerala model of development," also known more simply as the Kerala model.

This triumphant narrative once dominated imaginaries of the region. Outside Kerala, it has circulated widely across sites as varied as public health reports and the travel section of the *New York Times*.[26] Within Kerala, it has been promoted by development theorists, technocrats, and reform movements alike. While this story of Kerala's exceptionalism is a compelling one, it is a particular kind of story about the region, one that within the state is authored and authorized by elites. In recent decades, this story has come under intense scrutiny and debate and has been challenged from several angles. As has now been pointed out, the story is deeply ideological and rife with elisions. Radical feminist, *dalit* (ex-untouchable), and *adivasi* (tribal or indigenous) assertions in the Kerala public sphere have powerfully articulated the ways this narrative of the region privileges a hegemonic developmentalist agenda, assumes an upper-caste *(savarna)* Hindu male subject, and masks forms of patriarchy and inequality on which Kerala modernity was built.[27]

The claims of the Kerala model narrative have been radically disassembled. At the time of my fieldwork, many in the capital city felt deeply ambivalent about the claims of this progressive narrative. Yet ideas of exceptionalism persist in uneven ways at the level of individual and community identity, continuing to define for some both in and outside Kerala the very sense of what it means to be "Malayali." These ideas also serve as the implicit backdrop against which high suicide rates come into relief as a particular kind of phenomenon: one of paradox.[28] This particular framing accounts for the difficulty met by friends and colleagues in reconciling suicide with the idea of progressive Kerala.

More striking than this cognitive dissonance is the moral offense expressed by others. A conversation with a physician who was born in New Delhi and is now settled in the United States comes to mind. In response to learning about Kerala's high suicide rates, she recounted for me her impressions of her intelligent, accomplished, and confident Malayali classmates from her college days in New Delhi. "These are the people committing suicide?" she asked in disbelief. Replicating a hegemonic development-defined Malayali identity, she commented that it was "such a shame," given that "Malayalis have overcome the public health challenges that continue to plague other regions of India." While Indians in states like Bihar are dying from lack of clean water, she said shaking her head, Malayalis are taking their own healthy lives.[29] In certain rhetorical contexts, some among the educated elite in Thiruvananthapuram similarly condemned the "shamefulness" of Kerala's high suicide rates, juxtaposing the disappointments of Malayalis to the abject conditions ascribed to "the rest of India." In the most unflinching terms, Malayalis have been freed, I was told, of the struggles for existence amid the grinding poverty and disease that have kept other Indians in the cruel grip of death, only to self-destruct over problems brought upon themselves.[30] Viewed this way, suicide in the developing world appears, at best, as the squandered efforts of the state and, at worst, as the indulgence of the privileged. Development creates particular obligations to the nation to stay alive.[31]

Srirupa Roy has noted the global hegemony of a construction of India in terms of its "essential lack."[32] This concept of lack was not newly invented in the postcolonial state. Rather, it is intimately related to colonial discourses that elaborated a hierarchy of difference between the colonial self and the backward, primitive, and uncivilized Other.[33] Through this defining feature of lack, Roy argues, India continues to be configured in political imaginaries as a needy nation. Comments about the shame of Malayali suicide suggest that this construction also shapes dominant assumptions about how death "should go" in postcolonial India. In the needy nation where death is recognized and defined as biological life that fails to survive, life that is willfully destroyed confounds the logic of postcolonial needs discourse. The vexing problem posed by Malayalis destroying the life that other Indians "still" struggle to possess points to the moral, spatial, and teleological confusions posed by suicide in a nation of lack: Malayalis are not dying "in need" but are in fact refusing life. Framed this way, suicide is less a paradox of the state's developmental achievements than a moral violation of the implicit neediness of the nation as a whole.

Discourses about the shame of Malayalis refusing, in Lisa Stevenson's phrase, to "cooperate in their own survival" are haunted by colonial and developmental concerns for population survival as a key mode of governance.[34] Speaking of suicide in Kerala therefore demands grappling with broader regional and national histories in the governance of life and death in postcolonial India and the dominant assumptions these histories carry. It prompts us to ask what lies behind the desire to condemn "Malayali suicide" as extravagant and wasteful and what drives the (ambivalent) imperative that follows to save lives in the developing world from their own destruction.

When framed as a regional pathology and a national blemish, suicide in Kerala appears to some observers as shameful, but in Thiruvananthapuram the explanations I heard for the suicide crisis were typically far more complex. Many city residents construe the contemporary suicide crisis to be less the cumulative failures of Malayalis themselves than the signature injury of historical developments in the region. Particularly when discussed not in the anonymous terms of a suicide epidemic but on the scale of the individual case, suicide can generate reflective commentary and debate about the social and political dimensions of desire, aspiration, and progress. Every so often, highly publicized suicides like that of Rajani Anand in 2004 provoke such heated debate about class, community, and collective struggle that they spark moral outrage and political violence across the state.

### LIFE NOT WORTHY OF LIVING?

On July 22, 2004, in the thick of late afternoon traffic, a young woman jumped to her death from the seventh story of a building in the heart of Thiruvananthapuram. The sparse contents of her purse identified her as Rajani S. Anand, a twenty-two-year-old computer engineering university student from the village of Vellarada. Just moments before she jumped, she had been refused a bank loan. Investigations later revealed that this was the last in a line of rejections that the young woman had experienced in applying for an educational loan to continue her studies at a "self-financing" engineering college. A low-caste dalit woman from a poor family, "Rajani," as she came to be known in households across Kerala, had been receiving governmental educational assistance. The funds, however, had been insufficient to cover the full costs of her studies. Violent reverberations immediately followed her death. Cities across Kerala burned under the fury and the bottle bombs of political protestors and leftist student activists. North of the capital, protestors in the municipality of Adoor, in Pathanamthitta District, smashed windowpanes and broke furniture at the engineering college where Rajani had studied. In the harbor city of Kochi, pro–Congress Kerala Students Union activists stormed the office of the city branch manager of the nationalized bank that had rejected Rajani's final request for an educational loan. In the capital city, members of the All India Youth Federation held the commissioner for the Welfare of Scheduled and Backward Communities hostage in his office. Meanwhile, hundreds of male students gathered at the Thiruvananthapuram University College campus, set government vehicles ablaze, and clashed violently with police as they marched to stage a *dharna* (sit-in strike) in front of the secretariat. Having arrived in Thiruvananthapuram a few days prior, I, along with the rest of the city's residents, remained indoors from morning till evening for a week, immobilized by the agitations spreading through the streets and the statewide *hartal* (general strike) that brought life in the city to a tense standstill.[35]

Life and death, as many scholars across the disciplines have noted, are increasingly matters of contemporary political concern. Power exercised in the name of "life itself," often as a core component of liberal politics, protects and optimizes human life on the one hand while it neglects and even actively eliminates populations on the other.[36] As the willful destruction of a life by one's own hand rather than its loss through some outside force, suicide appears to present a unique problem to the governance of life and death. If, in Achille Mbembe's words, "the ultimate expression of sovereignty resides, to a large degree, in the power and capacity to dictate who may live and who must die," then what of the arrogation of the decision to die by the individual?[37] Scholars have argued that by dictating the terms of self-destruction, the suicide bomber, for example, divests sovereign power of its object by destroying the possibility of biopolitical regulation and control while also granting the bomber the status of sacrifice.[38] The political implications of suicide would appear to sharpen in light of claims of Kerala's developmental achievements. If a thriving population has been a crowning success in the Kerala model narrative, what does it mean for an increasing number of Malayalis to willfully end the very life that has been so aggressively promoted?

Indeed, when read as the expression of free will rather than the fault of pathology, the public act of self-destruction has been positioned by scholars and philosophers as the ultimate form of political protest.[39] Compared, for instance, with suicides committed in the privacy of the home, public suicides—particularly acts of spectacular violence—can lend themselves to being read as clear-cut acts of protest or resistance authored by individuals and as transparent and meaningful in intention.[40] Yet there is nothing inherent in the act of public suicide that determines its message. Neither motivation nor meaning—nor even the fact of self-determinacy—automatically unfolds from the event itself.[41] For through the interpretive lens of investigating police officers, medical examiners, journalists, and the watching public, the body that destroys itself is necessarily constructed as a gendered, sexed, and classed one. Rajani's positioning in the media as a young, unmarried, and poor dalit woman structured the field of meanings and motivations ascribed to her death. Consider how in the heavy media coverage of the suicide, one image became iconic of the event itself. In a photograph taken at the site of the suicide, a pair of sandals lies dispossessed of their body, haplessly strewn across the pavement. A male officer gazes down on them. Rajani's body escapes the frame of the photograph, but in its evocation through the pair of sandals it is keenly present as a gendered and (hetero)sexualized body. This unseen yet hypervisible body framed the debates that waged in the media, in politicians' speeches, and in the speculative talk around my neighborhood. On the one hand, a young woman's public suicide captivated people for the very fact that it so violently and spectacularly transgressed local ideas of the respectable, contained, and carefully controlled female body.[42] On the other, it was the largely male student protestors and state officials who would determine the meanings that were attributed to the suicide and that circulated in the public sphere.[43]

The body and its willful destruction can matter in highly contested ways. In the weeks that followed Rajani's death, a flurry of speculation and debate blanketed the media and neighborhood conversation regarding the young woman's motivations, emotional state, and personal troubles. Some commentators spoke in a language of deprivation, welfare, and the responsibility of the state to its most vulnerable; others spoke in the individualizing terms of psychological defeat, moral weakness, and intellectual failure. One script circulated by opposition-party politicians and student activists positioned Rajani as a martyr who sacrificed her life to protest the commercialization of higher education in the state.[44] Reproducing a governmental construction of dalits as passive recipients needing the intervention of elites, technocrats, and the state, others positioned her as an abandoned supplicant.[45] Here, Rajani's claim to welfare rested on the complete denial of her own agency. Others went so far as to shift the terms of the young woman's death to that of homicide.[46] Public accusations made by opposition-party leaders that in failing the young woman the state had in fact "murdered" Rajani were quickly transmuted into a public witch hunt for those officials "responsible for the suicide."[47]

Friends and neighbors had their own interpretations to share. One afternoon at her kitchen table, the fifty-four-year-old Chitramma recounted for me an interview with Rajani's father that she had heard on the evening news. It was just over a week since the young woman's death. "It seems Rajani had gone to see a holy man when her financial troubles became very bad," Chitramma said. "This holy man told her that because she was poor, she shouldn't behave this way, she shouldn't aim for things like being an engineer. He told her that she shouldn't have such hope *(pratheeksha)*." When I asked Chitramma what she thought about what this holy man had said, she shook her head. "A person may be poor or rich, but the hopes are the same, no? It was good she wanted to study and to help her family this way." Chitramma was clear who was to blame: the loan officer at the bank who rejected Rajani's application had blood on his hands. After a pause, Chitramma added, "And she was intelligent, too. That's what her neighbors said."[48]

As a middle-class, college-educated Hindu of the Ezhava community, formerly an untouchable caste, Chitramma spoke from a particular vantage point on the good life.[49] With her husband now a retired government-employed engineer and her son a software specialist in New Jersey, Chitramma has seen the gradual mobility of her family over the span of several generations, progressing from the low-status "traditional" occupation of tending coconut gardens to government employment and transnational migration. Her family is emblematic of an experience of social and economic mobility "away" from practices of untouchability claimed as part of a broad community-wide project of social reform among the Ezhavas since the turn of the twentieth century.[50] Chitramma's contention that the rich and poor share not only the same hopes but also an equal entitlement to them expresses faith in an "optimistic master narrative" of development.[51] Defined as access to education and social mobility, this master narrative has been a critical part of a modern, self-created Ezhava identity and has brought the community into the mainstream Hindu fold. In promoting education as the path to the good life and extending it as a rightful claim to Rajani, Chitramma spoke from within an elite narrative of development promoted by the state government, development academics, and reform movements.

Yet Chitramma's master narrative enacted a striking amnesia. In proclaiming the same hopes for all regardless of gender, community, caste, or class and localizing blame for Rajani's death on one individual's actions, this narrative elides the reproduction of inequalities that has characterized the higher education system following India's liberalization. Privatization has created a largely bifurcated system of higher education in Kerala, with high-quality institutions catering to an affluent few on the one hand and low-quality institutions reserved for the general population on the other.[52] As the affluent gain access to management courses and to engineering, computer, and other technical courses, the rural poor remain restricted from these routes. Even the principles of equity and access taken to define government-run and government-aided private institutions like the one where Rajani studied have their limitations, as typical scholarships under government schemes are insufficient to cover the full costs of higher education.[53] While Chitramma extended her vision of the good life to all, the gesture obscured the decisive exclusion of Rajani and many like her from this vision.

If Chitramma read a particular story of development into Rajani's suicide, others turned their gaze on the young woman herself. A month after Rajani's death, I visited a senior police officer to speak with him about his extensive experience in investigating suicide cases. As his office assistant shuffled listlessly in and out of the room to deliver stacks of paperwork, he broached the topic of Rajani's death. There had been little to investigate in that case, he explained, since the desperation that had driven the young woman to suicide was no one's fault but her own. As a woman of "poor intelligence" who secured a chance to study only because she was a dalit favored by the government's reservations policies, Rajani had broken down under circumstances she proved unable to handle.[54] Without a doubt, he said, Rajani had suffered an "inferiority complex" (using the English term) that stemmed from her intellectual deficits and from the daily humiliation she must surely have felt studying alongside upper-caste students. Politicians, he told me, had manipulated her death to serve their agendas. But the simple truth, he explained, was that Rajani had been a poor student, a "dropout" who had ended up where she did not belong.[55] Using a language of popular psychology and meritocratic entitlement that only thinly veiled a virulent casteism, this police officer spun a morality tale about the risky pretensions of an aspirant low-caste woman and the injudicious beneficence of the state.[56]

Others interpreted the suicide in generational terms. To some mental health professionals I spoke with, Rajani's death warned of the poor psychological fitness among Malayali youth today. Read as the fault of emotional frailty, the young woman's suicide generated talk among experts about an epidemic inability among the rising generation to endure frustration and disappointment. Such accounts psychologized a widespread experience of uncertainty that has generally characterized the lives of youth in Kerala, not only those among the rural poor. Reports in the media also illustrated the ways dead bodies are made to emit signs. Speculations that Rajani had killed herself over an illicit love affair and others that suggested she was pregnant at the time of her death diffused political agency through truths that appeared to automatically unfold from the body itself. Here, the dead body was read as heterosexual, unmarried, and the subject of illicit passion, signs that cohered in the act of self-destruction. Some even demanded an examination be conducted on the body to "prove" Rajani's virginity at the time of death, suggesting that eligibility for state welfare demands evidence of female sexual purity.[57]

One of my key concerns in this book is how speculative tales and moral commentaries like those that flourished in the wake of Rajani's death are laden with history and power. Far from being a transparent act of political authorship or of self-determined will, Rajani's death served as the highly contested "ground" upon which ideological and political debates were waged.[58] Differently positioned actors read divergent moral lessons about rightful entitlement, intemperance, and reckless pretense into Rajani's pursuit of the good life. In this way, these accounts say far more about social histories of class and community struggle and about those speaking of the dead than anything about Rajani herself. Whether valorized as sacrifice, framed as murder, or dismissed as personal weakness of body and mind, Rajani's suicide illustrates how meaning and agency are ascribed, denied, and debated in ways that defy any easy recuperative gesture to "discover" willful intent in the act itself. In Thiruvananthapuram, tales told about the dead enact powerful cultural politics over visions of the good life and who has a rightful entitlement to that life. These are not transparent reflections of longing and disappointment among the once living. Rather, tales about the dead are social and moral interpretations of what constitutes reasonable and responsible living in a time of suicide.

## THE GOOD LIFE

Suicide has altered meanings and ways of living in Kerala. In the capital city, suicide, construed as a "problem" of aspiration, provokes reflection on what ought to define the good life at the crossroads of development, liberalization, and global change. It generates debate about the aspirational struggles of individuals like Rajani and my friend Amita; it also raises questions more broadly about the promises and failures of historical trajectories and collective struggle in the region. As commentary in the wake of Rajani's death illustrates and as we shall see throughout this book, struggles for the good life and contestations over who may rightfully strive for it are powerfully shaped by social histories of community, caste, class, and gender.

In the dominant developmental imaginary in Kerala, access to education as the path to social mobility and progress has long defined ideas of the good life. While promoted by the local developmental state and the people alike, this path is one to which communities continue to have uneven access, as we have already seen. Some have suggested that in the liberalizing present, Kerala's educational achievements, while lauded in development circles, have not undermined long-standing inequalities (for instance, of caste) but have in fact stratified groups in newly mediated ways.[59] Even for those able to pursue these opportunities, the promises of formal education have dramatically eroded as transitions into adulthood have become increasingly uncertain. As in other postcolonial contexts, there is an unsettling paradox felt by many young adults in Kerala: at a time when mainstream schooling has been extended to an increasing number, salaried work has significantly declined and deteriorated across social groups and classes.[60]

Kerala's ever growing unemployment is the highest in the country and is shouldered most heavily by educated, unmarried youth.[61] Experiences of unemployment among the educated and of periods of "waiting" and of doing *timepass,* which lengthen the process of youth transition, are now prominent features of many young people's lives.[62] Exclusion from salaried employment stalls achievement of local notions of maturation. Among young men, for example, this can often mean not being able to marry or to fulfill expectations of masculine adulthood and social reproduction in the form of the established householder.[63] Developmentalist promises that education leads to social mobility no longer hold in any easy way, as Rajani's death makes tragically clear. Nonetheless, young people see and hear stories of success among those able to gain social opportunity and wealth through formal education and entry into new forms of white-collar work. This reinscribes the importance of higher learning on the road to the good life while magnifying feelings of stagnation, frustration, and powerlessness.

At the same time, cultural practices, material markers, and visions of the good life are undergoing significant movement and differentiation. During the 1970s and 1980s, a relatively coherent understanding of middle-classness was embodied by a Nehruvian civil service–oriented salariat that enjoyed the stability and prestige of government employment. Today, the government service work once esteemed by older generations and associated with a particular vision of the good life is growing obsolete in the ambitions of young people in the capital city. Ideas and practices of middle-classness are broadening. Liberalization reforms have brought with them ideas of the "new" consumerist Indian, together with a rapidly expanding universe of commodities and mass-media images of urban Indians zipping around in foreign-brand cars and occupying homes appointed with modern gadgets.[64] In Kerala, migration to work in the Persian Gulf countries following the 1970s oil boom, as well as migration to other regions of the world, has enabled formerly lower-class and lower-caste groups to access middle-class lifestyles while escaping local unemployment. Meanwhile at home, the rise of India's information technology (IT) industry, trumpeted as the sign of the nation's rise as a global superpower in the knowledge economy, has been strongly associated with an idealized "new middle class" among younger generations.[65] This new employment niche and its associated lifestyle are highly visible and widely coveted in Thiruvananthapuram, the home of Technopark, a colossal and growing IT business park.

These dynamic transformations have enabled new values, practices, and upwardly mobile communities to enter the middle-class social field.[66] People aspire to and identify projects of worth within this widening field in different ways shaped by their particular social locations and histories of mobility. As anthropologists Ritty Lukose, Filippo Osella, and Caroline Osella have shown, in Kerala lower-caste and lower-class young people, for example, have engaged consumption as a site of agency, desire, pleasure, and self-fashioning in ways that shape and are shaped by local gendered moralities and histories of community struggle.[67] The broadening of cultural practices in the constitution of middle-classness has offered critical opportunities for individuals and communities earlier underrepresented to forge claims for status, citizenship, and social power. This means that what defines middle-classness and who can rightfully claim it has also become a stridently contested field.

Suicide registers the disenchantments that arise in struggles over visions of the good life. It does so in a number of ways explored in this book. For aspirant individuals like Rajani and Amita, who pursue educational and social opportunities but with partial or limited access to economic, cultural, and social capital, suicide marks in stark terms unequal prospects and exclusions in the quest for better living. These are exclusions shaped by individuals' distinct social locations and by the broader contradictions of Kerala's postcolonial present. Suicide marks disenchantment in other ways. The widening of the field of middle-classness has generated intense anxiety for urban conservative elites in the capital city. As claims for status and social power among earlier underrepresented groups inspire reproach and envy, higher-status elites, like the police officer who blamed Rajani for bringing disappointment upon herself, reassert social hierarchies by stigmatizing suicide as a social pathology among those who "inappropriately" aspire. Claims to the good life are multiply haunted by suicide as the fallout of aspiration.

Construed as a symptom of widespread moral crisis, suicide in Kerala generates other ideas of the good life. Prevention efforts under way among a growing cadre of mental health experts in the city prescribe how Malayalis *ought* to live as a reasonable, responsible, and healthful enterprise in this time of suicide. "Good" living in this sense involves moral notions of virtuous restraint. Mental health professionals endeavor to save lives by scrutinizing and recalibrating the ways people strive in their everyday lives. In doing so, they prescribe not a stark asceticism but rather a cultivated capacity for moral distinction: the ability to decipher false aspiration from "good" projects of daily living, many of which, we will see, focus on the reform of the family.[68] Although these ideas propose "new" and healthier ways of living in the liberalizing present, in fact these prescriptions draw on longer regional and national histories in the virtues of restraint.[69] They are also inflected by social histories of community, caste, class, and gender as they come to bear on notions of deservedness and the moral capacities of individuals. In promoting ideas of healthy and responsible living, suicide prevention and reform efforts serve as a critical site for the cultivation of ethical, life-avowing subjects in postcolonial India.

In other rhetorical contexts, suicide in Kerala is understood in the urgent terms of public health crisis. Read this way, suicide engenders other ideas of "good life" projected at the scale of populations. Fears of an unfolding epidemic and of dead-end futures have provoked population concerns about a new generation ill prepared to face the psychological challenges of contemporary living. Mental health professionals, educators, parents, and state officials alike worry that today's young people are not only overambitious but also emotionally weak in facing an increasingly uncertain and global future. Read as a barometer of some failure of the population as a whole, suicide, understood as life ill prepared for the times at hand, demands new forms of subjectivity, intervention, and management. As we will see, efforts to prevent suicide are therefore not only concerned with saving life; they are, more critically, focused on producing "good" life as *fit life,* that which is durable enough to survive the disappointment, contradiction, and uncertainty that have emerged as preeminent features of postcolonial urban life. The threat of dead-end futures promotes new kinds of life in order to save the future.

## LIVING IN A TIME OF SUICIDE

As an anthropological study of suicide, this book is among rare company. While suicide served as a keystone topic through which sociology established itself as a discipline with distinct empirical methods, historically suicide has attracted little attention from anthropologists.[70] For many decades, anthropology's contributions were limited to a handful of articles that extended into different cultural contexts hypotheses from sociologist Émile Durkheim's canonical study of suicide.[71] With few recent exceptions, anthropology as a discipline has been largely silent on the contributions ethnography might make to the systematic study of suicide.[72]

In bringing anthropological methods and questions to bear on the subject of suicide, *In Pursuit of the Good Life* begins by reconceptualizing the object of suicide itself. It challenges the commonsense assumption that suicide necessarily marks the failure and destruction of the social and only that. In clinical and sociological approaches as much as in popular imagining, suicide has been traditionally conceived as a marker of poor social cohesion, the annihilative act of the atomized individual cut loose of the ties that bind to family, community, society, and to life itself.[73] Rather than begin with the premise that suicide is "anti-social" in the many senses of the term, this book instead recognizes the ways suicide may be generative of social, political, and moral life. Writing about the AIDS pandemic in Africa, Jean Comaroff notes that "as fetish or taboo, disputed truth or irreducible reality," AIDS has generated "new etiologies, utopian vocabularies, and visions of apocalypse," producing "desperate forms of inventiveness, representation, and enterprise."[74] Influenced by the work of Marx and Foucault, Comaroff suggests that the pandemic has been "prolifically productive" of socialities and forms of signification. Whether as fear, empirical fact, or contested truth, the suicide crisis in Kerala also breeds new meanings, languages, visions of past and future, and ways of living. Drawing on mixed ethnographic methods and moving between the public and the private, the institutional and the intimate everyday, the expert and the vernacular, and multiple media contexts, this book explores the prolific life of the suicide crisis: as object of intervention and prevention (as acted upon by experts); as fear and fantasy (as spoken of in everyday discourse); as sign of moral and cultural power (as represented in film and popular media); and as dystopic vision (as configured in public discourse).[75]

Suicide also makes multiple claims on reality. These claims depend on how suicide is enumerated, classified, explained, discussed, targeted for prevention, and experienced. Annemarie Mol notes, "No object, no body, no disease, is singular. If it is not removed from the practices that sustain it, reality is multiple." These realities are "not given in the order of things" but rather are "brought into being, sustained, or allowed to wither away in common, day-to-day sociomaterial practices."[76] Rarely if ever do suicide's multiple realities align neatly with one another; often, they openly conflict. Child suicide in Kerala, for instance, has become a preeminent concern among state officials, educators, and parents, catalyzing an array of reform efforts, but in a manner vastly disproportionate to epidemiological numbers on the phenomenon.[77] Meanwhile, the taxonomic categories of proximate cause of suicide as classified and reported by investigating police officers to the state may stridently contradict the accounts of surviving kin. Mental health professionals insist that suicide is a problem of the middle class and that the poor never kill themselves, but the desperate fact remains that the poor end their lives, too.

Faced with these multiple realities, I do not intend to reconcile their incongruities by weighing truths against one another or by filtering out those narratives that do not "fit." My objective is not to present a coherent or fixed object; nor is it to present an array of viewpoints and interpretations that somehow, treated as neutral and transparent, add up to suicide as Durkheimian social fact.[78] Instead, I take seriously the ways different sociomaterial practices sustain different truths, all of which have some grip in shaping experience, meaning, and practice. At times, these truths may jockey openly with one another; at others, they coexist in mutual ambivalence. This is where the particular methodological strength of anthropology lies: ethnography is able to capture the multiple, moving, and contradictory realities of suicide as they are simultaneously lived.

This book also asks how suicide bears intimately on individuals and their families. People lived alongside and cohabitated with suicide in innumerable forms: as disquietude in the face of threats; as indifference to passing jokes; as unrelenting defense of a dead loved one; as the tormented spirit that returns to dwell; as fear that suicidal thoughts might be passed into the womb. Dreaded possibility, thwarted event, defensive narrative, unsettled soul, and tragic inheritance—these were some of the many presences that suicide commanded in ordinary life, between bodies and across planes of existence. But suicide was also lived in other ways by the living. For my friend Amita and others in these chapters, speaking of, fantasizing about, and yearning for death from within life, sometimes without announcing "suicide" explicitly, could be a mode of maintenance. For some, approaching death was a way of getting by or existing differently; it could also be a means of altering relationships and commitments between loved ones. While potential distinctions can and have been made between such practices and suicide as "completed" act—distinctions that sort behaviors and feelings in hierarchies according to "sincerity," gravity, or diagnostic import—these are not the guiding criteria I take for what matters. Ultimately, this book holds together all of these phenomena as equally important to understanding how suicide finds traction in the everyday and shapes ways of living. Suicide, after all, matters not through the degree of its "event-ness" alone but through its multiple and enduring presences as material, psychic, and social reality.

*In Pursuit of the Good Life* is organized in two parts. Part 1 explores dimensions of the "problematization" of suicide as an issue of aspiration. Chapter 1 examines how people in the capital city construed contemporary suicide to be the signature injury of failed collective struggles in the region. Chapter 2 journeys into the clinic to explore how mental health professionals read the lives of patients and their kin to discern false aspiration and suicide risk. Chapter 3 extends these concerns beyond the mental health encounter to examine how deaths around the city and in the neighborhood where I lived were read for signs of wayward striving in the speculative tales and rumors told by the living.

Part 2 of the book takes up the ways people lived with suicide as ever-present possibility in the intimate spaces and practices of daily life. Chapter 4 grapples with women's allusions to, jokes about, and fantasies of willful death. Chapter 5 explores the role of space and migratory aspiration in the ways young people experienced hope, hopelessness, and life's critical limits. Chapter 6 examines the reform of middle-class parenting in light of fears about child suicide. The afterword concludes with comments on the anthropological study of suicide. The materials in this book draw from interviews that I conducted in either Malayalam, or English, or, as was most often the case, a blend of the two, depending on the educational background, class, and social status and the preference of my interlocutors. I have indicated language use where it was significant to the social positioning of the person speaking or important to the ethnographic context or both.[79]

## ACCOUNTABILITIES

The 2004 Malayalam film *Kadhavaseshan* (Epilogue to a Life Lived) begins with three brief consecutive scenes. A young man rises from bed and walks to the bathroom to brush his teeth. It is 6:30 in the morning. The scene dissolves. At 7:30 A.M., the same man stares out the window of his apartment, drinking coffee in silence, absorbed in his thoughts. The scene, too, dissolves. In the next, the camera opens up focused on the floor, where a chair lies knocked over. As the camera pans up, we see the feet, legs, torso, and face of our unknown protagonist hanging from the ceiling fan in his bedroom. It is 8:30 A.M.

The young man, we learn, was named Gopinathan. He was to be married in a few weeks' time. The remainder of the film revolves around his ex-fiancée's efforts to uncover the reason for Gopinathan's death. *Kadhavaseshan* is styled in the genre of a detective mystery, with the audience sharing in the female lead's chance encounters, revelatory discoveries, and retrospective insights into Gopinathan's life. At one point in the film, her efforts deliver her to the bright, modern interior office space that a prominent signboard on the far wall announces as a "suicide investigation agency." Here, women dressed in crisp navy dress suits and paper hats—bearing a striking resemblance to airline stewardesses—mechanically type away behind rows of computers, evidently engaged in the technoscientific pursuits of "suicide investigation."[80]

I first saw this film in a Thiruvananthapuram movie theater, accompanied by friends who suggested it might be helpful to my research. At the time and several times since, I have wondered if word of my research inspired visions of me, the anthropologist, engaged in similar investigative pursuits. Many did assume that my research on suicide involved such endeavors; these assumptions often persisted in spite of my explanations to the contrary. On occasion, I was asked to weigh in with my "expert" opinion regarding the "real" cause of a suicide reported in the news. Some around me expected ethnography-as-psychiatric autopsy, the investigative application of anthropology to unlocking silenced secrets. While suspicions (and actualities) of anthropologist-as-spy abound within and beyond the discipline, the figure of anthropologist-as-sleuth—whom her interlocutors endow with detective powers that border the heroic—is less traveled terrain. This was the position in which families, casual acquaintances, and colleagues sometimes placed me. Along with sincere concerns expressed by neighbors and friends that exposure to so many stories of suicide might unconsciously elevate my own self-destructive drive, there was a powerful assumption that suicide is studied through one means only: investigation.

How do we write and speak about violence if not through the modality of investigation? Some anthropologists have mobilized ethnography as a mode of what Nancy Scheper-Hughes conceives as "bearing witness" to suffering and violence rendered invisible in everyday life.

Conceived as an ethical and political bidding, ethnography is recruited in an effort to speak truth to power, a critical commitment and tool in the liberal project to mobilize against the cruelty and indignities suffered by humankind.[81] This is ethnography as a mode of witnessing grounded in Christian theodicy, namely, in the desire to discern within the pain of suffering a narrative of redemption, hope, and collective transformation.[82]

While these efforts have their place, anthropologist Veena Das offers insight into a mode of ethnographic witnessing that I have found more useful for my own work. Attending to the ways the violence of the partition of India and Pakistan shapes subjectivity, Das suggests that the role of the ethnographer is not to ask "what happened?"[83] Rather, it is to consider the ways violence acts upon people's capacities to engage with everyday life. Traumatic memory of violence, writes Das, cannot be understood "as a direct possession of the past."[84] When perpetrators, victims, and witnesses all come from the same social world, violence animates the ways people live (or fail to live) with themselves and others as they labor to remake and presently inhabit that world together. Ethnography becomes less about an originary moment of violence than about a "descent into the ordinary."

Like Das, in both writing and in conducting fieldwork, I have refrained from beginning with the question "what happened?" While news of my research circulated among friends and neighbors, never did I seek out individuals and families for the suicide others spoke of as gossip, for the deaths reported in the news, or for the incidents clinicians had recorded in their patient files.[85] The stories and accounts shared here unfolded out of my evolving relationships with individuals and their families and the incidental ways I came to pick up on the threads of suicide in their lives: in the form of the photograph of a brother I never met, passing reveries during conversation over tea, or the first-year anniversary of a death. These were not windows onto an event, narrowly defined, as much as they were openings onto the ways individuals and loved ones labored to make meaning in the wake of death, lived in disquietude and fear, and lived with one another. Attending to the ways suicide is folded into the everyday is not to avoid the materiality of violence itself. Instead, it reflects my hesitancy to prioritize death events over the multitude of ways suicide shapes life among the living. Rather than speculating on what "really" happened or how "truly" sincere a feeling or word was, I instead yield to my own deep uncertainties around much of what I observed. This is part of my effort to acknowledge the limits to ethnographic knowledge and to keep at bay the desire to designate transparency and fixity to that which may have many lives or may be incomprehensible.[86] It is also an effort to take seriously the power of uncertainty itself to transform reality and relations between people.

While ethnography offers useful methodologies for developing an anthropological approach to suicide as a shifting, historical, and multiple object, Das's meditations on violence and subjectivity remind us that ethnography is also a form of practice and mode of engagement embedded in human relationships. Although I refrained in fieldwork from asking, "what happened?," some wished to begin with precisely this question. The insistence and importance of this question for family survivors of suicide could be all consuming. It was a particular framing of violence foisted on them by medical and legal entities, but one that many also claimed for themselves, driven by a desire for closure. In speaking with me in the register of "what happened," some did so in the hopes that I could help decipher a mysterious death or distill a different truth, one that might put their minds at peace. My hesitation to speculate on the motivations and thoughts of individuals I never knew in life stood uneasily alongside the desires of family members and friends for some sense of an ending. Apologies that this was beyond my capacities and training were irrelevant and disappointing to some. I fear that for others, they were taken as dismissive. Some pressed with urgency and directness: after having researched suicide for so many years, couldn't I help them find the answer they were seeking? Self-assurances that talk could be therapeutic were dangerous and flimsy: even in recounting details of "what happened," loved ones tugged at loose threads, threatening to unravel entirely the delicate fabric of truth they had woven in the wake of rupturing loss. What constitutes accountability in such terrain? How do we make a place for ethnography in the face of mourning?

There are neither easy nor absolute answers to these questions. The best, if sometimes deeply unsatisfactory, recourse I have been able to figure is to prioritize, in fieldwork and in writing this book, the ways suicide shapes people's capacities to engage and live in the present and what happens when that capacity founders. I explore this question in the everyday lives of attempters, survivors, and witnesses of suicide, as well as among those who are not directly touched by suicide but who nonetheless live in the long shadow that it casts in Kerala. I focus on the lives of disparate and competing truths about the dead, tracking how relations of power endow certain accounts of suicide with more authority than others. I explore the symbolic violence enacted by clinical and bureaucratic explanations for suicide and by the ways the living judge the dead. I highlight the effects that such explanations have on the ability of family survivors to claim the integrity of love and of the remembered past. I seek, too, to make a part of the text itself the tensions between fieldwork and the demands for truth made of me in daily life. For me, living alongside, speaking of, and writing about suicide have not only concerned the production of "good enough ethnography," in Nancy Scheper-Hughes's phrase.[87] Ultimately, they have also been about the production of good enough truths.

# PART ONE

# The "Problem" of Striving

# 1

# Between the Devil and the Deep Sea

The opening remarks of R.L. Bhatia, then governor of Kerala, were brief but galvanizing. Having set the tone for the seminar on governance and development, the governor proceeded to formally inaugurate the event by lighting the large brass lamp located center stage. Enthusiastic applause erupted from the audience, but it died out awkwardly as the governor struggled to light the last wick on the far side of the lamp. Despite the governor's strained efforts with a rapidly disappearing match, the wick refused again and again to light. A young man eventually entered from stage left, carefully resoaked the wick, and, to the relief of the strained necks in the audience, finally set it alight. With renewed applause, the seminar was now set to begin.

Over the course of three days in December 2005, the national seminar on Kerala's developmental experience attracted politicians, community organizers, scholars, and public officials from around the country to the leafy suburbs of Thiruvananthapuram. Participants were given an ambitious agenda: to discuss new orientations for Kerala's developmental and governmental future. A sense of urgency charged the seminar atmosphere. Many spoke in the dystopic terms of crisis and decline, referencing high suicide rates, the "disease" of consumerism, aimlessness among youth, the moral breakdown of family life, and rising violence against women. A few were more optimistic, configuring the present as a turning point. What kinds of horizons might be imagined at this critical moment in Kerala's history to move the state forward to a brighter future? Could

Kerala's former international status as a so-called model of development be recaptured, this time in novel and visionary ways?

Although the seminar's objective was to envision new political futures, the past was what featured most prominently in the opening speeches and discussions that first day. References to Kerala's earlier achievements on the world stage of development were prominent in the welcome speech made by the seminar's chairman. But if "the Kerala of the past" had once been widely praised by Western scholars, that Kerala was no longer, remarked the chairman. The earlier gains of the Kerala model, once celebrated by scholars around the world, were being rapidly undermined by globalization while the developmental horizons that had once delivered the region to international acclaim were receding into obscurity. Symptoms of social and moral breakdown were everywhere. Now was the time to forge new trajectories for the state, he declared. Rallying his audience to action, the chairman urged that if the economists, social scientists, and politicians among them were to accurately assess the needs of the people to envision better futures, then conventional metrics such as the state's oft-cited high literacy rates had to be abandoned altogether. Such indexes were insufficient to capture the "reality of Kerala" at a time of globalization. "There needs to be less talk about the GDP," quipped the chairman, "and more about the state's GDH." GDH, or "gross domestic happiness," would reveal the "true condition of the people," a condition that had become "most miserable" in the last decade, as suicide rates made clear. Even with all of their material comforts, the chairman observed in his speech, Malayalis were unhappier than ever before. Indeed, by the metric of happiness, the people of Kerala ranked among the least developed in the world.[1]

## BITTER FRUIT

In Kerala public discourse, high rates of suicide reported since the 1990s have gained widespread visibility as the preeminent symptom of an ailing social and political order. Explanatory narratives for these unhappy developments abound. In the capital city of Thiruvananthapuram, many discussed the suicide crisis in ways that extend beyond individual pathology to implicate broader political, economic, and social developments in the region.[2] Much as the seminar chairman did that December morning, city residents spoke in terms of historical contradiction, crisis, and decline to account for the social and moral ills they linked to contemporary

Kerala life. But explanatory narratives for what ails Malayalis today are not merely tales about past and present. More critically, they are important at the level of identity and experience. In warning of a GDH deficit, the seminar's chairman spoke of the failure of a particular dream of progress. By his account, this has caused a dramatic shift in regional identity and experience: if an idea of the "Kerala people" was once linked to exceptional development, it is presently characterized by unhappiness and suicide. Narratives such as this one are also political and moral claims. They position disillusionment, frustration, and suicide as the bitter fruit born of historical trajectories and projects of modernity in the region.

This chapter explores perceptions and experiences of betrayal, contradiction, and decay in Kerala's postmillennial time. Through narratives about the past and the declining present, Thiruvananthapuram residents I spoke with during my fieldwork reflected critically on the postcolonial condition in the state, a conjunctural condition shaped by regional and national development, liberalizing reforms, transnational migration, and global change.[3] They also made sense of the present as a time for suicide. In the capital city, many construed the suicide crisis to be the historical product of collective struggle and the tragic fallout of the misperceived aspirations of the people. Explanatory narratives for these developments were therefore a critical means to articulate anxieties and contested ideas about horizons of progress and modernity and to assert the psychic injuries these horizons have produced in daily life.

City residents I spoke with understood and experienced the declining Kerala present in myriad ways. Individuals and communities claimed different relationships to migration, globalization, the local developmental state, and the promises of the Kerala model. Older-generation upper-caste elites, for example, tended to align themselves with a nationalist ideal of state-centric development and with a once-triumphant tale of the Kerala model. Through narratives of moral and social decay, they accused a "new generation" made up of consumerist, globally oriented youth of undermining Nehruvian socialist ideals and the developmental achievements of the past.[4] With the diversification and widening of the middle-class social field in Kerala, many of the upper-caste elite also perceived social crisis through intimate urban living with the upward mobility of formerly lower-class and lower-caste communities. Meanwhile, young people facing uncertain futures often spoke critically of the contradictions and failures of development. In doing so, they gave temporal depth, political meaning, and moral force to everyday experiences of unemployment, social vulnerability, frustration, and powerlessness. Through explanatory narratives about the ambivalent postcolonial present, young people made sense of the uncertain.

These anxious times feel very different, then, from differing social vantage points. At the national seminar that December morning, the predominantly male technocrats, politicians, and developmental academics in attendance perceived the present through a particular elite discourse about Kerala's ascendance and decline on the world stage of development. The shared tone was one of lost bearings. If record educational achievements and low infant mortality rates no longer captured the "reality of Kerala" in the present, as the seminar's chairman suggested, what suitable metrics could measure "happiness"? To be able to progress toward it in the making of new futures, how would happiness be recognized? If the Kerala model was now obsolete, where did the future lie? True happiness, many agreed, would not be found in moral surrender to globalization, the most prurient symptom of which was said to be the "disease" of consumerism spreading in the state. The Kerala present, they seemed to say, faced two impossible paths: one marked by the invasive and morally suspect forces of globalization, and the other by a receding developmental horizon. This predicament recalled for me the words of twenty-four-year-old Priya, who once described her life as trapped between two dead ends: between the pursuit of a first-class life that risked drowning debt and suicide on the one hand and the failure to keep up with social expectation on the other. She described it as being caught between the devil and the deep sea.

## UNHAPPY DEVELOPMENTS IN INDIA'S DEVELOPMENTAL MIRACLE

In his comments that December morning, the seminar's chairman pressed for an alternative metric that might capture the state of disenchantment in Kerala today. By promoting the need for a happiness index, he criticized the failure of standard yardsticks of development, such as infant mortality and literacy rates, to register the collective malaise in the state. He also faulted development itself for failing to deliver on aspects of living rather than merely improving chances of survival.[5] In the Indian state once hailed a developmental miracle, biological life has been made to thrive, and successfully so. Yet by the chairman's assessment, something has been critically missed if, however "developed," Malayalis are in fact so very unhappy.

While dressed in the new garments of an emergent science of happiness circulating in policy and governance frameworks, the chairman's critical commentary on development in Kerala was itself hardly new.[6] Disillusionment with the so-called Kerala model of development—a model based on the state's achievement of significant improvements in material conditions of living in spite of its relatively low per capita income—has been voiced from many angles for some time. Whether they charge the model for failing to deliver meaningful and radical change, for not yet realizing its promises, or for bearing poisonous fruit, ongoing debates over the merits and claims of the Kerala model have had profound effects on cultural and political imaginaries of the region.

As J. Devika observes, "The desire for 'Development'—often defined vaguely, working as a catch-all term for economic growth, social welfare, and socialistic redistribution of resources—has been intimately linked to the construction of the idea of a 'Malayali People' as a distinct sociocultural entity in the post-Independence period."[7] In the 1970s, dreams of Kerala's developmental exceptionalism appeared to many within and outside the state to have been achieved. Widespread popular support for the Family Planning Campaign was read by the Malayali press as evidence of everyday people's commitment to the goals of population reduction as prosperity. State-led land reforms fueled dreams of egalitarian development. Infant mortality rates had dropped, literacy rates were rising, and the other progressive social indicators for which the Kerala model has come to be known were emerging into view. By the 1980s and through the 1990s, however, enthusiasm for the Kerala model would become increasingly muted. A looming fiscal crisis, concerns for the environment, political stagnation, and acute levels of unemployment were raising difficult questions about the sustainability and fundamental merits of the developmental dream. Although international scholars continued to remain optimistic, policy makers and scholars in Kerala were declaring a state of crisis.[8]

In the wake of concerns about the viability of the Kerala model, an assortment of explanations and responses has proliferated. Some scholars suggest that the state's worsening fiscal and political crisis is the result of factors endemic to the Kerala model itself.[9] In making sense of these experiences, many have framed Kerala's successes and failures in the language of "paradox."[10] Others have retooled the claims of the model to emphasize its positive attributes. This discourse of "progressive Kerala" highlights the state's social developmental achievements as notable in their own right rather than as merely ancillary to economic development. Some are actively working to develop a "new" Kerala model that might reconcile social, labor, and environmental objectives at the local level.[11] Still others have hopefully declared a turnaround.[12] Radical critiques have focused on the ways the Kerala model narrative of social progressivism obscures inequalities and important elements of the history of modern social reform in the region.[13]

As optimism for the model waned through the 1980s and '90s, the sociologist Joseph Tharamangalam noted the crushing feelings that emerged among technocrats, social reformers, and development academics. When it became clear that the model was "in the throes of a major fiscal, economic, political and cultural crisis that threatens, not only its future development, but the sustainability of what has already been achieved," these troubling realizations provoked "soul-searching self-analysis and self-criticism that has often sunk into the depths of despondency and despair."[14] But these disappointments were never the domain of academic or policy circles alone. Uncertainty and skepticism for Kerala's developmental future and for the sustainability of past achievements have generated "near-frenzied and compulsive dystopic visions" that have been the defining feature of public discourse since the 1990s.[15]

That the dream of developmentalism has been thrown into crisis strikes at the very heart of, in the words of one journalist, "what it means to be Malayali." In a newspaper editorial by the same title, the political columnist T. J. S. George boldly declares that misery is the defining feature of being Malayali today. George is clear about the origins of this unhappy state: it lies in the "tragedy" of Kerala's fall from grace on the world stage of development.[16] "What it MEANT to be a Malayali would have been a pleasant topic to think about. What it MEANS today to be a Malayali is not such a happy subject," George begins (emphasis in original). "This is because the progress of the Malayali in the last thirty years has been downward. All that made us a proud and civilized people was lost." Plotting this precipitous turn of events, George observes, "Fifty years ago, Aikya Keralam was flush with hopes. . . .[17] And excel we did. Literacy broke all records. Primary health centers opened up in every village. Electricity became available in all nooks and corners. Population statistics turned the Kerala model into a world phenomenon. Educational levels became the envy of others." But this ascendance would not last, says George, lamenting "the great tragedy that we could not sustain this astonishing progress." He concludes with a grim pronouncement: "What it MEANT to be a Malayali? Proud. What it MEANS to be a Malayali? Miserable." George's account of Kerala's decline before an international audience configures a regional identity defined by misery in the present, one that he ultimately attributes to political stagnation and rampant corruption. The betrayal of past hopes and achievements is a most unhappy subject in the pages of Kerala's recent history, one that has produced, in the eyes of this journalist, unhappy subjects of the state.

Whether presented in the guise of utopia unfulfilled or the reversal of gains made, narratives such as this one are built on a particular idea of the linear progression of Kerala modern history. They reflect the developmental telos that has been central to a dominant construction of the region and that plots Kerala modern history as the progressive advancement against the forces of backwardness. By these accounts, developmental markers were "achieved," inequalities "overcome," primordial attachments "replaced" with the allegiances of modern citizenship, and the oppressed were "emancipated"—only for these gains to be "lost" in the present. Discourses of progress and decline like the one above see regional history from the eye of the Kerala model discourse and its beneficiaries, its proponents, and even from the eye of many of its opponents—those who may dismiss the model yet reinforce its master telos by lamenting the failure of its promises. This is a version of Kerala modern history that also claims to speak on behalf of a unitary and singular "Malayali" experience while rendering invisible the upper-caste Hindu male subject that it privileges.[18]

So even though these dystopic tales appear as if to speak to a universal Kerala history, this is the past and present rendered from a specific vantage point. This narrative of decline belongs to particular authors: those who are privileged to claim a relationship to a dominant story of Kerala progress and are thus in a position to mourn its demise. The predominant makeup of the gathering at the December seminar, with which this chapter opened—state officials, policy planners, and preeminent figures of development academia—suggests some of those who have stakes in this version of Kerala modern history. The last few decades have seen the mobilization of radical feminist, dalit, and adivasi political struggles in the public sphere that have raised fundamental challenges to this narrative.[19] Dalit, adivasi, and coastal communities do not claim the relationship to these dominant constructs of the region that the authors and supporters of the Kerala model claim.[20] Nor do these communities share in the experience of ascendance and decline that shapes perceptions of the present for elites and new elites in the capital city.

The progressive narrative of the Kerala model has now been radically disassembled from many angles. Yet it still animates perceptions of the present in uneven ways in Thiruvananthapuram. Many older generation elites and new elites lament its unrealized promises; meanwhile, young adults and nonelites question its fundamental merits and claims. But dystopic narratives in the Kerala present are not only about development as lost object or failed promise.[21] Development persists as a recalcitrant claim and reoriented project in the liberalizing present, one that articulates in new ways with contemporary transformations. City residents express moral concerns for the ways globalization, liberal economic reforms, and transnational migration in the contemporary moment are shaping the legacies and emergent orientations of the developmental state.

Narratives of decline with regard to Kerala's developmental experience cannot be understood outside these transformations. Transnational migration, for example, has profoundly shaped the region's social, economic, and cultural landscape and has been looked upon by some scholars and state technocrats as a new route to development. Migration between Kerala and the Persian Gulf since the 1970s, as well as migration to other regions of the world, has been an important release valve for the state's high rate of unemployment and a needed stimulant for the economy.[22] Migration now features centrally in the horizons of expectation and projects of worth among young men and women. Together with migration, national economic liberalization has also encouraged an expanding circulation of commodities, money, and mass media images, fostering a now broad perception of Kerala as a newly consumerist society. These transformations and their reorientation of the developmental state shape the larger landscape in which city residents make sense of the present as a time for decay and suicide.

### CONSUMING DESIRES

During my time in the capital city, anxieties about suicide overwhelmingly focused on "consumption itself as a fetishized object."[23] Consumption has been recognized to be a critical site for debates and imaginings about values and identities in India's liberalization era.[24] Skepticism about consumption is neither new nor unique to Kerala. Yet the distinct contours of its threat are molded by the region's developmental and leftist political histories and by fears of an unfolding suicide crisis. In the Kerala public sphere, left-affiliated discourses have framed consumption as a manifestation of the growing reach of multinational corporations after liberalization. These discourses reflect concern that liberalization has wildly expanded the aspirations of everyday people, including the poor, to the point of self-destruction. Forwarding its own anti-globalization politics but in different terms, the conservative Hindu right has argued that consumption threatens Western adulteration of "Indian traditions" and "Indian values."[25] City residents across political and ideological divides blame debt from consumption as one major proximate cause of suicide, folding this into a broader discourse about the "problem" of aspiration in Kerala today. Suicide here, as one sociologist told me, begins with "big dreams and big purchases" and ends in sinking loans, unmanageable debt, and suicide.

Many in the capital city spoke to me of a historical and moral rupture from the temperance of Kerala's precolonial, developmentalist, or communist past to proclaim the dramatic effects wrought by conspicuous consumption in the present. They did so selectively, drawing on particular chronotopes and temporal maps that play up the state's "exposure" to the dangers of globalization after long periods of leftist rule, while downplaying, for instance, Kerala's place in a vibrant, centuries-long history of transoceanic relations.[26] Some, like Veliyamma, drew on ideas of Kerala as a newly consumerist society to rend a strident generational divide between regional and national political virtues associated with the past and constructions of globalized youth in the present. A sixty-three-year-old grandmother and retired government schoolteacher, Veliyamma belongs to a respected, upper-caste family. In the comfort of the well-appointed home where she lives with her daughter's family, Veliyamma spoke with me one afternoon about the greed (*aarthi*) that has taken over Kerala youth. Although some money is necessary to clothe, feed, and shelter the body, said Veliyamma, today that need (*aavasyam*) has turned into greed. By her account, greed is at the root of all problems plaguing Kerala society today. The greed that drives young men to rob women in broad daylight for their gold necklaces, said Veliyamma, pointing to the front-page story of the morning paper, is the same greed that drives whole families to debt and suicide. When I asked her to explain further the difference between need and greed, she spoke of the body. "The body needs eighty milligrams of vitamin C each day, along with other minerals and vitamins in their own exact amounts," she explained. Even if a person eats too much, taking up more than the body needs, the body will only absorb the eighty milligrams of the vitamin C that it requires. Rather than storing the excess, the body flushes it out. Like the person who eats greedily and stretches his stomach, Veliyamma said, today's youth are gorging themselves on fancy mobile phones, cars, and motorcycles. Not only are these items unnecessary to live; the energy spent "eating" excessively leaves the body wasted. That is why youth today are directionless and have no energy *(oorjjam)* to care for anything but consuming the latest gadgets. As a counterpoint to the greed she observed around her, Veliyamma recounted to me how she had donated her gold earrings and bangles to the national war effort during the 1962 Sino-Indian War.[27]

Veliyamma's comments fit with a broader discourse of consumption as a generational "problem" associated with a particular construction of globalized Indian youth. Her narrative of decline replicates a key binary in nationalist understandings of globalizing India, drawing an ideological, political, and lifestyle divide between the "new" and "old" generations.[28] Through her metaphor of nutrition and the body, Veliyamma spoke of basic needs in a manner that reflects the socialist-inspired ideals associated with Nehruvian development's focus on national eradication of famine and poverty, Gandhian notions of austerity, and Kerala's left-affiliated politics. She contrasted this with a popular image of intensively consumerist, capitalism-embracing, globalized youth today. In doing so, she replicated a pervasive discourse about a disengaged generation that has turned away from politics and service to the nation in order to focus on enhancing the self.[29] Such narratives gloss together youth, consumption, and globalization in a manner that positions an undifferentiated body of "youth" as an index of the reach and influence of globalization and as a barometer for social decay in the present.[30]

For Veliyamma, the greed she witnessed everywhere around her not only made everyday life in the city unhappy and violent; it also symbolized a dramatic loss of the nationalist values she associated with an idealized past, values that once led her to donate her gold in higher service to the nation. This vision of the "newness" of consumption is shaped by social and political histories that inflect the virtues of restraint.[31] Yet issued from her social position as upper-class and upper-caste, Veliyamma's critique also enacted a double standard. It selectively erased the contradictions in the ways she spoke passionately about austerity as a moral good and a higher duty while surrounded by the latest household amenities and two foreign-brand cars in the driveway.

Discourses about consumption, moral decline, and suicide were strongly inflected by the cultural politics of class, caste, and community. From the breezy covered veranda of her home, nestled in a quiet lane in one of the city's wealthier neighborhoods, thirty-year-old Gita outlined the problem of suicide and social decay from the specificity of her social position as an upper-class, upper-caste woman. "I belong to a middle-class Nayar family," she began in English.[32] "We are all well-educated, many of us have professional degrees. But we don't believe in accumulating or acquiring material goods. So we live a simple life." Emphasizing that her family has lived this way for "many generations," Gita spoke of how carefully she and her husband manage their finances, purchase only the necessities to live comfortably, and never borrow money under any circumstances. Condemning families that take out loans at exorbitant interest rates to purchase cars and jewelry, she preached, "If you cannot afford such things, you shouldn't buy them." Gita then began to whisper about the neighbors. "Nowadays, if my family has a car like a Sandro [a Korean car], these other people [gesturing to the house directly across the lane] are suddenly trying for the same things. They want to buy the same car to feel some 'in-groupness.'" By Gita's account, in seeking membership through intensified consumption, those who aspire to be upwardly mobile have brought problems upon themselves. "For my family, having such material things is something we are used to. But these other people will buy and buy, take loans, and won't pay them back. That's when they commit suicide," she told me. "That is what I think is the problem."[33]

Social histories of community, caste, and class were critical to elite discourses about decline in the Kerala present. The prestige of consumption in the region had historically been associated with upper-caste Hindu Nayar and "progressive" Christian communities, emblematized in the figures of the nineteenth-century Nayar landowner patron and the wealthy twentieth-century Christian entrepreneur successful in trade, commerce, and agriculture.[34] In her neighborhood, where upwardly mobile Ezhava families now live among Nayar and Christian families, Gita perceived social decay through intimate urban living with new elites. Speaking frankly of the upwardly mobile as "those other people," she made clear to whom she was referring. Pointing across the lane to the home of an Ezhava family whom she was aware I knew well, Gita unequivocally asserted the caste and class stakes of her experience of the declining present.

Social and economic mobility has been claimed as part of a broad community-wide project of social reform and development among Ezhavas since the turn of the twentieth century. Through strong anti-caste reform movements, together with the attainment of respectable employment, the accumulation of wealth, and alignment with upper-caste Nayars and "progressive" Christian communities, the Ezhava community has redefined itself as being no longer untouchable.[35] A consumer-intensive orientation has also facilitated the community's entry into a mainstream, middle-class Hindu fold.[36] Gita feared the moral and social decay of the present through the challenge this consumer-intensive orientation has posed to conservative class- and caste-based relations of hierarchy and dominance. New displays of wealth among the upwardly mobile—an intimate presence in Gita's neighborhood—inspired reproach and a tinge of envy. By framing suicide as a pathology of intemperate aspiration among new elites like her Ezhava neighbors, Gita retooled ideas of social hierarchy and difference by presenting herself in contrast as a responsible middle-class subject with the moral capacity to distinguish "good," restrained consumption.[37]

By contrast, Dr. Samuel, a psychiatrist in his fifties, spoke of consumption as the strange harvest of Kerala's developmental experience. From a wealthy, high-status Syrian Christian family that once owned extensive rubber plantations farther north in the state, Dr. Samuel drew on a hegemonic tale of Kerala development to explain what he called the "craze for consumerism" among Malayali youth today. "My feeling is that young people in Kerala today are very sensitive, very much affected by changes outside," reflected Dr. Samuel, speaking in English. "Their thinking is, 'I've heard this beauty powder is good for my skin, this nail polish is a bit expensive, but it's good for me.'" He contrasted this to elsewhere in India. "If you go to Tamil Nadu or Bihar or Uttar Pradesh, most people live in villages. They don't think these things. They only want to make both ends meet. If a multinational company goes there and says, 'Your skin will glow better if you apply this beauty cream,' they will say, 'My son is hungry and crying and would be happy with some rice.'" "But in Kerala," said Dr. Samuel, "we have enough food. We want to make ourselves pretty with lipstick and creams. Here, the priorities are different." Laughing and throwing his hands up into the air, Dr. Samuel declared, "Kerala people have always wanted to be on top of the world. These adolescents and youth are thinking, 'I want to be on par with the West!'"[38]

In no uncertain terms, Dr. Samuel characterized youth consumption as an act of moral surrender to the influence of multinational corporations. Malayali youth's unique sensitivity to global change, argued Dr. Samuel, is the direct result of development in the state. Freed of having to worry about the basic needs of living, they have the luxury to consume, aspire, and dream. In drawing a contrast between the priorities of Malayali youth and those of Bihari villagers, Dr. Samuel's national imaginary appears to resonate with left-affiliated discourses that critique the Indian state for the withdrawal of welfare provisions and growing support for neoliberal reforms. It seems to push back against the diminishing importance of basic priorities like alleviating poverty in India's liberalizing present. At the same time, the locus of blame in Dr. Samuel's critical commentary centers not on the state but rather on the ostensibly slavish desire and stubborn fixation among Malayali youth to be on par with the West.

Reading between the lines also reveals the subtle but important ways Dr. Samuel framed the problem of material aspiration as more than a generational or regional issue alone. Indexed by the use of cosmetics and beauty creams, consumption is implicitly imagined here through the bodies and practices of women. Dr. Bina, a psychologist in her forties from a high-status Nayar family, highlighted for me the gendered stakes of globalization and consumption in the Kerala present. One morning when I was observing Dr. Bina receive clients in the outpatient psychiatry department of one of Thiruvananthapuram's hospitals, a young woman entered the waiting room. Unlike many others her age, who, at the time of my fieldwork, mostly wore the *churidar* (long tunic with loose trousers, also known as the *salwar kameez*) in public, she wore jeans and a fitted T-shirt with the term *Fashionista* emblazoned on the front in pink sequins. At this government-funded hospital, where most of Dr. Bina's clients are of the lower-status working poor, the young woman attracted the psychologist's disparaging comments. "See this?" Dr. Bina whispered, nudging me behind the desk where we were both sitting. "This is the impact your culture is having on our youth today." Dr. Bina, whom I knew from our many hours in the hospital together to be a compulsive doodler, began drawing on the corner of her notebook a busty female silhouette complete with mini skirt and tank top. A few minutes later, she nudged me again. Pointing to her finished picture, Dr. Bina said that this was the reason why Kerala society was in decline. When girls begin to dress "without shame" *(naan-amillaattha),* values disappear and families break down. "Women should be the lamp of the home," Dr. Bina said. How could a girl dressed in such a way be the guiding light for family and society?[39]

Notions of Indian Womanhood became a major site of contention in colonial and nationalist discourse in India, in which women were often represented as icons of tradition and nation.[40] Women continue to be central to struggles over the cultural effects of globalization across political and ideological divides in India's liberalizing present. As part of these concerns, women's bodies and definitions of proper dress have served as critical domains for debating definitions of community and nation.[41] While leftist and conservative right discourses speak in different terms, Ritty Lukose has pointed out that there are important alignments in their postcolonial preoccupations with ideas of female respectability as they are linked to constructions of public and private and of modernity and tradition.[42] Like the nineteenth-century discourses promoted by cultural nationalists discussed by Partha Chatterjee, Dr. Bina's anti-consumerist stance framed women and the idea of Indian Womanhood as icons of the moral reproduction of home and nation, requiring protection against the prurient West.[43] Articulated from her social position among the upper-caste elite, Dr. Bina perceived the threat of moral and social decay through the newly consuming, lower-status female subject. The social worker's pictorial rendering of a curvy, full-figured female silhouette makes clear that this threat is linked to the expression of an overt (hetero)sexuality, one that defies the locally respectable, classed ideal of the contained female body.[44]

While many in Thiruvananthapuram spoke in the dystopic language of contradiction and decline, their perceptions of past and present were shaped by their social coordinates and by personal and community histories of struggle. Elites in particular drew on the "newness" of consumption as a central organizing theme to articulate the social and moral challenges created by liberalizing reforms and global change at an anxious juncture in Kerala development history. In doing so, they reflected on the particular stakes of class, caste, community, and gender that have shaped their experience of the declining Kerala present. As those like Gita, Dr. Bina, and Veliyamma spoke apprehensively of shifting political and moral values, lifestyles, and identities, they enacted powerful claims and counterclaims around the questions of what ought to define the good life and who are its proper claimants.

## A "RETURN" TO THE HAPPY FAMILY

In a time of decay and dystopia, where do city residents look to secure a better future? What hopeful horizons do they envision? At a time when the state's social welfare provisions are retracting and loss and failure appear to be the individual's alone, the elite discourses I heard often posited a solution, not in a turn to the state, but rather in the improvement of self and family. In popular discourse, families are increasingly called to reform themselves in order to mend the social fabric, salvage "traditional" values, and stem the suicide crisis.

Psychologist Dr. Biju once accounted for Kerala's high rates of suicide through a story about food. Describing to me the ways modern life has altered social interaction, Dr. Biju spoke of the deterioration of the family meal: "Scientific advancements have taken away the harmony and pleasures of sitting together. Even if it's not over bread, butter, and jam, we should all sit and eat together. Food is a symbol of love," he said, "but now most parents and children don't sit, eat, and share." For Dr. Biju, the shift from food as social practice for the nourishment of family life to food as foreign-identified marker of prestige symbolizes a broader dissolution of "traditional" values in contemporary Kerala. Observing that simple pleasures like sharing a meal have given way to the fast pace and materialism of modern living, Dr. Biju sadly concluded that in Kerala today, "the basic happiness of being alive is gone. And when life becomes miserable, there is always an option: I can commit suicide."[45]

In popular discourse, social decay has acquired its most troubling manifestations at the site of the family. Widely circulating media accounts of murder-suicide pacts among families escaping insurmountable debt, for example, link consumption gone awry to the wholesale destruction of households.[46] In targeting the nuclear family institution as the breeding ground for the problems plaguing modern life, the elite discourses I heard simultaneously heralded the rehabilitated family as the path to a suicide-free collective future. Consider Dr. Biju's optimism that, despite the grim state of most families in Kerala today, "basic happiness" can still be rekindled. Families only need to rediscover the intimacies "that were once there." Parents, he encouraged, have to learn once again how to talk with their children, not just about their test scores, but about their thoughts and opinions; likewise, married couples have to make space to reclaim "quality time" (using the English term) by taking walks together and speaking openly about their hopes. Dr. Biju's proposal to rediscover once again the basic happiness of being alive appears as a matter of simple revelation: the unveiling of a secret that has resided in conjugal and parent-child relationships all along but has been latent, buried under the modern-life rubble of television screens, computers, and atomizing individualism. By Dr. Biju's account, the path to happiness lies in the "return" to a seemingly pure and originary form of the nuclear family and its intimacies.

Yet if the antidote to modern malaise appears by such accounts to lie within easy reach, this "return" to the simple pleasures of the middle-class nuclear family is a mythological one. It conveniently forgets that there is in fact no pure or originary form of the family to return to. In a region once characterized by diverse patrilineal and matrilineal joint-family practices, social and legislative reform movements beginning in the nineteenth century gradually "modernized" these practices by shifting them toward legally recognized patrifocal residence, patrilineal descent, and patrilineal inheritance and succession.[47] Historian and feminist scholar J. Devika has charted the many forces by which the small, patrifocal, conjugal family form gained moral and practical purchase across social groups by the mid-twentieth century in Kerala.[48] This was a process driven by demographic anxieties, the production of modern citizen-subjects for whom "liberation" from the large family was considered fundamental, and colonial and postcolonial struggles to "civilize" matrilineal practices in the region.[49] As legislative interventions and economic transformations rendered earlier modes of family arrangement and inheritance unviable, the small, patrifocal family emerged as the reasonable, economical, and desirable life option. Dr. Biju's nostalgia for an originary nuclear family intimacy omits these histories of social and legislative reform. It forgets, moreover, that this class-specific dream of domesticity was never "had" in any straightforward manner by communities considered outliers of development. The past to which Dr. Biju encouraged a happy homecoming to save the future is an imagined one.

Proposals to reform kin intimacy as the solution to social decay circulate widely in popular discourse. They enact nostalgia for different imagined pasts. If Dr. Biju looked longingly upon a mythological nuclear-family intimacy in ways that erased histories of social reform and their exclusions, others cast their gaze on an idealized "traditional" joint family consigned to the past as the foil to contemporary nuclear family living.[50] Consider one newspaper article whose title staidly declares, "No More a Happy Family."[51] In the article, veteran journalist Leela Menon explains the rise of family murder-suicides in the state. Asking how such tragedies could ever come to be, Menon paints a grim picture of Kerala's nuclear families that references debt, marital mistrust, domestic violence, alcoholism, and depression. "At times it could be the wife of an alcoholic, depressed from years of torturous domestic violence, deciding to end it all, [who will] poison, drown, hang, or burn the children and commit suicide, ignoring the children's right to life," describes Menon. "Kerala, topping the chart in alcohol consumption, also has a population of Othellos, suspecting their wives of infidelity, and demanding DNA tests of children. Alcoholism coupled with suspicion leads to domestic violence, in which Kerala takes the lead. This breeds depression in women, sapping their zest for life."[52] In Menon's dystopic vision, kinship has been corrupted: mothers murder their children, husbands accuse wives of adultery, and fathers demand the incontrovertible evidence of genetic testing. The nuclear family appears as the social engine for depression, domestic abuse, and suicide, and it is women and children who must bear the burden of its violence. Concerns for Kerala's family murder-suicides are not misplaced. National crime statistics cited in the article reveal that Kerala has reported the highest number of family murder-suicides of all Indian states.[53] Debt from loans is a reason frequently reported in the media.

In counterpoint to Dr. Biju's nostalgia for a mythological nuclear-family intimacy that has "always" been there, Menon acknowledges that the small family is a relatively recent development in the region. Indeed, at first blush this account appears deeply ambivalent toward the institutional rise of a class-specific form of the nuclear family, particularly its gendered relations and forms of prestige consumption. The journalist's account of alcoholism, abuse, and depression aligns in this sense with efforts among feminist historiographers to recognize the gender inequalities on which the small family was built. Problematizing assumptions about Malayali women's "empowerment" that have been key to dominant narratives of Kerala development, these scholars have argued by contrast that gendered subjects and patriarchal inequalities were produced as a foundational part of the Kerala modernity experience.[54] Through the spread of modern domesticity and the small conjugal family, social reform and political movements inaugurated forms of patriarchy founded on the dichotomization of the male breadwinner and the female housewife.[55] In spite of the rising educational levels of Malayali women overall, this gendered division of labor has become further entrenched in recent decades among middle-class families.[56] Indeed, the relatively high educational achievements of Malayali women compared with those of their husbands, coupled with their limited agency in making household decisions and their disenfranchisement from inheritance, have been shown to render women vulnerable to domestic violence, dowry abuse, and suicide.[57] Menon's dystopic account shares in these concerns, appearing to question the notion of the small, conjugal, patri-focal family as an unproblematic social good. Nuclear family living seems less a middle-class dream than a nightmare.

In the end, however, Menon's critique stops short. Its locus drifts from the orchestrated violence and inequalities of modern domesticity to the mothers who ostensibly fail to adjust to its demands. Menon observes that it is ultimately mothers who are at fault: they are the ones who decide to kill themselves and who choose to take their children with them rather than abandon them to an unknown fate.[58] This may be a surprising development, says Menon, in light of ideas about maternal nurturance and protection: "This attitude of the mothers is in sharp contrast to the commonly held belief that mothers would endure anything to protect their children. Obviously there is a qualitative change in the value system in Kerala, which turns mothers into killers. It is a single-handed decision of the mother who tricks her children into death." Mothering here takes an aberrant twist, the extreme perversion of women's "natural" instincts.

In declaring "no more a happy family," this account implicitly constructs an idealized joint family of the past as the moral foil to the troubled nuclear family in the present. And yet Menon acknowledges that there is no turning "back." Instead, efforts must be made to make women better managers of the nuclear household, an institution that, Menon concedes, is a practical reality of contemporary life. Local women's organizations can prevent such death pacts by teaching mothers "strategies of stress management, healthy coping behavior, family economics and streamlining life within a budget to avoid a debt trap." The development of women's skills as household managers reshapes the scope and meaning of women's agency and domestic responsibility in this age of suicide.[59] Cast now in the language of popular psychology, good household management demands stress management, coping behaviors, and improved emotional health as protection against family suicide. The gendered stakes of these domestic projects are clear: it is a mother's charge and hers alone to ensure frugal accounting and defensive resilience on the course to a family that is "once more" a happy one. This is a classed discourse that presumes that the model housewife is the desired role that all can and must take. Reclaiming the happier family is a responsibility borne on the backs of mothers in a manner that produces classed and gendered domestic subjects against the threat of suicide.

Proposals to reform the institution of the family to stem social decay and salvage the future shore up classed and gendered ideologies about kin intimacy and household management. They also construct different imaginings of the past. If Dr. Biju looked to a mythological origin that never was, Menon looks ahead. Yet in some respects, their proposals to salvage the future are not so different. Like Dr. Biju, Menon enacts a pointed amnesia. By enjoining women to be consummate householders,

Menon proposes an optimized nuclear family as the path to happier futures, one that magically erases the inequalities, vulnerabilities, and conditions for violence upon which this very home is built.

## "WE GET AGITATED AT THESE DEVELOPMENTS"

Crisis-ridden narratives about the Kerala present and proposals for a better future like those above are important for the cultural and ideological work they do and the erasures they enact in public discourse. But they tell us little about how perceptions of past and present shape the experiential and affective dimensions of everyday life. Many young adults I spoke with, themselves in times of personal transition, actively drew on ideas of historical contradiction and decline to give political meaning, moral force, and temporal depth to everyday experiences of unemployment, social vulnerability, and frustration. In doing so, they reflected on the ways they were simultaneously enabled and hindered at the crossroads of development, liberalization, and global change.

Srijith claimed a deeply personal stake in a development-defined notion of progressive "Malayali-ness." It shaped his self-perception in powerful ways. A doctoral candidate in Malayalam literature, when we spoke Srijith was in the ninth year of his graduate program. The thirty-one-year-old had been taking on piecemeal teaching jobs for several years despite the unofficial completion of his dissertation. Srijith's extension of his student status reflects the uncertain period of "waiting" that characterizes the prolonged transition to adulthood many young adults in Kerala now experience.[60] As in other postcolonial settings, at a time when access to mainstream schooling is expanding, opportunities for salaried work have declined across social groups and classes, contributing to high rates of under- and unemployment.[61] Srijith's condition of educated unemployment may also reflect the postcolonial legacies of an educational system overbalanced toward forms of higher education mismatched, reformers argue, to the needs of a liberalized economy.

One afternoon over tea at the university canteen, Srijith drew on a dominant narrative of Kerala ascendance and decline to make sense of suicide among his peers. "The problem is that Kerala has become something else," he explained to me in a fluid mix of Malayalam and English. "Internationally, Kerala is considered a very developed state, the place where literacy is high, the place where people are aware [with an ironic tone], the place where people read the paper every day," he told me. "The state is now getting a very different face as the state that commits the most violence against women, the most suicides. And of course, Kerala is known as India's 'suicide capital,' so the whole face of the state changes, you know?" For Srijith, the crisis in a development-defined Malayali identity strikes at the very core of who he understands himself to be. "Those of us who have seen the progress, who have their own notions about Kerala, their own nostalgia—we get agitated at these developments." When I asked him if Malayalis still wished to believe in the idea of Kerala as exceptional, Srijith chimed, "Of course! The only people who don't believe in it anymore are those who commit suicide. For everyone else, at least in their subconscious, that particular model still persists. Somehow we want to hold on to this particular concept, destroy all doubts against it. We want to hold on to it and reinforce it from the outside."[62]

From a middle-class Ezhava family, his parents having secured the government jobs coveted by their generation, Srijith spoke that afternoon from the perspective of those "who have seen the progress." His faith in a hegemonic narrative of Kerala development emerges from his family's experience of upward mobility and access to social opportunities and from a self-created Ezhava community identity more generally. For Srijith, an idea of Kerala's exceptionalism was multiply mirrored across family, community, and region. The stakes of holding on to this facet of his identity are high: losing hope for Kerala's developmental dream means losing hope for life itself. Yet this is a shaky grip all the same. While Srijith claimed an idea of "progressive Kerala," his voice also expressed a tinge of irony when he characterized Kerala as a place "where people read the paper every day." In referencing in this way an oft-cited portrait of Malayali literacy, he reflected a critical awareness that the Kerala model ideal is itself a constructed discourse.

As Srijith struggles to hold on to a sense of what makes Kerala exceptional, he asserts distinction in other ways. He insisted, for instance, on the unique intelligence of "the Malayali people." The state's unparalleled educational achievements had endowed Malayalis with a special intelligence and resourcefulness, as their many achievements overseas could attest, said Srijith. Whether in the Persian Gulf or the United States, Malayalis found success all over the world. Through an updated narrative of transnational migration and global competitiveness, Srijith retooled the claims of a development-identified regional identity to construct a new sense of Malayali exceptionalism. Regardless of the state of the Kerala model, there were enduring attributes born of the state's past achievements that continued to set Malayalis apart. Srijith's evolving claims pronounced "the people"—and himself—as exceptional still.

Twenty-seven-year-old Philip spoke more critically of Kerala's development history to make sense of the frustrations and contradictions he felt in daily life. Upon Philip's request that we talk over lunch, I found myself one afternoon in a salmon-pink room with framed posters of Ravi Varma's iconic paintings covering the walls. Electronic instrumental versions of soft rock floated sleepily over the speakers. Philip had arrived early, and I found him busily texting on his phone. After ordering food, he began to explain to me in flawless English that it had been nearly a year and a half since the completion of his law degree. He was still searching for a job. Ideally, he told me, he would find a starter position with a reputable firm here in Thiruvananthapuram and leverage it into a position with an international organization in Canada or the United States. While frustrated by his fruitless search thus far, he was also hopeful. From a wealthy Syrian Christian family, Philip had security many of his friends could not claim. In the worst-case scenario, he told me, he could always work for the family restaurant business. For now, he was living at home with his parents and younger sister in a comfortably middle-class neighborhood in the city.

Mentioning his friends' similarly poor employment prospects as recent graduates, Philip began speaking more broadly about frustration and rising suicide among Malayali youth. These troubling trends, Philip said, were the direct result of Kerala's educational achievements. Alluding to the expansion of secondary schooling and the "high aspirations" of Malayali youth and their parents, Philip said that these days even children dream expansively of becoming engineers and doctors in places like London and the United States. But most, he said, would never realize their dreams, stuck instead in Kerala to compete for jobs that weren't there. For Philip, this gaping divide between opportunities and young people's horizons of expectation proved that education in Kerala has turned out to be "as much a curse as a blessing." Asked about the nature of this "curse," Philip answered concisely: "We know what others have that we don't."

The problem was that Malayalis were "too intelligent, too aware." Philip told me that Kerala had transcended the grinding poverty that afflicts "other Indians," since, "unlike Biharis, Malayalis have the luxury to think beyond where their next meal will come from." But when "compared to Americans like you," said Philip, educated Malayalis "know that they are deprived." He concluded, "That is the biggest problem, when people know that they legitimately have the right to be in a better position. That is a very specific problem to this state." This "relative deprivation," as he called it, creates the experiences of aimlessness and frustration he and his peers were now experiencing. Educated young people like him were well aware of the first-class life that others lived, and while equally if not more deserving of that life, they were stuck at the margins of its dominant articulations. Frustration and anger, together with the suicides that are their final result, were in Philip's powerful words, the "plight of the overeducated Malayali."[63]

If Srijith asserted the unique educational achievements of the "Malayali people" to cling to a life-saving narrative of exceptionalism, by contrast, Philip understood these achievements to be a curse in the present. He felt this curse in the ways his life had come to a grinding halt. For Philip, disillusionment and frustration among youth were the products of development "successes" coming home to roost. The heralded educational achievements of India's most literate state have structured the aspirations and horizons of expectation among educated youth like him, endowing them with a sense of efficacy and belonging. Yet many remain at the edges of the first-class life they aspire to. Philip claimed an experience of relative deprivation to express the felt contradictions that simultaneously station educated youth like himself at the center of development and at the peripheries of global modernity. Through the lens of his own search for adequate employment, Philip configured the present as trapped in multiple, nested disjunctures: between the Kerala model's receding development horizons and global capitalism, between educational empowerment and cultural marginalization, and between entitlement and deprivation. His critical reflections are a powerful example of what K. Sivaramakrishnan and Arun Agarwal call "stories of development": stories that not only challenge the hegemony of developmentalism but also draw attention to the ways individuals actively speak back to and make sense of development as discourse in the contexts of everyday life.[64] In speaking back to historical trajectories in the region, Philip questioned the notion of education as unproblematic social good promoted by development academia and by the state.[65] At once well-educated, disillusioned by employment prospects at home, and casting his fortunes on the chance to migrate abroad, Philip embodied felt contradictions and disappointments at the crossroads of development, liberalization, transnational migration, and global change.

Given that English-medium education has been a critical component of Syrian Christian advancement and identity in the region, Philip's criticism is a particularly trenchant one.[66] His sense of betrayal is also shaped by his desires for those professional occupations he sees appropriate to his education and social standing and their mismatch with the changing field of employment around him. Because of his access to resources in this period of posteducational transition, Philip has had more room to be critical and to hold out for suitable employment. When he updated me months later, Philip explained that he was still looking for salaried work. But in the meantime, he and his friends were keeping busy developing a modest, small-scale magazine publication. Targeting unemployed young adults like themselves, the magazine, Philip explained without irony, would feature interviews with employers and successful graduates, information about job fairs, and advice on every step of the employment process from how to dress for an interview to how to write a résumé. Philip's father had offered to front the start-up costs. Unlike Srijith, who defended the intrinsic worth of his education with little else available to him, Philip, enabled by cultural, social, and economic resources, exercised a greater freedom to impeach developmentalist claims about the value of education. If Srijith clung to an idea of Kerala's exceptionalism against the loss of hope, Philip criticized the failures of development with options before him.

Unlike Srijith and Philip, twenty-four-year-old Priya did not speak explicitly in historical terms to account for frustration and disappointment in her life. Yet the exclusions and contradictions she acutely felt as an underemployed, upwardly mobile lower-caste woman were also structured at the intersection of regional, national, and global trajectories. Having completed her college degree in history, Priya was navigating the terrain of labor conditions and marital life in an attempt to find work when I met her. Frustrations in finding a job had made it somewhat easier for strong-willed Priya to eventually relent to pressure from her husband and in-laws to remain at home. Six months pregnant with their first child when we spoke, Priya explained how she had cleverly worked around her in-laws' injunction against work outside the home and taken up a job as a medical transcriptionist for a U.S.-based company. Since this work could be done from home on their desktop computer, it was flexible enough for Priya to do on her own schedule and did not interfere with her household responsibilities. While just part-time, it brought in enough pocket money for occasional cosmetics for herself and small items for the household. Describing to me the tedium of sitting through hours of recordings and transcribing them into English, Priya expressed deep frustration over the futility of her degree. She had not expected her in-laws, who had earlier said they would permit her to work, to change their minds. As was the case for many middle-class and aspiring middle-class families I met in Thiruvananthapuram, for Priya's in-laws the domestic ideal is the educated housewife who channels her capital toward raising quality children and a well-managed household, rather than toward economic gain outside the home.[67] These expectations shaped the disappointments and exclusions Priya experienced as an underemployed college graduate.

Priya also felt the loss of her education and labor potential in another way. Now that her husband, Sabu, had started a position at the government medical college as a physician, she told me that they both felt intense pressure to live up to the consumption standards of Sabu's colleagues. One afternoon, after discreetly shutting the bedroom door so her in-laws wouldn't overhear, Priya went into this subject with me in great detail. "Right now we need money," she explained in Malayalam, sitting cross-legged on the cot in the corner of the room. "We need money for different things. And it's only because of the class difference—the way his friends are living. We can't reach their level. They are all very posh!" Switching from Malayalam to English to mark the discourse of her husband's peers, Priya said, "And you know what? Many of his friends, they take vacations in Dubai, Singapore . . . just to shop! They say, 'Oh this life! It's so boring. The college, clinic, the patients. We have to escape for a week!' So to get rid of their tension they go abroad to have a good time, spend lots of money, and then come back.[68] That is the way of life for most of his friends."

Despite their best efforts, the young couple's inability to keep up with the consumption standards of their peers continually reminded them of their precarious status. She explained to me that as low-caste (scheduled caste) Hindus, she and her husband felt pressure to keep up with Sabu's high-status, upper-caste Hindu and Christian peers. Describing for me how the young couple had carefully saved up over several months to buy Sabu a new pair of brand-name Woodland shoes, Priya said how disappointed they were when none of Sabu's colleagues had commented on the purchase. "They cost almost twenty-five hundred rupees," she told me, a significant portion of Sabu's salary for the month. "They are very, very expensive, and they look so nice, so nice. He wore them to work. When he came home that evening I asked, 'Did anyone say anything about your shoes?'" Priya shook her head in frustration. "He told me, 'Who would look at them? Everyone else has the same on their feet. They probably have two or three more pairs at home.'"[69]

Priya's phrase that is the title of this chapter captures with eloquence the particular predicament she perceived in her life at the time we spoke. Priya described being trapped between two dead ends: between the pursuit of the posh life that she felt was expected of her family and that she herself desired on the one hand and the risk of debt and suicide on the other. In navigating this trap, Priya was both facilitated and hindered. Endowed with a college degree, yet struggling to claim social and economic mobility through her husband while prohibited from working herself, Priya experienced the contradictions of the postcolonial present through the specificity of her gender, class, and caste location.

Shaped by development and globalization's structures of aspiration while situated at their edges, Priya, Srijith, and Philip spoke eloquently of the promises and exclusions they experienced in their everyday lives. Each felt enabled and disenfranchised in particular ways as they drew on available resources to navigate economic and social uncertainty. When I visited with Priya several years later, she proudly showed me the new car she and her husband had purchased with the help of a bank loan. The month-to-month payments at high interest rates were difficult, Priya confessed, particularly now that she had given up her medical transcription job. But it was worth it, she said, smiling. For her husband to show up at the medical college in a motorcycle like those his students took to class, Priya said shaking her head, was simply unacceptable.[70]

## DISORDERED STATES

" 'God's Own Country' has been forfeited to the devil." Inverting Kerala's well-known epithet and state tourism brand, Prabhu, a retired government servant in his seventies, made this comment to me with staid pessimism.[71] Like Prabhu and others introduced in this chapter, many in the capital city announced an unhappy Kerala present, one marked by the failures of collective struggle, and uncertainty about the future. In accounting for contemporary suicide as the bitter harvest of historical trajectories, city residents spoke back to political, economic, and social developments in the region. Their explanatory narratives about the anxious present offer powerful insight into how projects of modernity and their disappointments feel and are made meaningful in ordinary life.

Many in Thiruvananthapuram now express deep skepticism for the Kerala model and its claims and do so from a variety of angles. The exclusions, contradictions, and betrayals people perceive in the present produce both ambivalences and opportunities. Some lament the inexorable decline of an ideal; others draw on historical narratives to make sense of personal frustration and uncertainty. Individuals and communities experience these anxious times in ways shaped by their particular social positions and by their perspectives on the past. And in doing so, they struggle with the question of what ought to define the good life today and who are that life's rightful claimants. In this time of suicide, the stakes behind these questions could not be higher. For some like Prabhu, they wager no less than the forfeiture of God's abode to the devil himself.

## 2

# Gazing at the Stars, Aiming for the Treetops

The English word *overambition,* used regardless of how much or how little English one spoke, surfaced often and widely in my conversations about suicide with mental health professionals in the capital city. Dr. Cheeran elaborated the meaning of this word for me in his own terms one morning as we prepared to receive clients in the psychology department of Trinity Hospital. "Imagine," the psychologist said, speaking in English, "the typical Malayali, someone of average height but not very tall. This is the man who fights to become a star basketball player. It's simply unrealistic." Access to education has proven a fundamental good in Kerala, affirmed Dr. Cheeran. But it has also led to a phenomenal expansion of aspirations among the people, sometimes in ways that surpass talent and ability. Dr. Cheeran imparts this advice to clients who come to him in such circumstances: "I tell them that happiness first demands understanding one's abilities and limits. There must be a level of aspiration that is realistic." Unrealistic aspirations, he warned, lead to unhappiness and suicide. "There are so many people these days finding it difficult to achieve their aspirations, and they feel miserable. But they shouldn't need to! Do your best and be happy with the result. If you're gazing up at the stars, just aim for the tree tops."[1]

The previous chapter explored the ways Malayalis in the capital city have made sense of suicide as the bitter fruit born of historical trajectories toward progress, development, and modernity. Many understand suicide today to be the preeminent symptom of an ailing social and political order, one that registers the failures of collective struggle in the region. In this chapter, we shift to the clinic. Here, too, suicide emerged as a problem of striving but through different modes of attention and practice on the scale of individuals and families.[2] Dr. Cheeran's comments begin to orient us toward the ways clinicians I observed scrutinized aspiration in the lives of patients and their kin to discern suicide risk. As they "read" lives for signs of false ambition, clinicians like Dr. Cheeran focused on a number of domains of everyday striving: from education and work to love and parenting.[3] These were the intimacies and projects of worth that mental health professionals assessed for their feasibility, worth, and latent perils.

Earlier, in the introduction to this book, I described the linking of suicide to aspiration that was pervasive in the capital city at the time of my fieldwork as a form of "problematization."[4] Foucault's concept highlights how an issue comes to be defined and acted upon *as* a problem of social concern. The framing of the suicide crisis as a problem of aspiration shapes how suicide is understood and experienced; it also necessitates forms of subjectivity, management, and intervention as life-and-death necessity among the living. The clinic is a rich site to explore how patients and kin are taught to live in new ways in light of this framing of the suicide crisis. Mental health professionals like Dr. Cheeran were carefully attuned to both the presence of aspiration in patient lives and the circumstances of their aspirations. They held desires up to the light, scrutinizing them and checking them against patient biographies, family situations, and social histories to separate dangerous excess from reasonable claims. But if clinical attention flowed along particular channels in the effort to prevent suicide, it often did so at the expense of other patient narratives and experiences. By examining how domains and aspects of patient and kin life are subjected to heightened scrutiny in the clinic, I also consider what may sink into invisibility and silence.

In this time of suicide, where do clinical attentions fall in determining who may reasonably aim for the stars and who should settle for the treetops? How do these evaluations take shape in the situated interactions among clinicians, patients, and kin? The "provisionality" of psychiatric diagnosis, to use Elizabeth Davis's phrase, has received significant attention in light of the epistemic ambiguities of psychiatric nosologies, a problem of knowledge recognized as a characteristic of the field more generally.[5] Anthropologists have also shown how histories and ideas of social difference shape the ways diagnosis and therapy are relationally constructed between mental health professionals and their patients.[6] In Kerala's capital city, where many psychiatrists and psychologists draw from higher status elites, the mental health encounter is a dense site to examine how ideologies and histories of social difference related to gender, community, caste, and class shape therapeutic interactions. At a time when the upwardly mobile are claiming social power through the widening field of middle-classness, gendered moralities are being reworked across transnational landscapes, and a gaping generational divide appears impassable from either side, clinical concern for suicide as a problem of striving enacts powerful cultural politics over who may rightfully aspire and to what ends. As clinicians scan patient and family histories for signs of dangerous aspiration as markers of suicide risk, they sort and stratify visions of the good life and their proper claimants. Their assessments are shaped by the particular social locations from which clinicians, patients, and family members encounter one another in the institutional setting.

While risky striving and its drawn links to suicide do often "stick" to certain bodies and experiences in the clinic, assessments of patient aspiration rarely unfold in any straightforward manner.[7] Nor do relations of power and ideas of social difference in the clinic simply manifest as the automatic effect of hierarchies of domination or institutional authority. Rather than fixed or pregiven, alignments and assumptions in the clinical encounter are shaped by moments of lived, situated interaction, moments that are often improvisational and shift precipitously in the resource and time-strapped institutional settings of mental health care in Kerala.[8] If in editorializing registers clinicians like Dr. Cheeran make broad statements about the unrealistic ambitions of Malayalis today, at the level of therapeutic practice they assess and manage the aspirational lives of clients in ways that prove far more complex and uneven.

## THE MAKING OF A CRISIS

On a busy Monday morning in the psychiatry unit of the publicly funded Central Hospital, three clinicians, together with a few nurses, were handling more than sixty client cases with sink-or-swim efficiency. Shoulder-high plywood screens demarcated Dr. Susan's door-less "office" from the adjacent waiting room. Despite the architectural gesture, the psychologist's consultation area offered little privacy. Over the course of the morning as their numbers grew, waiting patients and their family members gradually edged toward the backs of the chairs of those in consultation. As patient histories were taken and narratives of troubled relations unfolded, I watched shifting shadows of disapproval and surprise take shape on the faces of bystanders. They unabashedly listened in on the stories of confessing patients, much as if they were watching any one of the popular teleserials beamed into homes in the evening hours.

It was approaching one o'clock in the afternoon—time for the rush of exiting staff ending outpatient service hours for the day. Dr. Susan had started to pack up her things when the nurse entered with one last patient, out of breath from his sprint from the bus stop. Dressed in faded but well-kept shirt and trousers, the young man had arrived in the unit alone. In an unusual request, he asked if the three of us might move to somewhere more private. He would be able to talk more freely, he said. As Dr. Panicker had already left for the day, we shifted to the psychiatrist's office and shut the door.

"Where to begin?" asked Harish, eyes downcast. He took a deep breath. Dr. Susan encouraged him to begin with his background information. "I'm twenty-two, unmarried," he said, starting where it was easiest. As is standard practice on the unit, Dr. Susan inquired with bureaucratic directness after the young man's community and caste identity, and noted "Hindu, Ezhava" on the clean patient history sheet in front of her.[9] "Education?" she asked. Harish had ended his studies after seventh standard. "I wasn't a very good student," he said. "Family?" Father and mother were agricultural laborers; his young sister was still studying. Harish had come into the city alone on the hour-long bus ride, without his family's knowledge. It was this point made in passing, as Dr. Susan would later explain to me, which first signaled to her that something was not right. At Central Hospital where the majority of patients are brought in or accompanied by kin, Harish's arrival to the unit alone, together with his request for privacy, sparked concern that he had something to hide.

"Employment?" prompted the psychologist. His voice breaking at the edges, Harish let out that he had spent the last two years working as a construction worker in Dubai. But for reasons unspoken Harish had lost his job. Forced to return home, he had arrived in Kerala three weeks before. Dr. Susan sat up in her chair—something had caught her attention. I watched as she penned in capital letters and boxed the term "Gulf returnee" under the "Symptoms" portion of the sheet in front of her. She inquired further: what had been his mental state *(maanasikaavastha)* since coming back? Distraught over the loss of his job, Harish confessed he had turned to heavy drinking. Smiling faintly and mumbling now to his feet, he said he was in such a sorry state on his return flight from Dubai that he had boarded the plane with several duty-free cartons of cigarettes, a bottle of Black Label whiskey in his back pocket, and little else. Since returning on the first of January—a symbolic start to the new year, Harish sadly joked—he had no motivation to find work and had squandered all of his savings.

Dr. Susan's concern was visibly rising. Turning to me, the psychologist now referred to Harish's condition in English as a "crisis situation." "The patient," she pronounced with palpable urgency, "needs immediate attention." Looking confused and concerned at overhearing this aside, Harish interrupted Dr. Susan. He did not want to take medications, he told her. He feared addiction and other side effects. In a clinical setting where drug-oriented therapy is standard care, Harish's reservations offered weak deterrence.[10] As if to decelerate the conversation's driving momentum toward medication, the young man shifted his tone, assuring Dr. Susan that these were only recent developments and not typical of his nature *(swabhaavam)*. He had been happy and active during his school years, Harish insisted, forcing a smile. He had been hopeful about the prospect of working in the Gulf, and all had been going well up until recently. Dr. Susan nodded her head empathetically: "Yes, exactly. You had many high ambitions and big dreams, but now they are gone." The psychologist asked if he had had any thoughts of suicide, recently or in the past. Harish shook his head no. While he recognized himself as "depressed," using the English term, he told us plainly that he had never had thoughts of suicide.

Dr. Susan turned to Harish's family history. Did he know of any suicides or mental illness in his family? After a brief pause, he mentioned the suicide of a distant cousin several times removed on his mother's side. That had been five years ago. He hardly knew this cousin, he added, nor did he know anything about the circumstances of her death. The air of urgency that had been gradually building took a sharp turn. Dr. Susan picked up her phone. Within seconds, she had staff psychiatrist Dr. Panicker on the line. Harish and I looked at one another, confused. "There is a young man here at the hospital suffering from depression. He needs to see you immediately for medications and maybe for admission," she declared into the phone. The state of emergency was palpable. Nervous and alarmed, I looked again at Harish, who now, too, seemed frightened. Hanging up, Dr. Susan commanded Harish: "You have to take mood stabilizers immediately." Harish expressed once more his concerns about taking medications. Perhaps he could begin with counseling, he offered weakly. But the psychologist interjected, impressing upon him once again the urgency of his situation. "With counseling alone, your life will be under threat. You must immediately start with medication," she repeated, this time in English and with greater force. "You are depressed, and you are feeling this way because you have returned and because of your family history." Relenting, Harish finally agreed to allow Dr. Susan to drop him off in her car at Dr. Panicker's home and private practice.[11]

### At the Razor's Edge

Among patients seen to be riding the razor's edge between lofty dreams and drowning loss, clinicians scanned lives for sudden slips and the acute distress they implied. What they found could precipitate dramatic shifts in the clinical encounter, transmuting interview into pressing emergency, sometimes against the words and testimony of the patient. As Dr. Susan would explain to me when we debriefed the following morning, the path to action had been laid once she learned of the nature of Harish's homecoming. For Dr. Susan this premature return signaled a particular experience of "failed migration," one characterized by dashed hopes, massive loss, and the failure to fulfill the social and economic mobility expected of the "successful" Gulf migrant.[12] Dr. Susan narratively figured for me Harish's trajectory as if it were a curve plotted on a graph: rising steeply, it peaked with Harish's "high ambitions and big dreams" in the Gulf and ended in the free fall of his failed return. What we observed yesterday, she explained, was the young man hurtling to the depths of acute distress, substance use, and suicide. The final push in the making of this state of emergency came with the revelation of a suicide buried deep within the chapters of Harish's family history. The urgency of patient signs, both social and biological—first, of "failed return" and, second, of family history—set the path of clinical response as immediate drug intervention.

In the areas of both social commentary and therapeutic practice, clinicians scrutinized aspiration among Gulf migrants and their family members with particular tenacity. They often spoke of the predominantly nonelite migration to the Persian Gulf as risky business driven by false ambition. In this elite discourse, Gulf migrant laborers are seen as chancing it all by taking tremendous loans, leaving their families behind, sometimes traveling by illegal means, and risking injury, disappearance, or even death—all for questionable gain.[13] In the observations of Dr. Mary, a psychologist who has worked extensively with the children of

Gulf migrants, migrant parents leave in the name of improving their children's lives but in the end "sacrifice their children's sense of security and their mental health" by disappearing for years at a time. Powerful associations between Gulf migration and dangerous striving are evident in the catch-all term *Gulf Syndrome,* a pliable umbrella term used to capture a range of migration-related social pathologies: from the "craze" among nonelite youth to reach the Gulf at any cost, to the loneliness and mental health problems suffered by wives and children left behind, to the adjustment problems among returnees. While cast in the concerned terms of the social and psychological welfare of migrants and their families, these moralizing discourses construct "Gulf migrants," "Gulf wives," and "Gulf families" as generic categories that erase the heterogeneity of their experiences.[14]

Concern for the acute distress of patients like Harish is also shaped by the particular locations from which clinicians view the mobility of others. Dr. Susan's perceptions of the risky business of Gulf migration stood in relief against the clinician's own migration biography. From a high-status Syrian Christian family, Dr. Susan spoke often of her family members abroad. Her physician brother had settled years before with his family in California, and her first cousin had married and moved to Malaysia, offering reference points on migration as the path to permanent settlement and the united household. This family history of high-skilled professional migration diverges significantly from the nonelite, temporary contract work that characterizes much of the movement between Kerala and the Gulf. Dr. Susan's heightened concern for Harish's status as a "Gulf returnee," as she configured it in the language of the file, may have been fanned by the comparative manner in which she sees Gulf migration as an irregular, desultory, and haphazard way to make quick money—or to lose everything.

For those dwelling between Kerala and the Gulf, the challenges are indeed very real. Temporary contract labor in the Gulf can be a precarious endeavor whose stakes are high for those facing unemployment and social vulnerability at home and who wager family savings and take on heavy loans for a chance to work abroad. Facets of life and work among the millions of contract workers in the Gulf have now been documented: dangerous and exploitative labor conditions; orchestrated violence under the *kafala* sponsorship system; dynamics of class, race, and nationality that keep migrants physically and socially isolated.[15] The hardships met by both male and female migrant workers in the Gulf have gained visibility in the Kerala public sphere through media, literature, and film. Suicide among Indian migrant laborers in the Gulf is an issue of growing concern.[16] Yet for all of Dr. Susan's vigilance, on the afternoon that Harish came to the hospital, his experiences in living and working in the Gulf remained the unspoken presence at the margins of the psychologist's driving lines of inquiry. The making of the "crisis" in Harish's case did not emerge out of the complex realities of his experiences *as migrant* or as an underemployed man of lower social and class positioning more generally. It hinged most critically on Harish's "failed return" as a discrete event and clinical fact.

My point here is not to contest Dr. Susan's vigilance in this case, though it is clear that this state of emergency left little room for Harish to negotiate treatment. Rather, I wish to highlight how patient traits and fragments of experience—the fact of "failed return" and the label of "Gulf returnee"—can be reified in the clinical quest to discern suicide risk. This fractures patients' life histories and the complexities of suffering into clues and telltale signs that mystify the domain of human experience as a whole. The dangers of fracturing experience this way are great for Gulf migrants, who are already homogenized as a category in the service of pathologization and whose movement is often fragmented from the broader conditions of uncertainty at home that can make migration a project of necessity. Rather than prompting exploration into the particularities of Harish's experiences of social and economic vulnerability, including, but not limited to, his unexpected return from Dubai, the assessment of a failed return obviated further questions and made immediate action imperative. As Dr. Susan set urgently down the path of intervention, left behind was all that remained unspoken, all that lay just beyond the pale of clinical investigation.

While concerns for aspiration and drowning loss cling to Gulf migrants and their families, members of migrant households are understood to bear these vulnerabilities in different ways. For comparative contrast to Harish's story, in which clinical attention to his precipitous return made for a state of crisis, I turn to the management of striving and its consequences at the site of women's subjectivities, this time through the medium of a psychologist's advice column in a local newspaper.

*The Faustian Bargain of Transnational Households*

A thirty-seven-year-old mother of three calls herself "M.A.K." In her letter to the columnist and psychologist Dr. Sreedhar, she recounts the mental problems *(maanasika prasnangal)* she has been suffering since her husband left for the Gulf. "After he went and it suddenly fell upon me to handle everything, I suffered both mentally and physically," she writes. "Despite all this, it is me alone who must look after and raise three children. When I think about all of these problems, I get a headache and I become physically exhausted. I get into a state where I can do nothing. If my husband were here, this would distress him." In addition to having to quit the job she enjoyed as a result of the added responsibilities created by her husband's absence, there are other problems:

> When I experience any sort of stress *(maanasika sangarsham)*, I immediately leave the house and go to temple, to do some shopping, or else I will go to my sister's house. After some walking, I will find a bit of mental peace. But the neighbors gossip about my going out. Because my husband is not here, they feel that I should live simply. Everyone looks at me as if I were an indecent woman (Ellaavarum mattoru tharatthil enne veekshikkunnu). But only I understand my mental state. It is a state without my husband and in which I must bear all responsibilities. The responsibilities of caring for the children are distressing. Then there is the pain of giving up my job. Everything taken together makes for an indescribable state. I cannot look after my children's schooling or raise them well. If I control my mind to not go out and instead sit in the house, I take out all of my anger on the children. I cannot show them more love. In this mental state, what should I do to control my mind, doctor? After having studied my postgraduate and worked for 8 years, to have to sit uselessly in the house is a state that causes me incredible distress. I wait expectantly for a solution to my mental state.[17]

In response, Dr. Sreedhar reflects upon M.A.K.'s situation as a telling example of the problems he believes to be endemic to Gulf migrant families. On this topic, he has much to say. "Psychologists do not see this development to be a trivial matter," writes Dr. Sreedhar with regard to the rise of transnational households. "To move forward, a bullock cart needs two wheels. If a wheel is sold to feed the bullock, can it take the cart forward? A cart with a fed bullock and with a wheel lost can only go in circles. It can't go forward. In the case of the joint family, there were six wheels. Even if one was lost, the cart still moved forward. For the nuclear family, the only two wheels are named wife and husband." He addresses M.A.K. directly: "If one person tries to carry the burden of life which two people are meant to carry, that person will not be able to bear it. If you take on a burden you cannot bear, body and mind will tire. Expert opinion says that the absence of a life partner produces great difficulty *(budhimuttu)*." Nor will the problems that result be hers alone, warns Dr. Sreedhar. "When one person disappears to go abroad and make money, will the family chariot move forward?

Isn't the problem you are experiencing, sister, the circling of your one-wheeled family chariot?"[18]

While the psychologist blames the compromised structural integrity of the family as the proximate cause of M.A.K.'s troubles, he also makes clear that at their root is a more insidious problem: the failure among Gulf families to distinguish between true happiness and its false counterfeits. "Do we realize the truth of the fact that more money does not make for more happiness? We don't realize this," writes Dr. Sreedhar. "If we get ten rupees, we want a hundred. . . . However much we get, will man be satisfied? Contentment can no longer be defined for anyone."[19] Viewed in these terms, M.A.K.'s experiences today are the result of a poor choice made in the past, one that sacrificed at the altar of material pleasures the values of good, healthy, and happy family life. Dr. Sreedhar frames the aspirational pretensions of Gulf migrant families such as M.A.K.'s as a kind of Faustian bargain: money over love. This is a powerful and moralizing elite discourse, one that blames the poor "choice" of families and communities seeking social and economic opportunity and that obscures a dire unemployment scenario at home.

To the extent that the psychologist sees the retrieval of happiness to be possible in the Gulf migrant family, he proposes strategies to another wife of a Gulf migrant that might help to salvage flagging relationships. In response to this young wife's admission to thoughts of suicide, Dr. Sreedhar suggests that finding female friends to confide in can be healthful. "With this, stress will be reduced and your mind will feel lightened." But in the next sentence, he acknowledges these strategies carry potential problems, as they may encourage gossip or the concern of in-laws. To quell any problems resulting from "possible rumors or false comments by others" like those faced by M.A.K., Dr. Sreedhar reminds his readers that it is the duty of the conscientious Gulf wife to actively dispel worry and suspicion that can arise in a husband's mind. Thus, he advises that she report all of her day's activities and interactions in letters written nightly to her husband. This kind of transparency, says Dr. Sreedhar, is the only foolproof way to put her husband's and in-laws' doubts to rest. "From today forth, whenever you go to see the doctor troubled by illness, to do shopping, a report containing all of this information should be sent to your husband," advises Dr. Sreedhar. "There should not be any reason for your husband to have any doubt (*samsayam*) in his mind."[20]

In the medium of letters, the psychologist's attentions are of a different performative nature, therapeutic intent, and temporality from those in the institutional mental health encounter. Yet these written exchanges are still important for what they reveal about how the lives and testimonies of these women are read and evaluated. Dr. Sreedhar appears less concerned with the specific content of these letters than with the moral tale they can be made to tell. These wives speak pressingly in the language of distress and suicide, yet Dr. Sreedhar's discourse is entirely different from Dr. Susan's in the case of "failed" migrant Harish. Attention to the problem of striving does not precipitate intervention as it did for Harish but instead encourages the boundless adjustability of women, in part as the cost that those like M.A.K. must now bear for having aspired unwisely in the past. If by this account the ambitions of Gulf migrant families are ill-conceived, the path to rehabilitation is clear: wives are enjoined to reaffirm their conjugal commitment to their husbands in absentia by conscientiously dispelling fears of rogue sexuality. Classed and gendered moralities are reworked across transnational space, here in full view of distress and suicide. Salvation of minds and lives rests in the protection of female respectability as the cornerstone to the reproductive family unit and to "healthy" relations between spouses, even when miles apart. Together with Harish's case, these letters suggest the uneven manner by which the problem of striving and its psychic repercussions become visible to clinical attention in the context of transnational living.

If clinicians scrutinize with particular vigilance the aspirations of individuals and communities seen to be riding the cusp of aspiration and loss, the problem of striving proves far more ambivalent with regard to others struggling, perhaps more quietly, for a livable life. Here, we return once again to the outpatient psychiatry department at Central Hospital.

## IDEALIZATIONS OF THE CONTENTED AND INVULNERABLE POOR

The client handed over the neatly folded plastic bag previously tucked under her arm. Greeting Dr. Leela and nodding to me, she took a seat next to her husband. The plastic bag, swiftly and unceremoniously emptied onto the psychologist's desk, revealed a colorful confetti mix of handwritten doctor's notes, records, and prescriptions. Its sheer bulk told of a long patient career. Stealing sidelong glances at me, the foreign presence, the neatly dressed woman waited silently as Dr. Leela thumbed through the bag's contents and reviewed her own notes from their last consultation three weeks prior. Dr. Leela summarized for my benefit:

Chukki is a mother of two in her thirties, diagnosed with depression. Eyes now on her paperwork, the psychologist asked her patient if she had been taking her medications daily as told. Chukki nodded, and her husband confirmed. "Every day?" Dr. Leela asked again, jotting down notes. Another nod. Dr. Leela's questions were economical and symptom-focused. Had sleep improved? Any stomach upset? Chukki mentioned mild nausea. More writing.

Dr. Leela glanced at her watch. With the waiting area already standing room only despite outpatient service hours having just begun, the psychologist was on target to wrap up this case in an economical handful of minutes. But she chose instead to slow things down, noticing as she did a teaching moment emerging. Placing the therapeutic encounter on momentary hold, Dr. Leela's tone shifted to a pedagogic one, signaling that she was about to explicate an instructional case for me, the anthropologist and student. Continuing to speak in Malayalam but talking now of Chukki in the third person, Dr. Leela briefed me further on her case history. "The patient is an adivasi, a tribal woman," she began as Chukki looked on silently. "She comes from a very poor family. She has traveled a long way to see me." Chukki, Dr. Leela explained, has endured many difficulties that the psychologist now enumerated: an abusive father, an alcoholic husband, the death of a child, unsteady work. Such were her many troubles in life. What was to be learned from all this? Dr. Leela asked rhetorically, pausing for effect. In spite of the difficulties this woman has met, in spite of all the torture she has suffered over the years, "she holds on to life" (Aval jeevithatthe muruke pidikkunnu). Hers was a tenacious grip, said the psychologist, as evidenced by the client's careful adherence to her drug regimen. Smiling at Chukki with genuine praise, Dr. Leela declared, "She is a model patient."

Watching us impassively until then, Chukki interjected. Her voice tremulous, she started into a different account, explaining that on occasion she still has thoughts of suicide that will "quickly" *(pettennu)* come and go. Chukki locked eyes with me, asking with her direct gaze that I listen carefully. Though silent, I had emerged as the third-party arbitrator.[21] Now it was Dr. Leela's turn to interrupt. Turning her body squarely toward me, Dr. Leela declared that while the patient might have passing thoughts of suicide from time to time, they were only thoughts *(chinthakal)*. She would never act upon them. "Such people are like this," insisted the psychologist, switching now from Malayalam to English and gesturing at Chukki across the desk. "They possess great strength." Affirming Chukki's status as model patient once more and promising that with time such thoughts would cease with medication, Dr. Leela sent her patient off with a reminder to return in three weeks for follow-up.

By conscripting my unspoken authority as foreigner and peer and by distancing the clinical "object" with the use of English and the third person, Dr. Leela asserted a transcendent authority on the matter of suicide among "such people."[22] Rather than generating alarm, Chukki's thoughts of suicide were rendered normal psychic chatter, white noise to the background of daily suffering, harboring no significant threat. After Chukki left the unit with refilled prescriptions in hand, I asked Dr. Leela how she could have such decisive confidence about her patient's future. "This woman has to walk ten kilometers from her house every day just to get a bus to the city. These people are used to such things," she maintained. "In Kerala, we do not see suicide for trivial or impulsive reasons among poor people. They know what a hard life is. And they don't have any other high aspirations in life. Such people will use the resources they have, whether physical, mental, or biological." Dr. Leela insisted, "Rarely do these poor people commit suicide."[23]

### Immune to Desire?

As a rhetorical device, Dr. Leela's declarative faith in her patient's endurance may have had therapeutic purpose. Now as I reflect back on their consultation that morning, it occurs to me that perhaps such words were intended to "boost confidence," to use Dr. Leela's phrase, "emplotting" Chukki in a hopeful narrative structure of clinical time in the uncertain terrain of symptom management.[24] At Central Hospital, these words may have also been meant to reinforce Chukki's continued drug adherence in an institutional setting where clinicians spoke with frequent concern of "noncompliance." But when taken alongside Dr. Leela's commentary on "the poor" shared with me after Chukki's departure, such configurations of the differential vulnerability of communities to suicide as a problem of striving demand a closer look. Dr. Leela was hardly alone among mental health practitioners I met who, at least at the level of social commentary, were as quick to glorify the anti-suicidal endurance of the "the poor" as they were to attribute suicide to "the middle class." In Dr. Leela's words, "The middle class in Kerala wants to live in a better way; they have high ambitions, but they also lack economic stability and opportunity. This creates problems." By contrast, those whom Dr. Leela glossed as "the poor" were configured as free of the desires that have left their counterparts vulnerable to dashed dreams and suicide. Such assessments dovetailed with ideas about psychological durability: while mental health professionals described the middle class in Kerala today as being emotionally weak and impulsively suicidal, the poor, I was told, are fully inured to the hardships of life. As reflected by Dr. Leela's confidence in Chukki's firm grip on life, the poor persevere against hardship, inoculated by the accumulated suffering of daily life, while the middle class, in these discourses, wilts in the face of minor frustration.

In the vibrant forms of editorializing social commentary that mental health practitioners shared with me, the poor/middle class binary was the preferred screen onto which experts projected differential risk for suicide, staging the two entities as the moral inversion of each other. Although a key rubric in imaginaries of suicide as a problem of aspiration, these reified constructions of class obscure much. Discourses of the middle class versus the poor configure homogeneous and stable entities in ways that mask critical hierarchies and distinctions of caste and community within them. These discourses also tend to say far more about clinicians themselves than about any sociological phenomena they purport to describe. A well-educated professional who strongly identifies as an upper-caste Nayar, Dr. Leela projected an idealized image of poverty onto Chukki that was shaped by her social vantage point. In figuring her adivasi patient as one among a generic and undifferentiated mass of "the poor," Dr. Leela positioned Chukki as an index of the margins beyond the adulterating reach of development and globalization. While updated in the psychological language of suicide risk, Dr. Leela's idealization of the poor resonates with a Kerala model imaginary that has viewed adivasi, dalit, and coastal communities as "outliers" of a hegemonic developmental experience.[25] But rather than viewing these communities as "victims" to the development experiences of others, as they are often positioned in mainstream discourse, here the poor are to be exalted for their immunity to desire and indomitable strength. In a time of soaring aspiration and suicide, Dr. Leela extolled these communities as the last refuge against the stormy waters of global change, waters in which others are now tossed about, unmoored in their wayward pursuit of the good life. This construction of the poor not only works to justify economic vulnerability; it also erases dynamic histories of political struggle and mobilization for reform among these communities by imagining the poor as quietly reposing in the "waiting room" of development.[26] In the sphere of the therapeutic encounter, for Chukki this meant that her own disclosures of brokenness evaporated into thin air, leaving behind only the sediment of presumptive and everlasting endurance.

Sentimental visions of the contented poor depict noble poverty as the chronological antecedent and moral foil to suicide as a problem of the middle class in contemporary times. They do so in ways that not only depict the poor as good suffering subjects; they also work to erase the heterogeneous nature of the diversifying middle-class social field in Kerala, where the broadening of cultural practices and values in the constitution of middle-classness is marked by unequal access to social, cultural, and economic capital.[27] Yet if clinicians like Dr. Leela were quick to draw on this class binary in certain discursive registers like the pedagogic one performed for the foreign anthropologist, such formulations were quickly confounded by the complexities and ambivalences of the therapeutic encounter. Some, like Chukki, for instance, spoke back. They interrupted clinicians' spoken and unspoken assumptions with varying degrees of success. The ambivalence of poverty in the clinic was moreover shaped by the practical demands and stark limitations of front-line care, where therapies are drug-focused, and time and resource constraints bear heavily on clinicians' sense of efficacy.[28] In the publicly funded Central Hospital, where many patients are of the low-status working poor, ideas that poverty inoculates against suicide were quite simply impossible to square with the stories of suffering that were the tempo of the outpatient unit.

*Eating Pills to Fill the Stomach*

Consider Ambu's story. A widow in her early forties, Ambu was first brought to the unit by one of her daughters who reported that her mother had hardly slept a wink the last eight days. They had traveled over an hour by bus. After a brief visit with staff psychiatrist Dr. Panicker, Ambu was diagnosed as having an "adjustment disorder with depressed mood" and was placed on medications. Two weeks had since passed, and she had returned this morning for a follow-up with Dr. Leela, accompanied once again by her daughter. In the manner of compensatory return to patient documentation that was the result of time and staff constraints in the unit, Dr. Leela had been asked this morning by her psychiatrist superior to flesh out the patient history component of Ambu's file. With the exception of Dr. Panicker's thin scribbles, it was largely blank. Dr. Leela began by inquiring after basic patient information. She promptly noted

"SC Hindu and BPL" in the file, using the government shorthand for "scheduled caste" and "below poverty line."[29] Widowed twenty years ago, Ambu had raised her two daughters on her own. Neither was married. The dowry demands made by the families of prospective grooms were beyond reach, she said. She and her daughters made what they could as spinners doing difficult low-paid work weaving coir rope at a local factory.[30] As her daughter listened, Ambu described how they worked seven days most weeks. Even then, they were barely able to make ends meet.

Picking up on a note in Ambu's file, Dr. Leela inquired after a past suicide attempt. That had been nearly ten years ago, said Ambu. She had jumped into a well. Ambu had nearly drowned before neighbors pulled her out. At the time, she recalled, she had been kept on the psychiatry ward of a different hospital for two weeks. "Why did you do this? What was the problem?" Dr. Leela asked. All of this, Ambu explained—her past and current suffering *(sangadam)* and that of her daughters—began when she lost much of their minimal savings in what turned out to be a fraudulent insurance scheme. Pulling a handkerchief from the waist of her sari, Ambu sobbed as she recounted the loss. Nearly everything she had saved after her husband's death disappeared overnight. Although a decade had since passed, she still had trouble sleeping at night, haunted by the thought of all they had lost. Her chest felt heavy and constricted at times. There were incessant worries, too, about her unmarried daughters' futures. "What will happen to them when I am gone?" she asked Dr. Leela, gesturing at the daughter who had brought her. The psychologist reached out and patted her hand. "What happened ten years ago has happened," said Dr. Leela. "You must accept that what is lost is lost." "But what am I to do?" asked Ambu. "The pain is still here," she said, her thin hand fluttering over her chest.

Ambu wept plaintively as Dr. Leela filled out her notes. Several minutes passed with only the sound of pen scratching against paper. Then, suddenly, Ambu spoke. At times, she thinks again about ending her life, she said aloud to no one in particular. Poison, she said, leaves less room for error than jumping. Ambu's daughter stared at her hands impassively as her mother's short monologue unfolded. The psychologist looked up from her writing. With blunt reason, Dr. Leela asked, "If you commit suicide, who will take care of your daughters? You say you are worried for their future. How can you leave them behind?" "I will take them with me," responded Ambu plainly. Her daughter glanced at me. Dr. Leela sighed heavily, her frustration palpable. She turned back to her notes. Quiet blan-

keted the four of us once again. As quickly as it had surfaced, talk of suicide was drawn down into a sinking silence. Rising now from her chair,
Dr. Leela poked her head into Dr. Panicker's office just a few feet away.
From her desk, Ambu, her daughter, and I could hear nothing of what she
was saying over the hum of the waiting room. She returned quickly, sending mother and daughter into the psychiatrist's office for a medication
consultation. Five minutes later, they reappeared at the psychologist's
desk with higher-dose prescriptions for diazepam (an anxiolytic), fluoxet-
ine (an SSRI antidepressant), and amitriptyline (a tricyclic antidepressant),
in addition to prescriptions for iron pills and a vitamin tonic.

As mother and daughter prepared to leave, Dr. Leela impressed upon
Ambu the importance of taking her medicines: "You must never skip a
day." Then recruiting Ambu's daughter in the effort, Dr. Leela said,
"You must help her with this."[31] Perhaps as proxy to fill the gaping
silence just minutes before, Dr. Leela took more time than usual to
remind Ambu of the role of the drugs in her treatment. Much like dia-
betes, described Dr. Leela, "your illness can be controlled with medicines." Just as insulin is injected into the body to correct blood sugar
levels, Ambu's medications worked to help correct chemical levels in
the brain. Using another metaphor, Dr. Leela said that in the same way
that Ambu must eat food, she must also "eat" her pills (Bhakshanam
pole thanne ningal gulikakal kazhikkanam). She sent mother and
daughter off with encouraging words that Ambu's depressed mood
would soon lift. Once they left the unit, Dr. Leela threw herself back in
her chair. "Poor thing," she muttered to herself, rubbing her forehead.
At the very least, said Dr. Leela, Ambu would have her medicines supplied free by the hospital. She would otherwise be unable to afford
them. "Did you notice how I explained why it's important to take the
medicines?" she asked me. "We must put such things in their terms."
Sitting up again as a nurse shuffled in with two more patients, she said,
"Beyond this, our hands our tied. We cannot do anything for economic
problems. Even if she has no food to eat, she must eat her pills."[32]

Where does Ambu's striving for social and economic security, along
with the suicide that marks its limit, figure in this clinical field of
vision—a field that discerns pathological aspiration in different terms
among different people? Here, exclusion from a livable life cast light
onto the darkened spaces and ambivalences of this field of vision. Seeing
her hands tied in the face of problems beyond the biological, Dr. Leela
circumscribed the limits of drug therapy while asserting its proper
domain. In that moment, and as she so often did on the unit, Dr. Leela

clung to a faith of necessity that eating medicines could be enough. She sought to bring her patient into the fold of that faith, one that demanded certain silences to appear life saving. If in one register Dr. Leela upheld an idealized vision of the noble life of the happy poor, in another she defensively reserved a place for therapy "outside" the structural violence she daily encountered as she struggled to maintain a sense of efficacy as a healer. Such was the equivocal presence of grinding poverty and social isolation in the clinic.

If Chukki struggled to make her counternarrative heard against drowning assertions about the boundless endurance of the poor, Ambu's story suggests that the muting of suicide and of the struggle for a livable life among the low-status poor is multiply motivated and multiply shaped: by the relational social positioning of clinician and patient, by practical therapeutic limits, and by the precipitous ways that emotionally charged interactions shift clinical attention and concern. Much as the confessions of suicidal thoughts made sotto voce fell outside the bounds of the formal structure of patient questioning, suffering declared itself but was quietly passed over. Even when a clearing was made in spoken and unspoken assumptions about the suicidal immunity of the poor, the practical limits of the therapeutic endeavor—limited by time and resources to the administration of drugs—served to wrench the realities of poverty and social isolation from suicide. This delinking turned poverty into something else entirely, the unwieldy presence in the therapeutic encounter, for which nothing can be done but fill the empty stomach with pills.

## THE "PROBLEM" OF SUICIDAL FRAUDULENCE

For the remainder of this chapter, I shift to a second clinical site to give further empirical traction to the ways that mental health professionals scrutinized patient aspiration, this time among a different clientele from that of Central Hospital. We move now to the privately funded Trinity Hospital, where it is nearing outpatient service hours in the psychology department. Patients and kin are waiting on chairs and benches in a neat queue that snakes along a well-lit, airy, and newly renovated hallway. Compared with Central, there are far fewer patients, and more time can be dedicated to each case. While treatment regimes at Central are decidedly drug oriented, patients who come to Trinity encounter a wider range of therapeutic options, including meditation and relaxation therapy. Trinity's more affluent clientele may consult with their preferred clinician. Such was the case with Sunita and her husband, Vinay, who arrived early one January morning to see Dr. Rajendran. Their half-hour-long consultation would unfold entirely in English.

Sunita and Vinay made a handsome couple. They had come seeking the psychologist's help, they explained, impressed by a recent television appearance in which Dr. Rajendran had spoken about marital problems. The young couple had been married for three years and had one son. "Arranged or love?" asked Dr. Rajendran. Theirs had been an "arranged-love marriage," Sunita explained. They had met while studying at the same college, Sunita majoring in literature and Vinay in computer sciences. Their families had approved the match in light of their compatible backgrounds as middle-class Ezhavas. Both were employed, Sunita as an office assistant at the state electricity board and Vinay as a bank manager.

Dr. Rajendran addressed Vinay first. "What brings you here today?" "She has been saying things," responded Vinay. "She keeps saying she will kill herself." The psychologist frowned. Turning to Sunita, he encouraged her to "come out" with her troubles. "I feel he is looking at other women," said Sunita. She described Vinay's flitting gaze—"jumping from one sari to another"—when they are out in public together. "Don't you know you must only do such things when the wife is not looking?" Dr. Rajendran ribbed, elbowing Vinay. Unlike most of the psychologist's efforts to buoy his clients' spirits with humor, this one fell with a dull thud. Sunita glanced at me uncomfortably. "Say more," he commanded. "Do you generally have a feeling of insecurity?" What at first appeared an accusation quickly registered with Sunita, who acknowledged, "Yes, I have some insecurity." Articulate and adept with the language of popular psychology, she speculated to Dr. Rajendran that early childhood experiences had created in her "some feeling of deep insecurity" because "attachment was lacking from the beginning." Her father had passed away when she was a teenager; soon after her mother married again, to a man who turned out to be cruel and unkind to them both.

Vinay was sent to the waiting room so that the psychologist could speak with Sunita alone. Much as Sarah Pinto has observed in the context of north Indian psychiatry, in which clinicians discern signs of illness by evaluating women's emotions related to marriage, Dr. Rajendran listened carefully to this young wife's fears with regard to her husband: her fear that Vinay wished he had married another; her worry that affection between them had changed with the birth of their son.[33]

Sunita blamed her worsening insecurity on a joke she had overheard Vinay make to his friends the day of their wedding: "I used to want a sexy wife, but I was always afraid that some other man might come along and steal her from me. Thank God I didn't get one." The joke still "burns in my mind," said Sunita. These days, when she noticed Vinay looking at other women, it sent her spiraling. She worried about keeping his interest. Would her husband get bored with her? Were such changes normal in marriage? she asked. Dr. Rajendran smiled. "A perfect marriage is a myth," he replied. "There must be some problems, some minor quarrels. Otherwise, life would be boring." He advised, "With time, you will have to learn that life is not about getting what you want; it's about liking what you get. Especially with these love marriages these days, young women like you have sky-high expectations."

Addressing her as "daughter" and thus drawing a generational divide between them, Dr. Rajendran began to disabuse Sunita of the myth of the perfect marriage. In contrast to their parents, who coped with the challenges of their arranged marriages, he said, "girls today" fantasize that their unions of choice will be effortless and easy. "Isn't that right?" asked the psychologist, not intending a response. As an educated woman, Sunita had probably sought a marriage of choice, thinking it might give her more freedom, speculated the psychologist. And perhaps because of the lack of a strong father figure in her life, he conjectured further, she had come to project unrealistic demands and fantasies onto her husband. Dismantling ideas of companionate love as the effortless alignment of stars, Dr. Rajendran spoke "realistically" about the need to adjust in marriage, "even in chosen ones." With regard to Vinay's wandering eye, he had this to say: "You must take it with a pinch of salt. Later you may come to appreciate such things as idiosyncrasies." By Dr. Rajendran's assessment, Sunita's troubles were the fallout of striving toward an unrealistic object: the fantasy of romantic love as self-actualizing, consummate, and perfect.[34]

Sunita was then sent from the room. Speaking with Vinay alone, Dr. Rajendran inquired further into their relationship and circumstances at home. Vinay let out that Sunita was "overly controlling," preferring him to stay at home than go out with friends. Sympathies over "controlling wives" were exchanged between the men. Taking his cue from the language now circulating, Vinay confirmed that his wife was indeed "very insecure," wanting always to "hold on to him and keep him close." Dr. Rajendran assured him that the problem lay with his wife's insecurities and her false expectations regarding companionate love and marriage. "Such girls are like this today," said the psychologist. "They think love will be perfect, life happy, but that they don't understand that marriage is not like that. There must be adjustment." Dr. Rajendran reminded Vinay that adjustment in marriage required the work of both parties: "Try to understand where she is coming from." Vinay nodded his head.

Almost as an afterthought, the young man asked if he should be concerned about Sunita's "threats of suicide." "Such behaviors are meant to get your attention," said Dr. Rajendran. "I've seen this many times. Once the wife threatens suicide, the husband fears she will do it again. At least 50 percent of these women are misusing these threats. After they threaten or make an attempt, they get lots of attention, lots of undue attention. They may try to use it in all sorts of ways." He warned Vinay, "Do not run to her or coddle her when she talks that way." Issuing the same advice he gives to parents whose children threaten suicide, he counseled the young husband against indulgent responses that might lead to "positive reinforcement." Yet at the same time, he encouraged vigilance. "Keep watch of her behavior," cautioned Dr. Rajendran, "but do not coddle her."

What Dr. Rajendran proposed was a careful balance between denial and vigilance. Concerns about not "positively reinforcing" women's suicide threats were common at Trinity. On a different morning, the psychologist explained to me why women's threats had to be handled with discretion, even a healthy dose of skepticism. "Here in Kerala," he said only half-joking, "the problem of women threatening suicide looks like this: A woman will take a bottle of pills from the medicine cabinet. She may look at her husband and say, 'I'll take the pills.' She has referenced the books. She has referenced the Internet, [so] she knows that up to five is okay on an empty stomach, and with [a] full stomach, up to ten is okay. She knows that, understand? So she's looking at her husband, swallowing one pill, two pills, three. Then finally the husband stops her and says, 'Okay, okay! I'll get you that new car!'"[35]

While hyperbolic in nature, Dr. Rajendran's caricature is important for the ways it configures women's suicide threats as flagrantly fraudulent. Here, women's threats are a problem insofar as they dupe fearful husbands and generate frustrations for overworked clinicians, who must now deal with managing insincere threats alongside sincere ones. Cast in the most unflinching terms as the housewife who manipulates her husband for material gain, the clinical imaginaries presented to me configured women's threats as a classed phenomenon: little more than bourgeois melodramatics. Cynicism was voiced among mental health professionals across the gender divide. As one female social worker put it, suicide threats have become so normalized among middle-class women that they are now part of daily interaction, as common as asking, "Would you like some tea?"[36]

If at the level of social commentary clinicians expressed skepticism toward a classed rendering of female suicidal fraudulence, management of women's talk of suicide proved more complex in the therapeutic encounter. As we have already seen in the setting of Central Hospital, women's admissions to suicidal thoughts could surface then disappear from the field of clinical concern, abandoned by shifts in attention, blanketed with drugs, or silenced with ambivalence. Among the more affluent clientele at Trinity, women's suicide threats typically acquired different contours from those at Central. For clinicians like Dr. Rajendran, who calculated that at least 50 percent of these women threaten suicide as attention-seeking behavior, threats like Sunita's were apprehended through a kind of double vision characterized by denial and vigilance. Dr. Rajendran cautioned Vinay that efforts not to reinforce his wife's behavior had to be exquisitely balanced against the possibility of unintended injury or death. While positioned on the one hand as harmless theatrics, women's suicide talk was seen on the other to harbor the possibility of the accident, where even the "insincere" gesture, committed in the wrong hands lacking the technical savoir faire to fake such acts "well," could turn fatal. While walking this careful line would be Vinay's responsibility in the home, Dr. Rajendran assured the husband that with regular visits, the larger issue of Sunita's diagnosed adjustment disorder would resolve itself. Over time, said the psychologist, "I can make her understand her problems." Clinical attention to the problem of striving inhered that morning in the domain of spousal intimacy and its aspirations to ideals of conjugal love. Emotions in marriage became the site of clinical scrutiny and management, delimiting possibilities for female subjectivity, experience, and personhood, yet their drawn links to "real" suicide proved equivocal, demanding a fine balance from a both blind and ever watchful eye.[37]

### PARENTAL ASPIRATION AND SUICIDE AS TRAVELING SIGN

In assessing patient and kin aspirations and their circumstances, clinicians focused their attentions on another domain of concern: children's education. At Trinity and Central Hospitals, children were often brought in by parents concerned about poor grades and school performance. At a time when child suicide has emerged as a prominent public concern—a topic addressed in the final chapter of this book—this issue has gained visibility in public discourse and in the media in part through the figure of the child who, fearful of parental disappointment, is driven to suicide over poor grades. These concerns peak every year around the release of the Secondary School Leaving Certificate (SSLC) exam results, a time that one suicide hotline volunteer grimly named Kerala's "suicide season." Concerns about academic pressure and child suicide strongly implicate parents. In the clinic, fear of child suicide often emerged less as a problem related to the competence or abilities of the child than as a sign of the unrealistic ambitions of mothers and fathers.

Dr. Heema patted the seat of the chair closest to her. Her invitation to the esteemed location by her desk was well received by a bounding eleven-year-old, who settled in comfortably. The doctor then gestured to the parents to have a seat. I watched Dr. Heema lean over to the boy. Smiling widely, she offered him a handshake and introduced herself. He smiled and, in a barely audible whisper, introduced himself as Chandu. The psychologist patted him encouragingly on the back. She then turned her attention to the parents. It was the boy's mother who spoke first. "My son has not been studying well," said Ambika, "and his grades are suffering." As she continued, we learned that Chandu had been born with structural abnormalities in his urinary tract, causing incontinence. He had undergone three surgeries, but the problem persisted, and he continued to have to wear a pad day and night. Ambika expressed deep worry for her son's condition and suggested that it might be the reason for his troubles at school and his misbehavior at home.

After allowing Ambika to air her concerns, Dr. Heema interrupted her gently to steer the conversation back to the mother's initial concern regarding the boy's study habits. Chandu's father chimed in now, explaining that his son used to study very well and had received full marks up until fifth standard, after which his grades began to decline. In addition, the boy could become unpredictably violent at home and, more recently, toward other children at school. Most upsetting was that Chandu had been talking frequently about suicide and about hurting others. As mother and father vented their concerns to the psychologist, Chandu silently traced his fingers along the edge of the desk. But now it was the boy's turn to talk, and Dr. Heema engaged him gently. "Is it true, Chandu, that you become angry sometimes? Is it true what your mother and father have just said, that you don't like to study?" The boy shook his head no, smiling demurely at Dr. Heema's questions. Changing her tact, she smiled back at the boy. "What do you want to be when you grow up?" she asked. Chandu told her he wanted to work in the computer field. She beamed widely and offered out her hand for him to shake. "Clever boy!" she exclaimed enthusiastically. "If you work hard, you can do it!"

Dr. Heema asked the boy's parents to leave the room so that she could speak with Chandu alone. She administered a short barrage of math and reading tests. A few minutes later, the parents were called back in. Dr. Heema assured them that Chandu was "bright and normal." What concerned her were the threats he had been making against himself and others, so she began to inquire further into conditions at home. With time, most of Dr. Heema's questions came to be directed toward Ambika, who returned to the topic of her son's health. Chandu's father interrupted, declaring that his wife worried after their son unnecessarily, bathing and hand feeding him even though Chandu was fully functioning. Revelations of intimate family life, exposed to clinical scrutiny, shifted alignments between parties. Ambika glanced harshly at her husband. Dr. Heema stepped in, warning Ambika against "over-pampering," using the English term.

If Chandu was the patient when this interaction began, the vector of pathology soon shifted. Dr. Heema began aligning herself with father and son, lightly teasing Ambika that she probably followed the boy around all day long, even into the bathroom. Soon, Dr. Heema began to ask Ambika about her own mental condition. As Ambika tried to deflect the questions by returning to her concerns about Chandu's behavior, her worries with regard to her son would become the evidence for her own illness. Dr. Heema explained to Chandu's father that Ambika suffered "masked depression" (using the English term) as a result of her constant and excessive worry about their son. Ambika's husband nodded affirmatively, piling onto the growing heap of "symptoms" that his wife also got angry easily. Was that a symptom *(lakshanam)* of this masked depression? Yes, said Dr. Heema. Ambika interjected: It was her husband who was at fault. He was the one who would hit their son when he brought home low grades. He was the one who got angry. "Is this true?" Dr. Heema asked Chandu. The boy sat silent. The father countered, accusing his wife of always comparing Chandu's grades to those of his cousins. Thus ensued a parrying back and forth between husband and wife.

Dr. Heema sighed. "Parents these days," she said turning to me, straining to be heard over the rising argument, "put too much pressure on their children to be scholastic achievers. No wonder these children threaten suicide." Interrupting the feuding couple, the psychologist told mother and father not to place excessive pressure on their son with regard to school. To make a point, and as she often did when parents brought their children in for consultation, Dr. Heema inquired after Chandu's typical school-day schedule. As the parents chronicled their son's daily activities, the psychologist drew a timetable, filling in slots for school, after-school tutoring, and scheduled homework time. Done, she held it up for them to see. Thin slivers of air peeked out between large shaded boxes. "The child is not getting enough freedom at home," she declared. "The child needs more time to be a child." If Chandu's study habits and behavior were to change, Dr. Heema made clear, both parents needed to stop placing pressure on his grades, and it was up to Ambika to stop indulging her son. By the end of the session, Chandu was prescribed more time to play after school, and Ambika was sent home with a next-day appointment with the psychiatrist. Both parents were warned not to place too much academic pressure on their son.

After the family left, I mentioned to Dr. Heema my surprise at how the consultation had unfolded: that although Chandu had been brought in as the patient, it was Ambika who went home with a diagnosis. Pleased by my observation, Dr. Heema underscored the responsibility of the clinician to be able to "unmask hidden pathology" in other family members. Pointing to the parents' "excessive attention" to the boy's grades and Ambika's "overprotection," she explained that Malayali parents today have become so entangled in their children's lives that they are unable to separate their own happiness from their children's successes and failures. Parents, she insisted, have become so consummately invested in their children—in their grades, in their competitive success—that they treat them as little else than "nationalized banks." Parents deposited their own aspirations and dreams into their children in the hopes of a profitable return down the line. But in striving through their children, parents risked their own mental health and that of their children.

Striving through one's child has its costs for all involved, said the psychologist. But by Dr. Heema's account, it is mothers who are at the highest risk of taking their children's failures badly, since they are "completely wrapped up in the lives of their children." As a mother already "prone to overpampering" because of Chandu's health, Ambika appeared to the psychologist as "the kind of person who will attempt suicide," "the kind who lives and dies for her child." "But we've intervened early in this case," Dr. Heema said with optimism. Usually with patients like this, she explained, only when they break down and attempt suicide do they seek help. Suicide risk emerged here as a relational sign, traveling from son to mother. Following Chandu's suicide threats back along a trail to the parenting behaviors seen to precipitate them, Dr. Heema "unmasked" Ambika's depression and suicide risk as the complications of impracticable parental ambition.[38]

## THE DEATH OF DESIRE

One February morning Dr. Cheeran invited me to join him on his visit with a patient. She had been admitted to the intensive care unit nearly one month before. As we walked across the west wing of the hospital, the psychologist caught me up on a few bare details. "She is sixteen, from a good, middle-class Christian family. But she fell in love with a Hindu boy, a Brahmin." When her parents discovered the illicit relationship, she was badly beaten. Two days later, she attempted suicide by dousing herself with kerosene and lighting herself on fire outside her home. She was admitted with burns covering half her body. "Her name?" I asked. "Theresa." With only this and her brief history to prepare myself, Dr. Cheeran and I entered a brightly lit room at the end of the hallway. A middle-aged man, reclining on the cot in the far corner of the room, shook off his nap. He stood to shake the psychologist's hand. A woman, her face drawn with sleepless nights, stood like a sentinel on the other side of the door. Dr. Cheeran asked Theresa's parents to leave the room so that he and I might visit with her alone.

Theresa was propped up on a cot by the open window, the flowered curtain billowing softly behind her. Wrapped in white gauze, her thin legs hung listlessly over the side of the bed. What remained of the young woman's hair had been tied back with a blue ribbon. Blood spotted the bleached white hospital sheets. Around Theresa's torso, a cotton cloth had been tied lightly around her upper body, her exposed neck like dried, broken earth. Dr. Cheeran introduced us. I was grateful for his composure. He asked how she was doing, smiling at her with kind eyes, his hand alighting softly on a covered arm. I winced. Theresa angled her head toward Dr. Cheeran. She had been waiting all morning for him, she said with urgency, skipping past his question. "I want to confess my sins," she said (Enikku ente paapangal ettu parayanam).

The young woman began to speak to Dr. Cheeran in the mode of confession: "In the past, I made a mistake. I loved a boy. I told many lies to my mother and father. I love my mother and father so much." She wept, her body racked with the pain of tremulous sobs. "It's not wrong for boys and girls to love one another," Dr. Cheeran reminded her in consolation, "but one must be the right age to be able to make such a mature decision correctly." One's desires should not contravene parents' wishes, he explained. In a manner ever more desperate, Theresa proclaimed again and again her love for her parents, while renouncing the boy she once loved. "Receiving" these confessions, Dr. Cheeran assured Theresa that God had surely heard her and would forgive her for what she had done. Sobbing, Theresa nodded her head. He asked her who would be able to help her get through this. "God and God alone," she said.[39]

Clinical excursions into the lives of patients scrutinize the many ways and sites in which people strive in their everyday lives: for love, for social and economic mobility, for their children's future security, for a livable life. Such were the many objects to which patients and kin oriented their lives in the pursuit of visions of the good. As clinicians evaluated aspirations, they made aspects of social life into sites of intervention, while clouding other experiences and violence within and outside the family. Some, like Theresa, yearned in ways that contravened the prohibitions of family and at the cost of staggering violence. In its wake, the management of life occurred once more through the domain of striving, this time exchanging the unsanctioned object of love for a new struggle for forgiveness in the eyes of God and family. But if Theresa's spoken sacrament and quest for redemption kept her in this world, they also make tragically clear that rejection, violence, and social death are all markers along suicide's path.

# 3

# Tales the Dead Are Made to Tell

A chime interrupted my sweep of the online news. It was a chat message received in real time on my laptop in California from a friend in Attingal, an hour outside Thiruvananthapuram. From the Internet café where he would while away the evening hours, Fayaz passed along casual updates about mutual friends: the upcoming marriage of one, the bid for a job in Abu Dhabi by another, and the recent birth of a healthy baby girl to a third. We were exchanging good-byes when he remembered why he had contacted me that evening. As part of his volunteered effort to forward news relevant to my research, Fayaz shared this account with me:

> *Fayaz:* I just heard that a young man killed himself. His mother refused to buy him a [motor]bike so he hanged himself.
>
> *JC:* How do you know this?
>
> *Fayaz:* It only happened a few hours ago. The police have just now gone to investigate. Many people have been talking about it.

I pressed my friend to explain further. Whom did he hear this news from? How did he know why this young man had killed himself, even before the police had started their investigation? Fayaz's response, laced with a hint of impatience at my apparent slowness, was simple enough: "Everyone has been talking about it." With his news delivered, he signed off.[1]

The exchange troubled me. Although I appreciated the sincerity of Fayaz's volunteered efforts, I was also disquieted by the way news of death had been sent through the ether as "yet another" datum point for the anthropologist. It appeared so easy—a young man's life and death, collapsed into a neat cause-effect equation, as if one sentence about thwarted desire contained all there was to know. And what of the young man's surviving family? What might such a tale mean for loved ones absent from this account of violence but for an act of refusal? How were memories and intimacies among kin rewritten in the public circulation of this tale of suicide?

We saw in the previous chapter how in the mental health care encounter, clinicians scrutinize the aspirational struggles in the lives of patients and kin in the pursuit to discern suicide risk. Clinicians evaluate domains like work, education, love, and parenting, assessing them for their feasibility and latent perils. In this chapter, we move out of the clinic but carry forth these concerns. We consider how the lives, deaths, and bodies of the deceased are read for signs of false ambition and risky desire, this time in the speculative tales and rumors told by the living.

During the time of my fieldwork, cases of suicide in the capital city generated steady streams of conversation, commentary, and rumor that were overwhelmingly social in nature. Just as Fayaz linked a young man's death to unsated adolescent consumption, casual commentators spoke less in the medicalized terms of aberrant neurochemistries or psychiatric illness than in the language of desire, deservedness, miscalculation, and loss. Stories of suicide were often reflections on the social dimensions of aspiration in new landscapes of risk, desire, and possibility in the liberalizing present.[2] They warned and instructed listeners against unscrupulous wagers—of hope, money, time, love—and the isolation and loss that trail close by. They served, in this sense, as morality tales, turning the dead into examples of what can go wrong at a time when gains and losses are steep. Stories and rumors of suicide judged the living, too. More than cautioning against the perilous investments of the departed alone, suicide commentaries spun outward to implicate the deceased person's social web. They often served as broader accusations about deficient love, poor care, and negligence that blamed inattentive parents, callous daughters-in-law, scornful lovers, and failed families. In this sense at least, the "problem" of aspiration was not the individual's alone but was shared across people and institutions. This meant that rumors and tales of suicide impinged on the living and on the capacities of surviving kin to inhabit the present.

My objective in this chapter is not to discern one "true" story from the haze that enveloped deaths like the one reported by Fayaz, searching for truth in the vein of a psychiatric autopsy. Nor is it to ask, "What *really* happened?" as if the answers are reposing somewhere, waiting to be found. These are ontological questions of a different sort from my own. I am concerned instead with how death and its uncertainties alter the ways people live and live with one another. I attend in particular to how rumors and speculative accounts act upon the capacities of kin survivors to engage the everyday present in the wake of loss. Following the work of Veena Das, ethnography here is not about an originary moment of violence so much as it is a listening for how loved ones live or fail to live in terrain overgrown with the easy speculation, poisonous cynicism, and accusations of others.[3] In their search for meaning and some sense of closure, the kin survivors I spoke with drew on different resources, forms of capital, and fluencies to resist, navigate, or strategically deploy bureaucratic and social knowledge of suicide as they sought to forward their own accounts. Called upon, often forcefully, to speak with and against stories about loved ones that were not their own stories, they labored in mourning to reclaim the integrity of the remembered past.

### INDIVIDUAL DEATH, SOCIAL PATHOLOGY

Fayaz's transmission provoked for me an uncanny moment of déjà vu in a manner that is telling. The story sounded so immanently familiar that for a passing moment I imagined I had already heard it from someone else. In fact, it was only that this account—that of an adolescent driven to death by unfulfilled consumer demands—reiterated a formulaic script of suicide with which I was already well acquainted. Fayaz's account was interchangeable with any number of identical ones I had heard in conversation and read in the papers, the only variant being that the noun *motorbike* might have been substituted with *sneakers* or *mobile phone.*

During the time of my fieldwork in the capital city, the impulsive, consumer-oriented child/adolescent was a highly visible archetype in media accounts of suicide and in the voluminous talk, speculation, and rumor that reported suicides generated in my neighborhood. This archetype kept company with others, as revealed by a sampling of newspaper headlines: "Man Driven to Debt Kills Himself and Family," "Medical

Student Commits Suicide from Stress," "Housewife Drinks Poison over Jealousy." Twinned to proximate cause and well-publicized through the mass media and other channels, suicide archetypes such as these circulate widely as cultural shorthand for perceived patterns of social decay. They both shape and are shaped by popular meaning around suicide and by the social and bureaucratic categories by which suicide is enumerated and reported. As such, these archetypes must be understood as well-circulated and overdetermined categories that have acquired a social life of their own rather than as straightforward indicators of epidemiological trends.[4] Each archetype sublimates particular fears about how misapprehended personal and collective struggles for "good" living in Kerala's postcolonial present have thrown social life out of joint in ways that court disappointment and death.

Archetypes such as these condense questions about striving that leap scales. In media and popular discourse, they mediate concerns between individual quests for visions of the good life and broader historical struggles for objects of development and progress. If they prompt scrutiny of how the individual lived life, they also generate evaluations of the social institutions of family, education, and work to which the individual belonged and the regional, national, and global trajectories that in turn produced these institutions. Embedded in Fayaz's account of a young man's suicide, for instance, are widely circulated issues of public concern, including the "disease" of consumerism among youth, defective nuclear families built on immediate gratification, and the wider moral and cultural perils of consumption in Kerala's liberalizing present.

In media accounts and in speculative tales I heard circulate in my neighborhood, individual suicides were commonly subjected to social amplification. Suicide was often read as a morality tale located on the broad scales of social pathology in a manner that pushed and molded the individual case to fit—and thus to stand for—aggregate trends at the level of populations. A suicide could thus become metonymic of ideas and categories of collective decline. This produces a circularity between different scalar phenomena: population trends inform the ways a suicide is read, and the individual case in turn serves as further evidence of the pattern for which it is taken to stand. This is a circularity that Annemarie Mol terms "mutual inclusion," in which "the elements create the aggregate and the aggregate informs the elements." Individuals and populations, notes Mol, "may get trapped in a circularity. They may loop. And spiral."[5] In Thiruvananthapuram, the circularity between individual and population meant that oftentimes casual commentators focused less on the particular details of the deceased person's life history than on the found body's fit with demographic patterns of suicide such as age, gender, method, and site. They did so in ways that sorted bodies, lives, and deaths into predetermined categories.

Among casual onlookers, this feedback loop between individual and population can make a suicide event appear familiar and self-evident. Sometimes on the basis of reported age group, gender, and location alone, the found body seems to testify to its own condition and reason for being. In this way, narratives and emotional reactions to suicide often flow from what seemed to be the events themselves. For Fayaz, a young man found dead in the home looked like "yet another" victim of the disease of consumerism; for others discussed in this chapter, a young man found by the railway tracks "always" meant a failed love affair. Charles Briggs describes this phenomenon as the agency of dead bodies "to 'speak' to discrete acts of violence and their motivations, where corpses can be their own discursive agents." He writes, "Their tales seem to unfold automatically once the proper human interlocutor is listening."[6] But a form of mystification is at work here. With respect to the suicide case in Thiruvananthapuram, the story of what happened may appear to follow automatically from the body itself and from an originary event. Yet it derives in fact from the ideologically weighted investigative practices, narrative accounts, and categories of enumeration of police, medical examiners, and journalists. Moreover, the facts the dead appear to tell with self-evidence—gender, sexuality, age, group, location, method of suicide—are themselves interpretive artifacts linked in chains of signification, produced and circulated across expert, media, and popular discourse. Often, these "facts" are read by casual commentators in ways that openly conflict with the accounts put forward by surviving kin.

The metonymy between individual case and population trend in interpretations of suicide is produced and sustained by diverse material practices, only some of which I endeavor to touch upon here. As mentioned earlier, the generic archetypes that populate the media—the forlorn housewife, the failed student, the impulsive child, the scorned lover—reinforce this metonymy. This looping effect must also be situated more broadly within colonial and postcolonial histories in the conception of suicide as a population concern. In India, suicide became "legible" to the state as a barometer of social health, to be regulated and controlled through technologies of taxonomic knowledge and record keeping initiated under British rule.[7] The quest for the predictable causes of suicide has its roots in what Ian Hacking has called the "avalanche of printed numbers" through which people and society came to be enumerated beginning in early nineteenth-century Europe.[8] Hacking explains that sovereign rule, once conceptualized around the maintenance of physical boundaries and territories, was transformed through enumerative technologies that enabled the control and management of subject populations and their behaviors. Numerical data served as the raw material for statistical laws of probability that were seen to govern societies in a manner analogous to the laws of nature. Statistics opened possibilities for social reform, and many of the first law-like statistical regularities to emerge were connected to deviancy: crime, vagrancy, madness, prostitution, disease, and suicide, the last commanding particular esteem as a barometer of social health. The enumeration and classification of suicide by proximate cause and other demographic markers enabled the ontological sleight of hand that transformed suicide from individual exception to controllable social reality.[9]

Numbers were central to the governance of populations in the empire abroad.[10] Colonial statistics, produced in negotiation with native elite concerns, sought to render indigenous realities calculable and thus reformable. In postcolonial India, crime statistics and bureaucratic categories continue to play an important role in framing legal, medical, journalistic, and vernacular accounts of suicide and its motivations. Suicide is categorized, enumerated, and made legible to the state through the First Information Report (FIR), the document prepared by police that summarizes investigation and autopsy findings. Every reported suicide in Kerala, as elsewhere in India, is assigned to one of twenty-six mutually exclusive categories of "suicide causes."[11] Suicide data is also broken out by parameters such as gender, age group, method of suicide, marital status, and educational level. Colonial and postcolonial enumeration and classification have therefore been critical to the visibility of suicide as a criminal offense and a social pathology.

State classification of suicide is also intertwined with the development of allopathic psychiatry in India. Michael Nunley has argued that psychiatry in India tends to favor what he calls an "epidemic view" of illness, one that accords with colonial and postcolonial histories of allopathic medicine.[12] Given that in India allopathic medicine registered its most visible successes in mass campaigns against infectious diseases, it follows, argues Nunley, that psychiatry would conceive of and act upon illness in similar public health terms. The comments I heard made by a senior psychiatrist at a state-sponsored suicide prevention workshop are illustrative. During the inauguration of the day's event, this psychiatrist called upon the state government to address suicide as Kerala's most pressing public health issue of the day—an epidemic that had come to replace "earlier epidemics of water-borne diseases like cholera."[13] Nunley argues that this epidemic view in Indian psychiatry supports the intensive use of psychopharmaceuticals. The heavy reliance on drugs that can be dispensed easily and widely is both a product of the framing of mental illness as a population concern and further reinforces that framing. Consider how one psychiatrist offhandedly commented to me that the quickest solution to Kerala's suicides would be to pour antidepressants into the water supply.[14] The importance of social interpretations of suicide in Kerala is not at odds with the use of pharmaceuticals, as we saw in the previous chapter. Indeed, social interpretations can strongly align with what Andrew Lakoff has called the "medicalization of social disorder," whereby framing suicide in terms of a social epidemic does not discourage the use of pharmaceuticals so much as endorse their broad application.[15] Synergy between postcolonial histories of state classification and psychiatry's public health orientation encourages understandings and treatment of suicide as a population concern.

What I have laid out here is only a preliminary archaeological foray into the sociomaterial practices that sustain the tight bundling of the individual and the social with regard to suicide.[16] Moreover, this brief discussion is not to argue that speculative tales about the dead unfold automatically from particular state categories or media archetypes. Categories of suicide differ depending on the commentator's social location and lived relationship to suicide. The hegemony of these categories within the popular imaginary also requires continual maintenance, as these categories are not static but instead shift in accordance with changing popular meaning, social knowledge, and moral anxieties. My point, then, is only to suggest that multiple forms of knowledge and practice encourage the easy metonymy between the individual and the social in the tales the living tell about the dead. What follows from this is a greater concern that drives the remainder of this chapter. While the dead are made to tell morality tales about misperceived objects of individual and collective struggle in these anxious times in Kerala, these narratives mystify the complexities of suffering and experience. They also charge surviving kin with the weighty task of speaking back to the assumptions of others in the overlapping spaces of mourning, rumor, allegation, and secrecy.

## AJITH'S MEMO

When Ajith and I were first introduced, he had recently returned to Kerala from New Delhi to facilitate ongoing investigations into his nephew's death. He was put in contact with me by a mutual colleague—a priest I had come to know through his work as a family counselor—who had assured Ajith that the foreign researcher studying suicide would be able to decipher if the circumstances surrounding his nephew's mysterious death pointed to suicide, murder, or accidental death. That Sunday morning I met Ajith in the entrance hallway of Father Mathew's church. It was only then that I learned of the ill-conceived hope motivating our introduction and took up the unhappy job of explaining to Ajith that this was something I was neither trained nor able to do. Yet even after explaining to him the modest objectives of my project, he entrusted me with an account of his nephew's death, in part, he said, to further my research and so that I might relay the facts to any experts willing to help. As we pulled two plastic chairs off into the far corner of the hallway to sit more comfortably, the wooden doors to the chapel shut with a sonorous thud behind the last of the morning mass stragglers. Ajith took this as his cue that we were alone to speak in privacy.

Ajith explained that a few weeks earlier, just before college graduation, his twenty-one-year-old nephew, Biju, had been found dead in his room at a men's hostel. According to police and postmortem reports, Biju had first slashed his arms and wrists multiple times, after which he had attempted to electrocute himself at the sink in the corner of the room. Both of those attempts had failed. But when friends eventually broke down the door to his room, they found him hanging from the ceiling fan.

Ajith initially referred to his nephew's death as a suicide. As he proceeded further into a tangled web of troubling details, he tacked seamlessly back and forth between calling the death a "suicide," a "murder," and a "suicide-murder." He spoke with staid composure, picking out a careful but tentative path through the confusing bramble of clues and leads. Highlighting certain details, cautiously bracketing others, and affirming those he knew to be simple fact, Ajith drew on various kinds of evidence and forms of knowledge, moving between intimate reflections about the nephew he knew and deeply loved and the language of experts. He used the technical English terms *material evidence* and *traces* when explaining to me the medical examiner and police reports' conclusion that Biju had made all three "attempts" within the span of less than an hour. The unspoken weight of this thought silenced us both. From upstairs, Father Mathew's sober refrains reverberated down into the empty hallway where we sat. Collecting himself, Ajith spoke again. Breaking from the earlier script of technical minutiae, Ajith admitted that the evidence put forth by the police investigation and postmortem were simply incomprehensible in light of the nephew he knew—happy, good-looking, with a supportive and loving family and a bright future that included employment after graduation. How could Biju have ever done this to himself? Ajith asked searchingly.

Exhaustion laced his face. Two weeks after Biju's death, the police and medical investigations had not decisively concluded if the death had been a suicide or a homicide framed to look like a suicide—only that the proximate cause had been "death by hanging." Ajith conjectured that the ruling political party might have pressured investigating police officers to manipulate or silence findings. With assembly elections around the corner, news of a student death might be used for political leverage by the opposition party. Ajith's concern was stoked by the highly politicized and publicized suicide of the university student Rajani Anand in 2004, which had sparked days-long protests that brought cities around the state to a standstill.[17] The lack of closure around Biju's death had led family to send Ajith to Thiruvananthapuram to collect more information from friends and mental health professionals willing to help. To facilitate the effort, Ajith had collaborated with two other relatives to produce a carefully crafted memo that summarized the case evidence, a copy of which he produced from his back pocket that morning for us to look over. Although Ajith sought new leads not yet pursued, the memo remained faithful to the police and medical reports, replicating their categories and interpretive frameworks.

Written in Malayalam with English phrases scattered throughout, the memo was organized into three sections: Academic, Financial, and Physical. The first stipulated in detail Biju's solid academic record as an engineering student. A copy of the young man's résumé and proof of his high grades were attached for corroboration. This was not a boy who had struggled academically in a field that had been his parents' choice, the memo emphasized, heading off assumptions about student suicide. Biju had not recently failed any exams. He had also had a good starter job lined up after graduation, its salary details provided. By these accounts, Biju's aspirations in the realms of education and employment had been achieved. It could therefore be concluded, said the memo, that nothing academic or work-related would have motivated suicide. The second section provided a similar inventory of points, this time related to Biju's financial situation. Describing the young man's family as middle-class Nayars, the memo included a copy of Biju's most recent bank statement substantiating the several thousand rupees available in his ATM account on the day he died. Biju had received a monthly allowance from his parents and never went without necessities. Yet neither was he a "spoiled" child, the memo made a point to state, discrediting reader suspicions and popular knowledge about consumer-avid, emotionally impulsive youth. Unlike the young man in Fayaz's account with which this chapter opened, the implication here was that Biju was not a child prone to impulsive acts related to consumption. In the financial and material realm, Biju was neither in need nor in excess. Taken together, summarized the memo, these facts were sufficient to rule out suicide related to financial status.

The final section of the memo focused on Biju's physical qualities. Fair in color, tall, and handsome, the young man would not likely have had any "confidence issues" with respect to his looks, it stood to reason. In its now established pattern, the memo once again headed off reader assumptions about male youth suicide by discreetly pointing out that while Biju had been well liked at school, he was not known as a "womanizer" or to have been involved in "love affairs" of any kind. The memo mentioned that Biju had suffered from a chronic skin allergy but had been responding well to homeopathic treatment. The boy, therefore, could not have been prey to "low self-esteem," expressed with the English term. In sum, there had been no social or economic status difficulties, no academic problems, no employment problems, and no love affair to speak of. By this account, too, Biju had been innocent of the risks of false ambition. This was a young man who had been competent, realistic, and confident across all domains of aspiration. Biju's death, concluded the memo, must therefore have been a homicide, framed to look like a suicide. It ended with a request that any information that might lead to the capture of Biju's murderer be forwarded directly to the family.[18]

Ajith's ability to navigate around the politically sensitive nature of Biju's death in the midst of election fever in the state suggests the forms of social capital this family was able to leverage to launch a parallel investigation. Thoughtfully crafted by Ajith and his relatives, the memo demonstrates how the educated elite are able to effectively deploy bureaucratic categories, expert languages, and popular archetypes of suicide, here to mobilize the help of experts and others. The family's second-nature fluency in the bureaucratic language of suicide was most apparent in the tacit logic that delivered the memo to its conclusion of homicide. This logic was rooted in the memo's organizational categories (Academic, Financial, and Physical) and in the proximate causes of suicide familiar to the memo's writers and, presumably, to its intended audience. In carrying over police and medical findings, Ajith's memo was strikingly consistent with the causes by which the state classifies reported suicides. The reasons for suicide that the memo systematically ruled out—academic difficulty, financial trouble, low self-esteem, and illicit relations—neatly align with four reasons among the twenty-four specified by the state: namely, "failure in examination," "bankruptcy or sudden change in economic status," "chronic illness," and "failed love affair." In its preemptive manner, the memo also anticipated and systematically dismissed "preferred readings" about the nature of young men's suicide in contemporary Kerala—assumptions about wayward material desire, thwarted educational ambition, and imprudent love affairs.[19] Through their fluency in social knowledge and popular meaning around suicide, the writers of the memo sought to channel readings of Biju's death in alternate directions.

Dictated by the categories of bureaucratic and popular knowledge, the memo was also striking for how it projected its tacit logic as adequate to the complexities of human experience and suffering. For what made the categorical disqualification of suicide possible at the end of the memo was a distinct form of deductive reasoning. Here, the systematic elimination of "all" the reasons why a young unmarried man would end his life became sufficient to the task of ruling out suicide. By disqualifying the young man, point by point, from membership in broad patterns of suicidal motivation among his demographic, the memo ostensibly ruled out Biju's death as a suicide. Thus, while it was purportedly about Biju, framed in social epidemiological terms, the memo was more precisely about a young man *like* Biju. Its carefully crafted argument unfolded less from the specificity of biographical details than from the dictates of bureaucratic categories and popular archetypes. When the personal details of this young man's life did emerge, they did so strictly as forms of evidence that placed Biju outside the trends among the aggregate of young men of which he was taken to be a part.

In spite of the conviction expressed in the memo, Ajith's continued struggle to make sense of his nephew's violent death was painfully apparent the Sunday morning we met. Upon Ajith's request that I seek the input of local mental health professionals, I shared the memo with

Dr. Fathima, a psychologist and trusted mentor. Scanning through the memo between client appointments one morning, her affirming nods suggesting its logic made intuitive sense, Dr. Fathima looked up at me suddenly. "It was drugs," she declared with staid certainty, setting the memo down on the table. Case closed. How did she know? "Because he was an engineering student," she stated simply. I looked at her confused, and she released a mild sigh. With the privatization of higher education and well-off parents now able to "buy" admission to prestigious medical and engineering programs, often against the wishes and abilities of their children, substance abuse and suicide were naturally on the rise among this population, Dr. Fathima explained.[20] Drawing on a widely circulated and publicized discourse about student suicide and parental pressure, Dr. Fathima accounted for Biju's death through a familiar narrative of parental aspiration, a phenomenon she framed as a wider social problem linked to the privatization of education in the state. The young man's multiple and consecutive attempts were consistent with the suicidal behavior of those who are high or under the influence, she continued. When I pointed out that the postmortem report indicated no presence of drugs or alcohol and that the family insisted Biju had chosen engineering for himself and had been a bright, happy student, she reminded me in a disabusing tone that official reports could not be trusted. Families, said Dr. Fathima, particularly high-status families like this one, often pay the police to conceal, expunge, or modify findings. This family, she said with a pitying look, has not told you the whole story.[21]

The familiarity and self-evidence with which Biju's death appeared to Dr. Fathima as "yet another" in a rising trend of student suicides illustrate the logic that Mol calls "mutual inclusion," introduced earlier. This is a logic wherein "a population is an aggregate of events that happen to individuals. But the events that happen to individuals are in their turn informed by the framing of the population they belong to."[22] The "whole" informs the individual element, and the individual element in turn becomes emblematic and further evidence of the whole. Dr. Fathima fit Biju's death into a preconceived category of suicide as a problem of parental aspiration, a category that has been widely publicized in the media and has acquired a social and political life of its own. This classed rendering of the suicidal student was widely discussed in mental health awareness programs that I attended in the city and has been politicized in the media and elsewhere among those critical of the privatization of higher education in Kerala's liberalization period. In "recognizing" Biju's suicide, Dr. Fathima fractured the young man's life and death into distinct clues and telltale signs. Read as a set of case attributes—young, male, middle-class, and engineering student—Biju in turn reinforced the suicide category for which he was taken to stand. The young man's apparent fit with a profile readily familiar to the psychologist, coupled with suspicion of manipulated evidence, was adequate for her to consummately disqualify all other details and family truths so painstakingly compiled in the memo. It obviated the need to know more or otherwise. For some like Dr. Fathima, this "fit" is the kind of knowledge of suicide that, at times, is knowledge enough.

Together, Ajith's memo and its easy dismissal by Dr. Fathima highlight the tacit ways that bureaucratic and clinical categories, expert languages, and social knowledge are used to decipher suicide as a problem of aspiration. These readings can easily conflict with one another, shaped as they are by the particular locations from which accounts of the dead are told. They also illustrate how educated elites draw on the languages and categories of suicide for different ends—for Dr. Fathima, to aid a family's pursuit of truth and to demonstrate her own diagnostic acumen; for Ajith, to mobilize the support of experts toward some sense of closure.

I turn now to the story of Kanthamma to further explore how those fluent in the bureaucratic categories and social knowledge of suicide are able to anticipate rumors and assumptions in order to strategically assert their own narratives. The final testimony of a dying woman, issued to pointedly refute suspicions of family abuse, illustrates some of the dominant social interpretations and legal implications of women's suicide in this context. Through the story of Kanthamma and her daughter-in-law Prema, I explore one family's efforts to defuse incriminating accusations that circulated in the wake of death, accusations that linked suicide to ill-conceived individual and collective struggles for the good life.

## KANTHAMMA'S TESTAMENT

As liquid beams of soft afternoon light streamed in through the curtained windows of her living room, Prema pointed to the large framed photograph of her mother-in-law hanging above the television set. She spoke of how beautiful Kanthamma had been: fair complexioned, with long, ink black hair (later regularly dyed with Black Rose powder, Prema whispered in confession, but beautiful nonetheless). She had also been generously kind. Gazing through the lens of her own marriage, Prema recalled how patiently her mother-in-law had taught her how to cook and manage the housework. She remembered with a smile how Kanthamma would greet her granddaughter at the doorway every afternoon when she came home from school, an apple outstretched in the palm of her hand.

It was eight years ago when Kanthamma, recently widowed, began talking about and planning her death. As Kanthamma's asthma worsened, causing her chronic discomfort, Prema took her mother-in-law's passing remarks about death as the customary discourse of an aging widow in the dusk of life—nothing to warrant action. Reflecting back upon the weeks before Kanthamma's attempt on her life, Prema recalled how no one in the family had expected what they would later find was unfolding. Kanthamma had purchased and hidden away a bottle of kerosene and a box of matches and had detailed in her diary her plans to free her family from the burden of her care.

The day Kanthamma died, Prema recalled, she and her husband, Manoj, were taking an afternoon nap in the living room. At the time, Manoj's brother and his wife were visiting from Dubai. Prema's daughter had just returned from school and was playing in her bedroom. Suffering from a bad cold at the time, Prema had taken a pill that put her into a deep sleep. After some time she roused, groggy from the medication. "I noticed a strange smell. And a tremendous breeze. A strange smell," Prema recalled. "When I checked inside the house, when I looked inside Mother's room, I didn't see her. I turned and looked out to the back of the house." Out in the yard, Prema saw what she thought was a man lying motionless on the ground. Had another roaming drunk opened their gate and stumbled into their yard? she wondered. She paused, looking more carefully this time. Prema's fears began to rise. Desperately, she began crying out for Kanthamma, checking again for her in the bedroom. Kanthamma was not there. "When I looked out in the back of the house again, my God—it wasn't a man," Prema recounted, her voice tremulous. "Her hair had burnt away."

Kanthamma was rushed to the government hospital with extensive third-degree burns. Prema recounted how the police came to interview Kanthamma in the hospital:

> *Prema:* The police came and questioned Mother. They made the rest of us all leave the room. The doctors, too, were sent out. Manoj, Manoj's brother—everyone was sent out. They asked Mother, "Why did you do this?" Mother said, "I want to die. I have a terrible illness."

*JC:* She told this to the police?

*Prema:* Yes, she told this to the police. I remember it well. I have a good memory. "I want to die." And also, "I have a terrible illness, really terrible asthma. If I lie here in bed like this, it's a great burden on my children. That's why I've done this to myself. My children—no one has done this to me. That's why you must not do anything to any of them," she said. So they immediately wrote all of this down. "All right," they said. The doctors, Manoj, all of us were brought back into the room. Then she said to Manoj, "My son, don't worry." Manoj really loved his mother. She said to Manoj, "Son, don't worry. It's because I couldn't bear it anymore that I did this. I am going to die."

Kanthamma passed away later that night.

Kanthamma's final testament was Prema's echoing refrain the afternoon we spoke. As a recorded declaration of her family's innocence, Kanthamma's testament points to the ways female suicide and self-injury in this context are taken to be intimately linked to, if not synonymous with, kin abuse or neglect.[23] In the Indian legal context, the so-called dowry death laws, for instance, raise the presumption of the husband's or the in-laws' abetment of a woman's suicide, particularly if it occurs soon after marriage.[24] In prompting overdetermined narratives about causality and female suffering in the home, legal, medical, and social techniques of investigation may in turn valorize suicide as an act of testimony for women. The equivalence between female suicide and kin violence may therefore encourage what Anne Waters, borrowing from Foucault, has called an "incitement to suicide."[25]

Fears that family survivors will stand accused in the wake of female suicide are very real. Kanthamma's death was no exception. To deflect police suspicions of abuse, Kanthamma made an explicit statement of her family's innocence. She directed the police to further evidence that might release her family from blame: the diary locked in the drawer of her bedside table at home extensively documented her suffering from asthma. Over time, Prema, too, had learned how to narrate Kanthamma's story and suffering to defuse spoken and unspoken suspicions of foul play. Citing her mother-in-law's dying words in first-person voice and authorizing her recall with declarations of steadfast memory ("I remember it well; I have a good memory"), Prema channeled the official voice of testimony to assert the family's innocence. "They [the police] wanted to open a full investigation, but Mother's words in her testimony were given utmost importance," Prema reminded me several times the afternoon we spoke. "What Mother said was simply this: 'I have done this myself. None of my children knew about it. They were sleeping. At the time my little granddaughter had just come home from school. After seeing my granddaughter, I did this.' That is what Mother told the police."[26]

### Rumors of What "Really" Happened

Ultimately, no police investigation was launched. Even then, rumors abounded in Prema's neighborhood. Gossip in the wake of Kanthamma's death invoked the specter of defective domesticities in the form of dispossessed elderly. An elderly woman's immolation may engender suspicion of kin for directly or indirectly precipitating death, suspicion that can be particularly incriminating for the daughter-in-law, who is said to return upon her mother-in-law the cruelties suffered as a young wife. Prema got wind of rumors circulating in the weeks after Kanthamma's death. She placed the blame for these rumors on the domestic workers who travel in daily from the outskirts of the city to clean and cook in the homes of her middle-class neighborhood. "We told everyone [what had happened]. But for some people around here, well, actually, mostly just those very *low-class people,* those domestic servants who come for housework—when a suicide like this happens, all of them say, 'My God! That's how she died! They killed her!' That's what they say." Such rumors reveal the fault lines along which social interpretations of suicide are produced and circulate. For Prema, gossip about Kanthamma's death emerged not from the specific details about her family—there were no incriminating details to speak of, she insisted—but rather from the desire among domestic workers to vilify their high-status employers. Among domestic workers both within and outside the middle-class households that employ them, rumors of the "real" reason for a mother-in-law's death could serve as a site for moral and social commentary about elder abuse and neglect as classed pathology. Such rumors can be performative, highlighting the moral failures and dissolute behaviors of the elite. Subaltern assertions of "what *really* happened" circulate with a volubility around the neighborhood that reflects the ideological power of discourse to produce subjectivities and sort them into social hierarchies.[27]

Prema spoke of other rumors. Gossiping neighbors, she told me, had blamed her for being selfishly and singularly devoted to her husband: "one of these young wives today," as Prema described it, "who only want to be with their husbands." The implication being, as she explained, that in her single-minded passion for Manoj she had pushed Kanthamma to the margins of the family's conjugal nucleus, making ever more tenuous her mother-in-law's position in the household. Whether this meant Kanthamma's death had been the end to a long history of quiet neglect or the result of a more forceful rejection depended on the version of the story told: Prema had heard both. Both laid blame on the affections of companionate marriage, figured in these rumors as excessive in degree and exclusionary in orientation. In their framing of Prema as "one of these young wives today," these speculative rumors leapt scales and people, moving from Kanthamma's death, to Prema's alleged selfishness as a young wife, to broader social commentary about the dispossessed elderly in modern life.

Judgments about young wives' selfish aspirations to companionate love were more than judgments about Prema alone. If these rumors blamed Prema's covetous affections for her husband, they also blamed the institution seen to have bred those affections: the modern nuclear family. Rumors are diagnostic of larger social projects.[28] Here, they challenged the conjugal, patrifocal family as an unproblematic social good, a notion that had long been promoted in nineteenth- and twentieth-century efforts to reform the region's diverse family and inheritance practices in the path to development. In raising the specter of the "bad" modern family here in the form of selfish and abusive daughters-in-law, speculative tales about the "real" reason for Kanthamma's death were as much defamations of Prema's character as they were critical commentaries on the failures of the small conjugal family form that has been a keystone achievement in the making of Kerala modernity.[29] In speaking of the precarious status of the widowed elderly and the misguided affections of young wives, neighborhood tales questioned a central object of collective struggle that has guided the path to progress and development in the region. Rumors here blamed a mother-in-law's death on a young wife's selfish aspirations to companionate love, seen here to be the unintended fruit born of the ill-conceived aspirations of "the people."

Rumors about Kanthamma's death that circulated in Prema's neighborhood emerged less in conversation with official police reports than by claiming transcendent knowledge over and above them. Rumors of middle-class murder often categorically disqualify official reports with allusions to the manipulation of evidence between police and families. In this way, they appear to open a clearing beyond authorized knowledge for vernacular assertions of "what *really* happened." Yet while such rumors claim to circumvent official accounts and see past the diversions of a corrupted system, they in fact reproduce the same bureaucratic categories and legal forms of attention by which female suicide is immanently read as the result of family neglect and violence.

### Ghost

Suicide commanded multiple presences in Prema's life beyond circulating rumors. One afternoon several weeks after Kanthamma's death, a domestic worker employed by a family down the street came to Prema with a premonition. "Daughter," the woman said to Prema, "I had a dream. At eleven o'clock tonight, there will be three knocks. When you hear these knocks, do not open the door. It is your mother coming back." That night Prema stayed awake with fright, imagining Kanthamma returning as the haunting, suffering figure in the hospital that she remembered so vividly. "When I heard that, I was so scared, so scared I couldn't sleep the entire night," Prema recounted to me. "I was filled with fear. I kept thinking to myself, 'She told me not to open the door. It's Mother's ghost *(pretham)*.'" In the end, Prema heard nothing. "She had said all this to frighten me."[30]

Yet in the days following, Prema could not shake the feeling that Kanthamma had indeed returned. At times, she would feel Kanthamma moving through the house. Her mind, Prema told me, would fill with fear whenever she approached the far bedroom, the room where Kanthamma had doused herself in kerosene before going out to the yard to set herself on fire. Prema's daughter, ten years old at the time, reported thinking that she had seen her grandmother pacing the far wall of the garden, just as Kanthamma had done in the evenings. During those weeks, no one in the family would venture into the yard after dusk. Deeply unsettled, Prema and Manoj invited a Hindu priest from their neighborhood temple to come to their home. For two days and two nights, *puja* (ritual of propitiation) was conducted to ensure passage of Kanthamma's soul from this world to the next.

After that, Kanthamma came to visit only in dreams. Now, Prema told me, she didn't feel frightened to see her mother-in-law when she appeared to her in the night. "Mother comes back in her original form *(roopam)*, not as she looked when she died. Fair-skinned, neatly dressed. With thick hair down her back. Nice black hair, nice long black hair. That is what I see." She closed her eyes, smiling. "That is how I see her," she told me. "Like that, she comes back to talk with me. How is my granddaughter, how is my son, she will ask. I will quickly open my eyes. Then she is gone." Kanthamma's soul, said Prema, had moved on and was now content. Through dreams and the conversations they had, Prema maintained an intimate relationship with Kanthamma as a physical and spiritual presence.[31] She did so alongside the rumors and speculative tales that, years later, became neighborhood lore. These were the multiple lives that Kanthamma continued to have among the living.

Murmurings about the truth of Kanthamma's death still surfaced from time to time during my fieldwork. While competing accounts of what "really" happened sometimes jockeyed openly with one another, as they did the afternoon Prema discredited the rumors she feared I had already heard, more often these multiple truths coexisted in mutual ambivalence—in the passing comment of a neighbor or in the knowing glances toward Prema's house as people walked by. While Prema's account never claimed complete victory over the rumors, both Prema and Kanthamma commanded a fluency in the bureaucratic languages and social knowledge of suicide that enabled them to effectively put forward their version of the event in the face of the law and in defense of each other. Leelamma's story, to which I now turn, suggests the stark limits of doing so for those with radically less leverage in their encounters with experts and the state.

### AN UNIDENTIFIED BODY

On a cool December morning, a body was found lying near the railway tracks on the outskirts of the city. Only a mobile phone, flung some ten feet away in an outcrop of wild grass, and a neatly folded letter in the front shirt pocket gave witness to the body's belonging in the world. Soon after, the event surfaced in the dry, clipped sentences of the local newspapers. "Young man's body discovered by railway tracks. Police report determines accidental death." The papers compensated for the thrift of the words with the disquieting intimacy granted to their readers through a small, black-and-white photo of the twenty-four-year-old.

While I was living in Thiruvananthapuram, parents spoke fearfully about youth desires for falling in love as a mode of being *modern* and independent. Concerned that a "new generation" is courting broken hearts and suicide in ways encouraged by the easy availability of technology, parents worried about adolescents hiding mobile phones and the secret relationships conducted through those phones. Particularly when linked to certain methods and sites, youth suicide appeared to speak to many of the perils of young love. In the words of a neighbor who responded to the news reported in the papers those days in December: "Around here, a body by the tracks always means a failed love affair." For my neighbor and many others following the story of the young man found dead, the already impoverished account reported in the news was distilled down to its trace elements:

> A young man's body was found by the police by the railway tracks.
> Young man's body by the railway tracks.
> Young man. Railway tracks.

These two elements, when united by violence, appeared to casual onlookers in the days following to speak to a discrete death event. When found along the railway tracks in Thiruvananthapuram, the body became metonymic of a particular act of suicidal violence and its motivation. Heartbreak due to unrequited or failed love was the reason for its being. For my neighbor who insisted that the reported story involved a suicide, even when he was given more details about the death than those given in the newspaper, the contents of the note discovered on the body were irrelevant. The physical condition of the body did not matter, nor did its exact location or positioning, only that it was the body of a young man, found along the railway tracks.[32]

While the details of the death mattered little to my neighbor, they were critical to Leelamma. It was Leelamma's son Prakash who was found that December morning. A practicing Pentecostal Christian of the low-status Pulaya (SC) caste, Leelamma had studied minimally to the third standard and had worked all her life as a domestic servant. At the time of her son's death, she was taking three connecting buses five days a week to do the cooking and cleaning for several families around the city. In the weeks shadowed by the first anniversary of Prakash's death, Leelamma pulled out a small square of newspaper from her wallet, softened from repeated folding and unfolding. It was a clipping of the photo of her son from the newspaper. Prakash had left the house as usual one Friday morning, heading, Leelamma had presumed, for the neighborhood bike shop where he had just recently started work as a mechanic. She recalled how she and her husband had gone to the police station that Sunday morning, two days after Prakash had gone missing, to file a report:

> The phone was ringing. One of the police officers picked up the phone. "There is an unidentified body lying on the railway tracks." They said, "There is a mobile phone lying there." When they took the body . . . they

found a note. A note was there. It had been on the body. My daughter's name. The three children's names . . . the three girls [Leelamma's grandchildren]. "Forgive me, Mother. Forgive me, Mother. Mother, I am going *(njaan pokunnu)*." The letter had been in the pocket. I said, "Sir! That's my son, my son! This is his name! [These are the names of] my daughter's children!" Then the sir immediately jumped up. He questioned the officer who had come from the scene. It had been one day since he died. Poor thing. An unidentified body.[33]

It was her son's unclaimed status that evoked such visible pathos in Leelamma that afternoon when we spoke. For an entire day and night, Leelamma's son had belonged to no one and nowhere.

Months after Prakash's death, Leelamma remained mired in speculation and in the retrospective insights of acquaintances, friends, and family. She continued to labor to piece together a coherent narrative of how and why her son had died. Years before, Leelamma recounted to me, Prakash had fallen in love with a girl in the neighborhood. Prakash came to learn that Tara had a *line* at the time, the man she later married.[34] Though heartbroken, Prakash remained in secret contact with Tara, aware of her deteriorating relationship with an abusive husband. One day while Prakash was traveling home by bus, Tara boarded and sat next to him. A family friend, seeing the two together, reported the incident to Tara's husband. That same evening, Tara was viciously beaten and subsequently cast out of her home. This, Leelamma suggested, was the event that triggered the cascade of problems that were the root of the severe mental troubles that plagued Prakash the last months of his life and that ushered in his untimely death.

On the way to work the Friday morning of his death, Prakash received a call from Tara. She said her husband had threatened to kill her. Frightened, she told Prakash that she was going to kill herself rather than face her husband's wrath. When Prakash promised they could run away and start a new life together, Tara gave him the address where she was hiding, several miles outside the city. Prakash arrived by autorickshaw to find Tara and her mother waiting on the doorstep of an abandoned house. Leelamma told me how, in a police interview, the driver of the rickshaw had said that Tara and her mother boarded his vehicle, leaving Prakash behind. Through his rearview mirror the driver saw four men emerge from the house. Leelamma said that Prakash had been beaten to death, having sustained massive injury to his head and body. Prakash's murderers had even thought to deposit his body near the railway tracks, knowing that the death would be read as a suicide. It was all planned, she explained, wringing her hands. Tara—all of them—had "cheated him" (Avar ayale chathicchu). When I inquired after the note in Prakash's pocket, Leelamma explained that it was her son's good-bye letter, written in the expectation that he was setting off with his love, never to return home.

In the wake of searing loss, Leelamma's struggle to generate closure for her family hinged on how successfully she could project her own interpretation of Prakash's death against others that threatened to colonize their lives and reputations in her community: "We told our friends and neighbors that he couldn't have committed suicide. They murdered him." Although the police reports determined the event to be an "accidental death," in crime parlance, many in Leelamma's neighborhood continued to believe his death was a suicide. Even those who knew him as a child, Leelamma told me in confused anger, whispered behind her back. In the months following Prakash's death, Leelamma conducted a parallel investigation of her own, talking informally with Prakash's friends and acquaintances. As details unfolded, she encouraged some of these young men to come forward to the police with their testimonies. But convinced they would be dismissed or, worse yet, harassed or punished by the police, they refused. Lacking the social capital and the fluency in bureaucratic discourse so artfully commanded by Ajith, Kanthamma, and Prema, Leelamma was unable to mobilize the help of experts or authorities to reignite a fresh investigation into her son's case.

Leelamma's efforts to project her own narrative of Prakash's death will never be complete. At stake are the reputation of her family, her faith in herself as a loving mother, and fidelity to memories of Prakash. Her efforts to forward a narrative of murder have also been caught up in judgments others have made about Prakash's behaviors before his death and about the failures of family. Leelamma recounted to me how, two weeks after returning to work, one of her middle-class employers tried to assuage Leelamma's sadness. She recounted the employer's words of consolation: "That boy was nothing but a great burden (valiya bhaaram) on you. He never had a proper job, roamed around, and caused you problems." Leelamma remembered her employer conjecturing that perhaps it was for the best, since now Leelamma could focus her resources on raising her daughter's children in a better way. Rumors about a failed love affair not only cast judgment on Prakash's pursuits in life but also left his mother's investments in relationships across the family vulnerable to questioning. Accusations of jobless loitering, troublemaking with boys in the neighborhood, and indiscretions in the realm of love have marked the young man's reputation in death as they have his family's in their ongoing life. The ability of Leelamma and her family to inhabit the present has been shaped by the commentaries of those like her employer, who sought somehow to assuage a mother's loss by casting death as a hidden boon. Tales of suicide can cut like a knife. They mark survivors and rend deep social divisions between people through judgments about what life was worth.

Leelamma worried what these rumors might mean years down the line when her granddaughters reach marriageable age. Would these slanderous stories stick like contagion? She was saddened, too, that gossip had generated cracks and fissures in the convictions of her family, to the point that her daughter had begun to question how well they had ever really known Prakash. Rumors had begun to colonize memories. As uncertainty and conviction gathered unevenly around the death of Leelamma's son, listening to her story demanded "listening for hesitation—listening for that which persistently disrupts the security of what is known for sure."[35] Leelamma herself vacillated as she continued to engage and forcefully postpone doubt: "It was murder. They took him and murdered him. That's what it was. But he did write a letter. That's true. [He had written] 'She called me. I am going with her. If I don't go with her, she told me she will kill herself.' That's why he wrote all of this. 'If she kills herself, I don't want a curse to befall my family,' he had written." Then in the same breath, Leelamma softly conceded, "But in what way we should think, I don't know."[36]

## "SOCIAL" SUFFERING

Arthur Kleinman, Veena Das, and Margaret Lock have usefully proposed the term *social suffering* to describe the "assemblage of human problems that have their origins and consequences in the devastating injuries that social force can inflict on human experience." The notion of social suffering seeks to recognize the often "close linkage of personal problems with societal problems" and thus resist the categorization of issues such as substance abuse, domestic violence, suicide, and depression as "principally psychological or medical, and therefore individual." It acknowledges the "interpersonal grounds of suffering" that are often erased in professional medical knowledge and official discourse.[37]

In speculative tales, commentaries, and rumors about the dead, bureaucratic discourses and popular knowledge of suicide enact the framing of a different "social" suffering. They cast suicide less in the medicalized terms of psychiatric pathology than in the social terms of poor investment, false ambition, isolation, and loss. In Thiruvananthapuram, suicide was widely read as a "problem" of aspiration, the fallout of miscalculated pursuits of such objects as illicit love, parental ambition, and success. Among gossiping neighbors and casual onlookers, Kanthamma's death, for example, generated scrutiny of intimacy and violence in the modern family, raising questions about a young wife's aspirations to companionate love and the modern institutions seen to have bred them. By Dr. Fathima's account, Biju's death warned of the incautious ambitions parents have for their children. Yet, insofar as the suffering in these accounts might be called "social," these social interpretations of suicide, understood here in epidemiological terms, fail to escape or resist the reductive effects of official discourse. They push and mold individual cases of suicide to speak to and stand for ideas of social pathology and regional crisis. For the families whose stories have been presented here, morality tales that locate the deaths of their loved ones on the broad scales of social pathology flatten the complexities of individual and interpersonal suffering into generic scripts. These scripts speak less to any distinct details about Biju, Kanthamma, or Prakash as individuals than to the characteristics of the aggregate populations to which they were taken to belong. Moreover, although these social accounts typically demedicalize suicide, they do not necessarily mitigate the use of pharmaceuticals. As previously mentioned, the epidemic view of psychiatric problems in the practice of Indian psychiatry in fact endorses the widespread and liberal use of drugs in the treatment of suicide as social disorder.

The "social," in this case, fails to account for the complex local worlds of individual and interpersonal suffering. Bureaucratic institutions, expert cultures, media representations, and social knowledge reify categories of social pathology around suicide while "casting a veil of misrecognition over the domain as a whole."[38] By reducing the act of suicide to one (or several) discrete social ills, speculative tales and rumors fracture the realm of everyday social life and suffering into discrete attributes. They shape the ways people live in relationship to the category and categories of "suicide" while deflecting attention from the powerful ideologies vested in reading suicide as such. In all of their claims to revelation, scandal, and exposure, bureaucratic discourses and social knowledge about suicide as a "problem" of aspiration also necessarily conceal and obscure. Suicide's categories are exposed and exploited as *the* secret at the expense of other narratives and experiences of social life—those marked by violence, social abandonment, despair, and illness as much as by love and care.

In suicide's wake, families struggle with the easy metonymy between lived deaths and social pathology in contexts of love and intimacy, care and grief. From Ajith's memo to Prema's recital of Kanthamma's last words, we have seen how intimacies among kin are placed on trial in very public ways for the surviving kin and the dead. Social and legal discourses of suicide, if not directly implicating kin abuse and neglect, call upon family members to testify against accounts that may not be their own. Social interpretations of suicide telescope the complexities of suffering, as well as the expansive histories and cosmologies of family life, into momentary acts of refusal and violence. Families bring different resources, fluencies, and forms of capital to forward their own truths. For both Leelamma and Prema, rumors worsened grief as they maneuvered truth toward closure and healing. By contrast, bureaucratic categories of suicide gave Ajith's family a language to rationalize a senseless event, providing a degree of closure around the conflicting details of a young man's death. For some, reading individual death up to broader scales of social pathology brought welcomed meaning to the otherwise inexplicable; for others, it brought down the heavy hand of the state.

The narratives that families struggle to put forth about the deaths—and lives—of loved ones reveal how streams of discourse flow together, pooling unevenly as fluctuating moments of ambivalence and certainty. The insistence of casual onlookers and commentators that they know the real reason for suicide can feel incontrovertible to kin laboring to forward their own narratives about life, death, and loss and can generate doubt about the lives of the loved ones they thought they knew. For those, like Leelamma, who endlessly shadowbox with the easy convictions of neighbors, acquaintances, and strangers, this makes the tales their loved ones are made to tell as real as any of their own.

# PART TWO

# On Living in a Time of Suicide

# 4

# Care-full Acts

Over tea, Kunjamma spoke of her youngest son's piecemeal employment since his return from the Persian Gulf three years before. As the
widowed grandmother in her seventies ran her thin fingers along the
base of her porcelain cup in quiet thought, the sounds of afternoon traffic floated in through the open windows of the front sitting room,
announcing the end of the workday. After just eight months in Bahrain,
Kunjamma's son lost his job as a hotel doorman. If only they could send
him back there, she said. Detailing for me the costs to arrange once
again her son's employment, visa, and travel—at an expense that far
exceeded Kunjamma's modest retirement pension—she told me that she
had applied for a bank loan but had been declined. The only option
now was to approach a *blade*, a private lending scheme floated by
migrant remittances offering quick loans at high interest rates.[1] With
that money, Kunjamma mused, she would send her son back to the Gulf
and then drink poison to escape having to pay it back. At her age, she
said to me in half jest, this was the best contribution she could make to
the family's future. Laughing now, she poured me more tea and patted
my hand for the look of concern, assuring me she was only joking.[2]

Kunjamma's comments dramatize a moral economy of care at the
shifting scene of middle-class family life in Kerala. They are reminiscent
of the "horizontal gift relationship" that Lawrence Cohen describes of
young men's fantasies of sacrificing a kidney for the economic reanimation of the family in Chennai, Tamil Nadu.[3] Cast in "the conservative

terms of a class-specific protection of the family form," young men's sale of the "other" kidney is tied to their economic ability to get sisters married off.[4] The attrition of the body through the sacrificial gift of the kidney facilitates the payment of dowry, the movement of women, and the cycling of family cosmologies. By similarly framing her life as capital for the financial rejuvenation of the family, Kunjamma proposed the ultimate sacrificial gift. Marking at once her economic limits and the value of her life in death, this gift declared Kunjamma's care for her family. But it also reflected in grim terms an aging grandmother's precarious place in the unequal distribution of care in this household: while attempting to provide a kind of care that would ensure the financial health of future generations, Kunjamma herself seemed little cared for at times. On the afternoon she spoke of sacrificing her life to send her son back to the Gulf, her hand rested gingerly on the swollen abdomen caused by a hernia that, for three weeks now, remained untreated. None of her children had the money at the moment to help pay for surgery, Kunjamma explained. Soon, she told me. Her words were punctuated by the click-click sounds of Kunjamma's teenage granddaughter typing away on a new desktop computer in the neighboring room—a purchase made just days before, Kunjamma told me happily, to help her get ahead in her studies.

With Kunjamma's story, we turn our attention to the concern that threads together the remainder of this book: how people live with suicide as an ever-present possibility in the intimate spaces and practices of daily life. Suicide as a possibility is folded into the everyday in diverse forms: forms as overt as threats directed at family members or as ambiguous as fugitive comment, fantasy, and passing joke. Kunjamma's remarks about sacrificing her life for her family begin to orient us to the ways that suicide is woven into the fabric of the domestic everyday. They also illustrate how suicide can insinuate itself into casual conversation, settle into the cracks of routine living, and take up residence in the home, sometimes without announcing "suicide" in any declarative or clear-cut manner. Yet even then, layered into ordinary life this way, suicide can powerfully alter how people live and live with one another.

Women's allusions to, jokes about, and fantasies of suicide surfaced with difficult regularity in interviews and observations of domestic life in the middle-class neighborhood where I lived. Kunjamma's musings on the value of her life in death, shared in passing allusion with (perhaps for?) an outsider, offer a pinhole view onto the broad repertoire of ways women invoke ending their lives in front of others, often as an ambiguous mixture of play, grave utterance, and citational performance. Such practices are a means to negotiate kin relations and women's place within them, in ways that can be profoundly unsettling. Invocations of suicide are powerful gendered responses to middle-class family life—its material, ideological, and moral injunctions, its dependencies and violence, and the vulnerabilities that women must bear in its everyday making. Often issued from a place of ambivalence, they reflect enchantments and disenchantments with a class-specific dream of domesticity.

These practices are also important to how women understand and construct themselves as gendered subjects, particularly as subjects caring for and needing the care of others. In his departure from anthropological and legal categories of kinship and marriage, John Borneman has proposed instead "a concern for the actual situations in which people experience the need to care and be cared for and to the political economies of their distribution."[5] Following Borneman, this chapter seeks to understand how invocations of suicide like Kunjamma's are critical to the enactment, distribution, and intelligibility of care and value within the middle-class household. Like young men's fantasies of gifting a kidney, Kunjamma's imaginings of sacrificial death were care-full: marked by discriminate and thoughtful planning and by concern for others. In this sense, these practices do not mark (or only mark) the failure of kin relations. Rather, they often work to catalyze or reconfigure the moral, affective, and material ties that bind. In their enactments, they evidence women's care for the reproduction of the family; in the responses they inspire, they can mobilize forms of attention and protection against injury or death. While issued from precarious locations in the household, women's invocations of suicide are often an amalgam of fear and pleasure. Concern for the actual situations in which women care and are cared for must therefore grapple with the difficult entanglements between desire, vulnerability, agency, and violence at the site of women's words and bodies.

## TROUBLING SUICIDE

In popular and scholarly discourse in Kerala, female suicide is often taken to signify the failures of a class-specific dream of modern domesticity in the region. Alongside mental illness and the rising visibility of violence against women, suicide has engendered ambivalence toward the middle-class family form and its material and ideological demands. Decentering the narratives of progressive "Kerala women" that had earlier dominated in political and popular imaginaries of the region, feminist historiographers have explored how modern Kerala history issued forth new patriarchal institutions and, with them, new gendered subjectivities and inequalities.[6] A hallmark of this process was the gradual "modernization" of the region's once diverse family and inheritance practices with a shift toward legally recognized patrifocal residence, descent, and inheritance, beginning in the nineteenth century. By the mid-twentieth century, the small, conjugal, patrifocal family became the economical, reasonable, and desired life option across social groups in the region. Social and political reform movements engendered new forms of patriarchy, instituting at the very heart of the modern family a dichotomy between the male breadwinner and the female housewife.[7]

But in scholarly discourse as well as in ordinary life, female suicide foments disenchantment with what had once appeared an unproblematic social good. Although women's access to education continues to expand in the state, this capital is increasingly channeled toward the role of consummate mother and householder rather than toward economic gain outside the home.[8] This orientation toward "informed" female domesticity has encouraged the withdrawal of educated women from the labor market.[9] Together with women's diminishing control over inheritance and limited agency in making household decisions, their rising educational achievement—at times rivaling that of their spouses— has been linked to domestic violence, mental illness, and suicide.[10]

Concerns for female suicide have also emerged in the clinical setting, though in different terms. Allusions to women issuing threats in the home surface in patient histories with unsettling frequency. Clinicians understand these threats to be a new phenomenon among the middle class. Such threats have become so common, I was told, that they are now part of the everyday grammar through which women negotiate family life. Sometimes read cynically as a means to personal gain, women's threats are seen to be damaging not only to self and marital relations; normalized in the home, they are also blamed for socializing children to impulsive and potentially fatal behaviors. I heard many clinicians declare their skepticism openly, characterizing women's talk of suicide as self-defeating, perverse, immature, and pathological practice intended to manipulate others. These behaviors emerged into clinical view through the lens of how genuinely—or, rather, disingenuously— "suicidal" they were understood to be.

Skepticism toward women's suicide threats is hardly new or unique to Kerala. As others have argued, the Western clinical literature carries with it a universe of implicitly gendered terminology around suicidal behaviors that do not end in death—that of the "threat," "gesture," and "cry for help."[11] Nonfatal female suicidal gestures are heavily weighted on the side of insincerity, manipulation, and false intent as contrasted to men's suicides, which are taken to convey self-determination and the will to "complete" the act. If men's suicides are typically seen as self-authored acts directed against impersonal adversities, women's suicides are read as impulsive or fraudulent acts gone awry and directed at personal troubles. In this sense, they demand skepticism as to "actual" intent. The feminization of nonfatal suicidal behavior is arguably grounded in empirical trends. Yet it is important to recognize that this construction is also ballasted by gendered ideas that "real" suicide—that which is committed with fatal intent to produce a fatal outcome—lies beyond the domain of female conduct, ideas that can be traced back to Durkheim's canonical study of suicide.[12] Such is the heavy baggage that nonfatal behaviors carry through the lens of female suicidal fraudulence.

Both frameworks—the clinical and the feminist historiographical—shape the larger terrain in which female suicide has been understood in Kerala. But acts like Kunjamma's do not fit neatly into either. Though Kunjamma spoke from her precarious position within the family and its stark inequalities of care and economic access—a position that must be located within the broader context of the historical making of the patrifocal family—suicide was not the drastic act to which she turned for lack of alternatives. Kunjamma's fantasies also confound any easy separation between life and death. In linking her imagined suicide to the economic reanimation of the family, her words suggest that death can be a mode of enhancing or building life. How do we account for the complexities of these practices without winding back into the bramble of assumptions about female suicidal fraudulence?

To sidestep the ontological and moral assumptions built into the clinical discourse in particular, I wish to release us from the tyranny of deciphering "sincere" suicide—a task and ontology of a different sort. I focus instead on the situations and contexts in which women enact these practices and the ways they reconfigure or redistribute care, concern, and attention among kin. Inspired by the work of anthropologist Ghassan Hage, I conceive of this broad regime of allusions to, jokes about, and fantasies of suicide as modes of "accumulating death."[13] I draw on this notion to highlight the myriad ways people accrue tactical vulnerabilities at the site of words and bodies and do so from within life itself. This notion is also useful because it attunes us to the possibility of what may be produced under the sign of death. The accumulation of death may, for example, enable women to produce themselves as moral subjects, mobilize others to respond with heightened care and attention, shift dynamics in the household to make domestic situations more habitable for a time, or serve to enhance the lives of family members. The accumulation of death, in other words, may be morally or socially productive.

This suggests that life and death may not always be diametrically opposed, as ordinarily assumed. By training our focus on the reciprocities between them, we open our analytics beyond polarizing dichotomies to recognize that accumulating death may in fact be a mode of affirming or reanimating life, that tactical vulnerabilities may create possibilities for agency, and that the indeterminacy of suicide alters ways of living. Ethnographic attention to the ways people accumulate death also allows sensitivity to events of different scales, ranging from the quiet, ambiguous, and fugitive to the openly declarative, dramatic, and performative. It broadens our field of vision beyond the singularity of suicide as "event," acknowledging that even playful gestures or jokes shape how people live with one another, sometimes setting new horizons of fear of a graver act in the near or far off future. Accumulating death thus exceeds, but does not exclude, death itself.

The notion of accumulation also situates these practices within a larger economy of value distributed across bodies and members of the household. In this time of liberalization and global change in Kerala, the ways women accumulate death to enhance the lives of others must be understood in light of new ideas and representations of embodied value.[14] Capital building at the site of the body is intensifying in the middle-class family, with value accrued by some members over others. The resources and energies of parenting, for instance, are increasingly funneled toward preparing children to become competitive, "high-quality" global workers and citizens.[15] Intensified child rearing through new regimes of educational, material, and developmental nurturance is now widely recognized to be a critical mode of value production in the capital city. As new strategies emerge in the building and valuing of life at the site of the middle-class family, value is often extracted from women's bodies to enhance the lives of others. Thus, a widowed grandmother stands to be sacrificed to set in motion a once-again migrating son, and the purchase of a desktop computer as a long-term investment for a granddaughter is prioritized over the remedial hernia surgery of the elderly. In the liberalizing present, the accumulation of death gives new material expression to value in the "shared" pursuit of the good life.

## A DECENT GIRL

It was just weeks into her college studies in Kerala's neighboring state of Karnataka when Kavitha's troubles began. When her cousin Meenu began dating boys on campus against the prohibitions of family, Kavitha became deeply distressed about the possible compromise of her own reputation as a "decent girl" *(anthassulla penkutti)*. As news of their quickly fraying friendship reached home, Kavitha's mother blamed her daughter for failing to be more adjustable. The timid, soft-spoken nineteen-year-old didn't feel she could tell her mother the truth: that the problems between the cousins had to do with Meenu's alleged indiscretions and the vicious *eve teasing* that Kavitha was daily suffering from male classmates as a result.[16] Despite trying to distance herself from her cousin, Kavitha found herself deflecting the overtures and aggressive comments of boys on campus. Explaining that her reputation was in jeopardy regardless of her innocence in the matter, Kavitha quoted for me the familiar Malayalam proverb describing the vulnerability of women, who must bear the cost when things go wrong, regardless of how or why. "Whether the leaf falls on the thorn or the thorn falls on the leaf," said Kavitha, "the leaf will have to suffer" (Ila mullil veenaalum mullu ilayil veenaalum, kedu ilakku thanne).

Hurt by her mother's harsh words conveyed through nightly phone calls, Kavitha weighed the options before her. As the situation on campus grew unbearable, she considered dropping her courses and returning home, a plan she ultimately dismissed as unwise, since in the minds of extended family and neighbors, only girls who fall astray are called back home without completing their studies. Concerns that girls will be "spoiled" in college, prey to influences that take hold in the absence of close family surveillance and protection, have been shown to shape family planning of female education in India.[17] Her parents' decision to allow her to study far from home had been no small matter, Kavitha explained. Her mother in particular had staunchly defended the decision to extended family. Kavitha had no intention of proving her mother wrong.

At the family's kitchen table on an afternoon her parents were at work, Kavitha recounted for me those difficult months. She was home from college on holiday, her graduation just on the horizon. It had been nearly three years since these events transpired, but Kavitha recalled those days with a troubled, restless urgency. Keen at the time to avoid the harmful rumors that would circulate with a premature return, she had considered her limited alternatives. Killing herself, Kavitha had decided in the midst of those torturous days, was most certainly the better option. It would, of course, have had to be disguised as an accident, she explained with a shy smile. Had it appeared as a suicide to others, they would have suspected a failed love affair or even pregnancy. That would have been far worse than returning home prematurely, she said, her eyes growing wide. She had no wish for such disgrace to fall upon her parents and brother. No, certainly not. Kavitha mentioned a steep bluff a few miles away from campus. During the rainy reason, its grassy slopes became slick. "If you fall from the cliff, it can look like you just slipped and fell down," she told me. "'She just slipped,' they can say."

With her memories punctuated by self-conscious, nervous laughter, Kavitha spoke of suicide as an escape. But she also spoke of suicide as an act of love. Ending her life would spare her family the pain of learning about the harassment she had suffered. Kavitha expressed the greatest concern for her elder brother. She hadn't wished to cause him any distress over her situation, particularly since at the time he was working his first job as an engineer in the United States. He had his own worries, she told me. "I never talked about any of these things with him back then," Kavitha said. "He would call me from Texas, but I would only talk about good things. How could I say anything to him?" It was Kavitha's brother who had been most staunchly against her studying so far from home. Several months of reassurance had been needed to win his consent.[18] Even after relenting, he continued to worry for his sister's welfare. "When I was in college," Kavitha recounted, "he was already so tense anyway, wondering, would I fall into any trouble? Would there be any trouble for me?" Growing quiet, she reflected, "If I told him about what was happening to me with the boys at the college, he might be so sad. So sad and unable to do anything."

Kavitha saw in her death the chance to release her family from the pain of troubling secrets, a death that was curiously emptied of the pain of mourning. Speaking in retrospect of those dark days, she framed suicide as an unavoidable sacrifice to protect those she loved most. Hers would be a most care-full death, one that would thoughtfully spare, by her account, the hurt feelings of others while also protecting her family's reputation in its deliberate execution as an accident. In constructing herself as a caring subject, Kavitha demonstrated her concern for her parents' welfare after her death ("he will look after them"). She also staked claims to needing care, positioning herself by contrast as little cared for—as having to turn to friends at a time when she felt most abandoned by her mother. Much of our conversation that afternoon revolved around Kavitha recounting how she had spoken openly about her thoughts of suicide with friends and their expressions of support and affection for her. When troubles at the college were running high, she turned to friends: "I used to talk to my friends about suicide and they would say, 'No, don't think about it.' I told them that my situation was so bad, that I can't bear it anymore, I'll do something. They would say, 'No, you shouldn't do that. If you do that, what will your parents' state be? What will your brother's state be?'" Kavitha's response to her friends underscores the relative value she attributed to her life as compared with her brother's. "'They have a son. He will look after them so they won't be that sad,' I would tell them. Then my friends would say, 'How can you say that? No, your parents need both of you.'" Reflecting on the solace she was able to find during those weeks, Kavitha emphasized that it was her college classmates, not her family, who were "really the ones supporting me at the time."

Accumulating death in this way, Kavitha galvanized sympathy, care, and concern through lateral peer connections. Fantasies of suicide were also autotherapeutic. They opened up an elegiac space in which Kavitha could imagine and mourn a world without her. In conversations with friends in which she staged the loss her parents and brother would suffer over her death, Kavitha rehearsed and reanimated the affective ties that tethered her to her parents and brother. Dwelling in this state of loss and fantasy, she channeled her frustrations with the young men at her college and the hurt over her mother's reproach into higher feminine virtue: that of self-sacrificing love for the family.[19]

Much has been written about the importance of ideologies of self-sacrifice to constructions of "Indian" femininity and their ties to discourses of cultural nationalism. Partha Chatterjee suggests that beginning in the nineteenth century, women and an idea of Indian Womanhood were positioned as icons of the moral and cultural reproduction of home and nation. As Chatterjee observes, this nationalist construct attributes "the spiritual qualities of self-sacrifice, benevolence, devotion, religiosity, and so on" to femininity, which comes to stand "as a sign for 'nation.'"[20] As Indian nationalisms of different shades have produced their variants of the good (Hindu) wife, themes of suffering and self-sacrifice have also been shown to operate as organizing tropes in political and legal spheres as powerfully as they do in idealizations of middle-class femininity in popular culture.[21] The icon of the self-sacrificing wife has emerged as an ambivalent presence in colonial and postcolonial discourses concerning the practice of sati, which have featured, among other ideological constructions, an idealized figure of the widow who "willingly" casts herself onto her husband's pyre out of selfless devotion.[22]

In the middle-class neighborhood where I lived, themes of self-sacrifice also emerged in the ways women understood and constructed themselves as gendered subjects. To suffer *(sahikkuka),* and to do so willingly and selflessly, served as a key trope in women's moral self-making. It intersected with the accumulation of death as a technology of the self that in the home could be as subtle as eating only after one's husband and children are sated and as brutal as suicide. But it is critical not to assume that "self-sacrifice" and its practices carry universal and already constituted meanings. These are not timeless ethical sentiments; nor are they the "innate" qualities of gender or culture. In instances in which the women I spoke with drew on ideas and practices of suicide as sacrifice to understand and construct themselves as moral subjects, these ideas and practices were fluid and shifting. Carefully designed to spare feelings and protect her family's reputation, Kavitha's planned death responded to particular conditions and pressures that threaten to warp class-specific notions of female respectability in contemporary Kerala. It navigated, for instance, the marked tension between increasing access to women's education and the moral anxieties in the family that accompany it, a tension that was shared across the household but came to bear most pressingly on Kavitha. In deeming her life eliminable in relation to that of her brother, the terms of Kavitha's sacrifice were also shaped by new ideas and representations of embodied value in a time of liberalization and global change. By Kavitha's calculus, sparing the emotional distress of her brother—a global worker with intensified resource-bearing capacities—took priority over her own sacrificeable life. As moral and material economies in the relationships between bodies and values are transformed in the liberalizing present, women like Kavitha spend ideas and practices of "chosen" death in new ways of enhancing others.

Through death, Kavitha imagined bearing the ultimate cost to spare others emotional harm and to protect the class-specific terms of her family's reputation. Like other women I met, she spoke of her death in the terms of care, producing herself as a moral subject caring for others and as a subject needing and deserving of care. Yet in framing her chosen silence and willful death as noble sacrifice, Kavitha elided the abuse and shame she may have met at the hands of family had they come to know the truth she had been hiding about her cousin. This narrative of sacrifice also transmuted into female virtue the profound humiliation that Kavitha felt in being the sexualized target of rowdy college boys and that further motivated her secrecy. It was also shaped by her acute sensitivity to her family's contentious decision to send her away for degree studies—a decision Kavitha's mother continues even now to defend to extended family members. Kavitha mobilized sentiments of love and concern to construct herself as a moral subject caring for family, but these same discourses veiled the coercive power relations upon which this loving home is built, relations that magnetized around the surveillance and potentially violent control of women's sexualities. Narrated as an act of care and the ultimate sacrifice, Kavitha's imagined suicide also disciplined the threat of rogue female (hetero)sexuality with the promise of death.

If at times the accumulation of death works to reinforce the affective and ideological scaffolding of the respectable family, at others it emerges at kinship's fault lines, exposing the quiet dissolution of intimacies and commitments among family members. Through the story of Lata and her mother, we next encounter the "internal precariousness" of kinship and the disappointments and failures that are the underside of accumulating death.[23]

## PRECIOUS CHILD

Lata awoke one morning to a knock on her bedroom door. In the early morning light, she discerned the face of her mother, Aleyamma, peering through the crack in the doorway. In her half-waking state, she vaguely heard her mother inquire after the step stool Lata had taken the day before to dust the shelves above her desk. When Lata asked her mother why she needed it, her mother replied simply, "I have something to do."

Days before, Lata's parents had learned of their daughter's relationship with a young man and their wish to marry. Although Kannan came from a respected middle-class family of government civil servants and held a master's degree in computer engineering, Lata's Ezhava family had firmly rejected the proposal, surrendering to pressure from relatives that Lata's marriage to a low-caste Pulaya man would shame them all. In the face of Lata's equally firm refusal to marry another, Aleyamma had spent those days trying to sway her strong-willed daughter but to no avail. Her attempts at reasoning with Lata eventually gave way to caustic words and, finally, to Aleyamma lying in bed for days behind closed doors. At the time, I had stopped by unannounced for a visit, unaware then of what was unfolding. Aleyamma's husband invited me in briefly, asking me to come by another day: "Auntie has a fever." In the eerily silent house, I could see piles of unwashed dishes in the kitchen.

Nearly two and a half years later in the comfort of Kannan's home, her one-year-old daughter peacefully napping in her arms, Lata recounted for me what had happened that early morning hour when Aleyamma woke her up. It was her mother's odd request for the stool that triggered Lata's suspicion. "When I asked her again why she needed it, she said she wanted something off the top shelf in the kitchen," Lata recalled. "But then I thought, she never stores anything that high up. So I thought I should take a look." As Lata descended the staircase, still groggy from sleep, she heard the loud whir of the ceiling fan set to maximum speed. In the kitchen, she caught sight of her mother perched precariously on the footstool, reaching up to the fan with the end of her sari, wrapped several times around her neck. By Lata's account, Aleyamma paused and turned to stare at her daughter. Lata calmly continued past the kitchen doorway to her parents' bedroom where she roused her father from sleep. He was the one who ran into the kitchen and drew Aleyamma down from the stool.[24]

Long before these events transpired and before Lata would run away from home in the middle of the night to elope, things had been different. On many afternoons, Lata and I would go on outings around the city together or read women's magazines and chat about campus life in her bedroom. On a handful of occasions, she would vaguely mention a "good friend" at her college whom she hoped one day I would have the chance to meet. On other afternoons, Aleyamma plied me with sweets and tea and told me stories about growing up in rural Kerala, her family, and her hopes for her children. Over the span of several years, I had grown close with mother and daughter, each in different ways. After they became alienated from one another, it was difficult and painful to negotiate these relationships. While they have since reconciled, there were many intervening years when each argued passionately to me that she was right and the other wrong. As Aleyamma tells it, her daughter drove her to desperation and suicide. As Lata tells it, her mother had different motivations.

On the afternoon that Lata chose, quite out of the blue, to recount for me the events with her mother in that early morning, I asked her why she hadn't intervened. By walking past the kitchen, Lata registered her stolid refusal to believe. Adamant that Aleyamma had staged the entire episode, she explained that her mother had planned to arouse suspicion by asking for the step stool. For in addition to the early morning disruption, what announced "suicide" in such certain terms for Lata even before she went down to investigate was the distinctive mise-en-scène implied in Aleyamma's request: the step stool indexed the means (hanging) and the place (the kitchen) conventionally equated with female suicide in this context. What Lata described was a gendered trope within an overdetermined visual economy of suicide, one immediately familiar even to me from Malayalam film and television. Lata claimed her mother was counting on her to draw these implicit connections: step stool, kitchen, suicide. Aleyamma had, by Lata's account, carefully laid out her props, not unlike a "scene in a film."[25]

Several months into their silence, on the first occasion I saw her after Lata's marriage, Aleyamma looked wearied and worn. She seemed to have aged overnight. Only in glimpses now did I see the ebullient woman I knew. Aleyamma and I spoke in retrospect about her desperate efforts to reason with Lata in the days after learning about Kannan. Over tea, she explained to me how she had chronicled to Lata all the comforts her daughter had been given growing up—nice clothes, a comfortable house, a quality education. At the very least, Aleyamma had begged, Lata should give up Kannan in recognition of how much—and here I was inventoried literal amounts in lakh rupees—her parents had invested in Lata's bachelor degree and now her master's degree in commerce. Aleyamma rendered a material and moral accounting of resources, time, and hopes invested in Lata, using a language of reciprocity to invite Lata to return in kind. In doing so, Aleyamma linked the fulfillment of Lata's potential to the forms of educational investment widely recognized as an important regime of value in Kerala. She also made clear that she tied this fulfillment to an Ezhava community ideal of upward mobility and social distancing from lower-caste groups.[26] By Aleyamma's accounting, Lata's costly postgraduate education and the family's wider endeavors at upward mobility would be thrown away with such an imprudent marital choice. If she chose Kannan, Aleyamma told Lata, all would have been for nothing.[27]

"If you marry such a boy, then what was the purpose *(uddesyam)* of all this?" Aleyamma recalled asking Lata, gesturing broadly at our well-appointed surroundings. Pointing to the material and symbolic home built with the express purpose of nurturing Lata to her highest human potential, Aleyamma suggested that it would all come crumbling to its foundations if Lata chose unwisely. The prospect that Lata's valuable life and the precious time, resources, and energy it signified would be squandered through marriage to a lower-caste man would mean that Aleyamma's own value as a mother would, too, be wasted. All of this had led to what Aleyamma used the English term *depression* to describe, the condition, she told me, that had pushed her to suicide. Accumulating death may have been Aleyamma's broken acceptance of the destruction of everything. Or perhaps it was the most powerful means she saw to compel Lata to choose the path to the social destiny Aleyamma had laid out for her. Maybe accumulating death was the only way for a mother to ensure the good life she had gifted her most precious child. The inscrutability of Aleyamma's intentions—intentions mistrusted by Lata, feared by Aleyamma's husband, and confusing to me still—would reorganize alliances and dependencies in the family in the weeks, months, and years to come.

The afternoon Aleyamma revisited those difficult days, our conversation was punctuated by long silences. She spoke achingly of her loss, a pain she felt as the heaviness in her chest, in her pounding and chronic headaches, and in the ghostly quiet of the home. All of Lata's things were still in the house—her books, her clothes—exactly where they all had been the night she departed. Symbolically left behind, it felt to me, for Lata to begin a new and different life of value. As they started to gather dust, the objects around Aleyamma announced a gaping absence. No Lata to keep her company in the kitchen in the early morning hours as she prepared the day's meals, sighed Aleyamma. No one to watch evening teleserials with. Losing her precious child, Aleyamma said, as if she were dead.

Aleyamma's inventorying of parental nurturance, now manifest in Lata as accumulated capital, should have inspired, in this mother's hopes, a reciprocal act of care. But rather than read into her education and comfortable upbringing an obligation to her parents, Lata had instead counted her master's degree among the privileges that would help her to elope and, if necessary, cut ties with her family. As she would explain to me on an afternoon long after these events had transpired, Lata had looked hopefully to her education as the means to a happy future with Kannan. Her educational capital was now hers to invest elsewhere, diverted from her natal family to the making of a new companionate life with her husband. At the time when they were planning to marry, Lata had been convinced that Kannan would be able to leverage his computer engineering degree into a high-paying job, maybe even one overseas. She hadn't felt reliant upon the dowry she would have otherwise brought into an arranged marriage. As new high-salaried careers in Kerala's IT industries enable young adults to attain financial solvency earlier, couples like Kannan and Lata are increasingly able to mobilize their own resources to support the marital life of their choosing, sometimes without the consent or economic support of family. For Lata, ideas of romantic love, paired with the possibilities for new forms of work and migration overseas, allowed her to see in her educational capital less an enduring obligation to her parents than the key to her emancipation.

Accumulating death can operate as an ambivalent mode of address: even though condemnatory, it may also contain within it the invitation to reparation and redress. This is an invitation not simply to concede or surrender to the other's will but, more powerfully, to legitimate and testify to the ties that bind past, present, and future selves together. Insofar as Aleyamma's act was an invitation for Lata to choose her parents over Kannan, it evidently faltered on recognition. Lata did not, and indeed refused to, see herself as responsible for Aleyamma's distress. It is here, in the fulfillment or breakdown of recognition, that the accumulation of death encounters its possibilities and limits. So incredulous was Lata that when Aleyamma later blamed her daughter's insolence as the reason for her suicide attempt, Lata returned a scathing retort. She urged her mother on: "Go ahead and kill yourself. You've had over fifty years of a life. I have only started mine." In declaring the relative value of her young life over her mother's, however, Lata also threatened to destroy it by her own hand, announcing in front of her parents that she, too, would kill herself if forced to marry another. But unlike her mother's, Lata had warned, her intentions would be sincere enough to succeed.[28]

Kinship relations are not fixed entities afforded transcendence through biology. Far from being a static and completed project as the anthropologist's webbed charts of squares and circles might suggest, kinship relations require ongoing maintenance. They are an everyday "doing" wherein "their order in the world is not a thing accomplished for all time, but an achievement needing constant recreation."[29] If hierarchies, dependencies, obligations, and affections must be continually renewed to maintain a working domestic order, Aleyamma's act brought this renewal process to a head. To the extent that Aleyamma's act summoned Lata to compensate for cares of the past with obeisance in the presence, it had evidently failed to deliver.

Lata's skepticism of her mother's actions suggests that in this case, the accumulation of death did not communicate transparently, nor did it reconfigure social relations in any predictable way. While Lata dismissed Aleyamma's morning episode as manipulation, news of it mobilized immediate action on the part of others, reorganizing care along other axes of the family. Lata's elder sister, married and living farther north in the state, withdrew her support of Lata. Pressuring Lata to give up Kannan, she issued a stern warning that if anything were to happen to their parents, the responsibility for "the two dead bodies taken from the house" would fall upon Lata's head. As Aleyamma's distress materialized in the otherwise taken-for-granted smooth running of the household—in mounting piles of unwashed dishes and late or missed family meals—her husband, too, expressed concern. He took Aleyamma to a psychiatrist.

Aleyamma once showed me the anti-depressants she had been taking regularly since that visit to the psychiatrist. Perching her reading glasses on her nose, she rifled carefully through an old leather purse repurposed to store the family's prescriptions. Finding the one she was looking for, she carefully unfolded the slip of paper and smoothed it out on the tabletop. A sample tablet removed from its foil and placed in my hand was presented as if to announce in material terms the suffering Lata had caused. Aleyamma reminded me that she had never before been to a psychiatrist, "only when I came to know about the secret of their relationship. My brother-in-law, he told the psychiatrist to help me because what Lata did was a very big shock to me. Lata was the reason." For Aleyamma, the accumulation of death catalyzed forms of pharmaceutical care and concern for her condition. It did so by mobilizing patriarchal relations in the family in a manner that positioned Aleyamma as injured, requiring the intervention of others. While antidepressants afforded Aleyamma consolation—"when I'm taking the medicines, the sadness goes away"—it was the label of depression that, in the eyes of extended kin, offered material evidence of what Lata had done.[30] As reproachable as Lata's pursuit of a love affair outside marriage was to gossiping family, it was her alleged neglect of her mother's suffering that aggravated charges of sexual laxity with accusations of carelessness, selfishness, and cruelty. Aleyamma's conscription into a pharmacological regime worked to realign economies of care within and between households, with Aleyamma consoled as the betrayed mother and Lata ostracized as the wayward daughter. If Lata's departure severed her ties to her parents, it also generated in its wake a web of reconfirmed commitments and forms of protection among those who remained behind.

## LOVE'S DISENCHANTMENTS

On a balmy afternoon in 2007, Shaila rolled up the sleeve of her *kurta* to show me four thin, discolored marks on the inside of her left forearm. During the tea break signaling the middle of her shift as a saleswoman at a clothing store, the twenty-four-year-old college graduate explained the cuts with surprising equanimity. "He hit me," she said. "I didn't expect he would do this, that my husband would hit me. When he hit me, to scare him, I went and . . . I did this to scare my husband." As we sat between towers of dusty cardboard boxes in the back stockroom, the languorous ceiling fan churning the afternoon humidity in thick circles above our heads, Shaila described taking a blade from her husband's shaving kit after one of the many arguments the couple had been having. After cutting herself, said Shaila, she had gone to show her husband what she had done.[31]

Recent newlyweds, Shaila and her husband, Sujit, had celebrated their "arranged love marriage" just three months before. Having serendipitously met, they fell in love and secured their families' approval given their compatible backgrounds as lower middle-class Nayars. Theirs was emblematic of what many young adults in the capital city told me was the ideal marriage—marrying someone of your choice, whom your family would have likely selected for you anyway. I was familiar with Shaila and Sujit's love story and how their paths first crossed, having been regularly updated on the courtship's developments over many months. Dropping by the shop on his motorcycle, at first once and then several times a week, Sujit would hang around chatting casually with the other salesmen and, eventually, with Shaila. Earlier the means for their clandestine courtship, Shaila's retail job was now a major source of tension in the family. Sujit's parents would have far preferred Shaila to be a homemaker than working in a service position in which she had to interact with strangers and commute across the city five days a week. Shaila herself had also hoped and expected to stop working once married. For now, however, the family simply couldn't afford for her to remain at home. It was only after marriage when Shaila learned that Sujit was several lakhs in debt. Much of it was the result of a high-interest bank loan he had taken to purchase the motorcycle that had first caught her eye when their courtship began.

When acts like Shaila's cutting surfaced within patient and family testimony in the clinic, mental health professionals I observed typically labeled them "impulsive." But judgments of impulsivity, with their temporal assumptions and built-in notions of unthinking irrationality, quickly appear inadequate. They fail to capture the care and control Shaila took in her deployment of cutting as bodily technique. Back in the storeroom, Shaila reenacted running the blade's tip across her skin, explaining to me in technical detail how she had used sufficient pressure to make herself bleed but not enough to tear any veins or muscles. As she glided the rolled cuff of her kurta back down to her wrist, I asked her why she chose to respond to her husband this way. "The reason why I did this is because he hit me," insisted Shaila. "I did this to scare my husband. I just made little cuts. That's all I did. I thought it wouldn't hurt much more than getting hit." Contrary to assumptions about women's impulsivity, the accumulation of death here was carefully produced. It also involved a fine calculus by which Shaila determined that injuring herself wouldn't be any more painful than the harm Sujit had already caused.[32]

The insights of feminist scholars and critical historiographers press us to consider the larger structures and social forces that shape possibilities for and conditions of violence and why it is that these structures and forces come to bear most acutely on women, including those like Shaila. As scholars point out, conventional social development indicators like women's impressive access to education in the state are inadequate for understanding the complexities of gender relations across public and private spheres in Kerala.[33] As a college graduate with a degree in philosophy, Shaila, for instance, was better educated than Sujit, who had discontinued his studies after failing his Secondary School Leaving Certificate exam. Even then, as a collection executive at a private bank, Sujit earned more than twice what his wife did working long shifts into the evening as a saleswoman. Moreover, Shaila herself desired to leave her job to be a full-time housewife. In this way, Shaila troubles any easy equation that might be drawn between women's education and "empowerment." Indeed, the widening lead of Malayali women in education, sometimes over their husbands, has also been positively associated with lifetime experiences of physical and psychological violence and with rising rates of suicide among women.[34] While the number one cause of domestic violence reported in Kerala, as elsewhere in India, is "disobedience" to one's husband, educated women's noncompliance in the face of the conservative attitudes of less-educated husbands and in-laws renders domestic violence in Kerala distinct from that in other states.[35] Long before the afternoon that Sujit hit Shaila, some of the most vicious arguments between husband and wife were sparked, Shaila confessed, when she baldly accused Sujit of loving his mother more than he did her. This was the case again the day Sujit hit her, and Shaila reappeared soon after with a razor blade in her hand. That it was Shaila's overt confrontation with her husband that precipitated his violent response suggests that this young wife had, from her husband's perspective, brazenly overstepped her place.

Women like Shaila are also increasingly disenfranchised from resources in the marital household. The dichotomization of the male breadwinner and the female housewife, instituted with the rise of modern domesticity in the reformed patrifocal family, has become further entrenched in spite of the rising educational levels of Malayali women overall.[36] Both domestic relations and labor conditions do not readily accommodate female employment, and women's workforce participation rates in Kerala have been among the lowest for all the states in India.[37] This withdrawal from the workforce—something that Shaila's in-laws ultimately expected and that Shaila herself desired—limits women's access to self-acquired income and thus their ability to make self-interested decisions within the household. Shaila's employment, however, did not guarantee her greater control over resources. Not only was all of her pay under Sujit's control; it was now being funneled toward the heavy consumer loans he had taken before they married.

Patrifocal forms of inheritance and succession that were legislated in the modernization of the family in Kerala have also disenfranchised women from immovable forms of property, such as land.[38] This trend has worsened as dowry takes on new contours. Dowry in the form of movable property, particularly in the forms of cash, gold, and consumer goods, has become the accepted social standard with the influx of migrant remittances.[39] Sujit's sale of Shaila's bangles within their first month of marriage to help defray loan repayments illustrates the ease with which gold can be pawned to support the needs of the husband's family. The liquid nature of such forms of inheritance further weakens women's ability to maintain possession of these resources or to determine how they are invested if and when they are taken away and has been shown to increase women's vulnerability to domestic violence and dowry abuse.[40] The ideological and material organization of marriage in the middle-class household powerfully shapes conditions for violence in the home for women like Shaila.

The unsettling exchange between husband and wife was also the culmination of Shaila's growing disenchantment with conjugal family life. Like many educated young women I spoke with in the capital city, Shaila had looked to an arranged love marriage to fulfill desires for companionate love. But as she confessed with aching sadness the afternoon she showed me the cuts on her arm, the love marriage she had envisioned during her courtship with Sujit had simply not come to be. Adjusting to a new life with her in-laws and husband had been difficult, she confessed. While Sujit had paid such devoted attention to her during the months when they were first getting to know one another, these days they managed little time together. What had happened to their weekend outings to the movie theater or their evening walks on the beach? What happened to their long conversations in the late hours of the night, when they stayed up whispering about their plans for the future? These days, Sujit was always tense about this or that financial matter, she said. He seemed distracted. Shaila felt isolated and alone in her husband's home, and Sujit refused to let her travel to visit her natal family as frequently as Shaila would have liked. She described to me barely keeping ahead of the cooking, washing, and cleaning—duties on top of her full-time employment made more difficult by her mother-in-law's exacting demands. As the family's financial hardships and Shaila's tensions continued to mount, the strains and disappointments of daily life drifted ever further away from her expectations of companionate marriage.

Shaila's act of cutting must therefore be understood in the broader context of the hierarchical relations, differential access to resources, and ideologies that shape middle-class family life. This is not to try to explain away an event and its knotted desires and vulnerabilities, rendering it transparent to history and ethnography. Rather, it is only to map the larger world in which Shaila's act responded to the "gendered fallout" of family life.[41] In accumulating death, Shaila forcefully expressed her deep disenchantment with a class-specific dream of domesticity. In its careful enactment, it also called upon her husband to respond.

Shaila's act sent vibrations across the folds of the family, some of which, she made clear to me, she had neither intended nor foreseen. While Sujit had chided her for cutting herself over a "trivial matter" (cheriyoru kaaryam) and would never explicitly raise the incident with her again, he had not laid his hand on her since that day. Her cutting also galvanized Sujit's concern and attention. With a bashful smile, Shaila noted to me that nowadays Sujit refused to leave her unattended when they were at home together. While earlier she would spend hours alone in the kitchen preparing the family meals, these days Sujit hung around and sometimes even helped Shaila wash and cut vegetables. "Even now," Shaila whispered to me with a smile, "my husband is scared. If I go here or there or do this or that, he keeps watch of me. He is that careful." Shaila confessed she enjoyed having her husband's attention. His doting behavior happily reminded her of the early days of their courtship. Yet if Sujit's concern for his young wife was indeed galvanized, it was under very different terms from those of Shaila's deeply held notions of companionate love. In the wake of Shaila's cutting, apprehension and uncertainty concerning her future behavior formed the basis of care. Sujit's attentiveness, as Shaila herself noted, evolved out of fear for his wife's emotional vulnerability and steely conviction.[42]

Anthropologists and others have commented extensively on the communicative nature of female suicide in South Asia and other contexts.[43] Where patriarchal power relations and local ideas of female respectability render women's overt physical violence toward others untenable, suicide may provide an "acceptable" means for them to express aggression.[44] Violence channeled against the self can be deeply interpersonal, for it not only communicates anger and grief; it can also accuse and punish those who were the victim's tormentors in life. Writing about troubling rates of female suicide in Sri Lanka, Malathi de Alwis observes, "One's intimates are perceived as extensions of one's self so that harming oneself is tantamount to harming them; they must watch you suffer, they must bear the moral burden."[45] Because a woman's suicide can precipitate the humiliation of her social antagonists, as well as more direct acts of retribution against them by the living, anthropologists have similarly suggested in other contexts that for those with limited agency, suicide offers a powerful means of resistance and even revenge.[46] In this sense, "suicide and homicide are much closer alternatives than we may ordinarily suppose."[47]

But attention to the subtle tremors and shifts that Shaila's act sent through the household suggests that accumulating death may not always be clear-cut in intent, message, or audience. Indeed, as we already saw in Aleyamma's case, accumulating death can be a highly ambivalent mode of address. What is communicated and to whom, and the response that accumulating death generates, if any, is rarely straightforward or predictable. Just as patriarchy itself is not a totalizing system, Shaila's response to her husband was not a transparent act of resistance that upended power relations. Nor was her act one that was straightforwardly and singularly authored as her "own": in surrendering her body to the command of another—it was Sujit who was made to grab the blade from Shaila's hand—the potential ending of the exchange was written in the moment, "chosen" by Sujit as much as by Shaila.[48] Her cutting might be usefully thought of as a mode of what Lauren Berlant calls "lateral agency." Moving beyond vertical constructions of the liberal subject that recognize agency only through the push against or throwing off of hierarchal power relations, Berlant argues that lateral agency "can be an activity of maintenance, not making; fantasy, without grandiosity; sentience, without full intentionality; inconsistency, without shattering; embodying, alongside embodiment."[49] Rather than a self-determined act committed for a prescripted conclusion, Shaila's cutting may have been a way of communicating as much as a way to feel different and be different.

As a form of lateral agency, Shaila's act reshuffled relations more than bringing them crumbling down. It did so in part by mobilizing certain patriarchal relations against others. Sensitized to Shaila's state, Sujit became her ally in the weeks following, interceding on her behalf against his mother and father to relieve Shaila's load of the cleaning and cooking responsibilities and permitting her more frequent trips to see her natal family. Household labor was redistributed among family members, and abuse was silenced across the folds of domestic life to maintain a working order in the home. By catalyzing relations toward the absorption and dissipation of violence and its destabilizing threat, Shaila's act afforded her more breathing space, if only temporarily, while maintaining the precarious functional working order of the household. It did so by positioning Shaila as a young wife needing the protection of her husband against the demands of her in-laws—the very same man who had hit her. In negotiating the dependencies of family life, Shaila's cutting mobilized forms of masculinist protection that allowed her temporary relief.

Shaila's act commanded an unspoken presence in her marital home for several weeks after. Her natal family never came to know anything of the incident. Sujit strongly warned Shaila against exposing what had happened to her brother and sisters, chiding her against causing them unnecessary worry and grief, especially, he impressed upon her, since it was over a trivial argument Shaila herself had started. The silencing response of both Sujit and his parents may have been motivated in part by the threat from without. Because the management of suicide is closely tied to the protection of middle-class respectability, fears about rumors concerning family dysfunction or mental illness, for example, can be powerful motivations for kin to conceal such acts to avoid the potential stigma.[50] These are fears, too, about public intervention. It was mentioned earlier in chapter 3 that in the Indian legal context, women's suicides are taken to be nearly synonymous with domestic abuse and dowry violence, particularly if a woman's suicide occurs soon after marriage.[51] Because the domestic, in this sense, is "always on the verge of becoming political," kin responses are necessarily forged under the reach of the law.[52]

## VANISHING POINTS

In rendering intelligible assertions of care and accusations of its lack, women's accumulation of death can force kin to evaluate lived commitments, reconfiguring rather than simply undoing connections among family members. As anthropologists have shown, care generated in conditions of vulnerability can remake possibilities for living in powerful ways.[53] Attention to how women accumulate death as a mode of altering ways of living or to enhance the lives of others may help to cut loose the tethers that so tightly bind suicide to the pathological, the irrational, and the anti-social. It also complicates easy assumptions that rising suicide is the result of growing atomism and individualization in modern life, for these stories suggest that these women sought death in part out of felt obligation to others.

But if the accumulation of death mobilized forms of care in the families introduced here, we must also ask what that care consisted of. In some cases, it generated attention mediated by pharmaceuticals. For Aleyamma, anti-depressants legitimated her moral positioning as the wronged mother. But for other women I met, psychiatric intervention brought exclusion, brute disciplinary management, and neglect. For Shaila, attention from an abusive husband was motivated in part by fear of stigmatizing rumors and the punitive hand of the law. Care from friends or kin could also facilitate women's endurance of violence by appealing to higher female virtue, as we saw in Kavitha's story. In some of these cases, accumulating death catalyzed forms of masculinist protection in ways that reinforced the conservative terms of gender hierarchies in the family. For instance, Kavitha's situation was ultimately resolved when she found the strength to tell her brother what was happening on campus. Her brother's response—immediate and, ultimately, effective—was to recruit friends back home in Kerala to intimidate and rough up the boys causing Kavitha so much trouble. Life, Kavitha said, became bearable again. What is the nature of care that is produced under circumstances of injured or threatened life? While offering means for women to negotiate the dependencies of family life, these accounts suggest that forms of care produced under the sign of death can quickly become complicit with coercion and violence within and beyond the household.

In addition, we should not lose sight of the incommensurabilities that render women's lives most valuable through and against the promise of death. That all of these acts and fantasies of suicide were themselves care-full in one way or another—oriented with concern and love for others—signifies how even in death these women bore the ponderous responsibility of ensuring the continuation of family cosmologies in ways that others did not. The insistent fact remains that Kunjamma, Kavitha, Aleyamma, and Shaila defined care at the point of transgression, where death revealed the singular magnitude of their worth. It was also where exclusion, punishment, and medical management stood close by. Women's accumulation of death may at times reconfigure or catalyze kin life, generating forms of attentiveness and care, but it also erodes in brute ways. This is the vanishing point of the domestic everyday, where the lines of life and death converge with each other.

# 5

# Anywhere but Here

"Malayalis only commit suicide in Kerala—never anywhere else." Sensing my skepticism, Krishna elaborated further. Take, for example, he said, the Malayalis working in the Persian Gulf. Despite their harsh working and living conditions, Gulf migrants never take their lives while abroad, the twenty-two-year-old contended. With the fruits of their labor to enjoy upon their return home, they have something to look forward to. "And here in Kerala?" I prompted. Malayalis stuck here in Kerala see that their futures are blocked, reasoned Krishna. "There is nothing to look forward to, nothing to help people through the hardships of life. That is why they turn to suicide," he concluded.[1]

From his modest home in Manacaud, on the southern side of Thiruvananthapuram, Krishna constructed a spatial imaginary that was at once global and distinctly regional, stretched between the two poles of "Kerala" and "the Gulf." In this mapping of hope and suicide, Krishna dialogically configured Kerala and the Gulf through moral assertions and empirical erasures. He translated Kerala's ignominious moniker, "the suicide capital of India," into geographic literalism: from Krishna's perspective, it is in Kerala and only Kerala that Malayalis take their lives. By contrast, he insisted that Malayalis never commit suicide anywhere else in the world, including the Gulf. In doing so, he masked an issue of rising concern among migrant workers.[2] In Krishna's spatial imaginary, the erasure of suicide in the Gulf, his ends-justifies-the-means view of labor exploitation, and his mooring of suicide to the place where he felt stuck, all worked to mark Kerala as a place of death and the Gulf as a hope-inspiring yet remote horizon.

Counter to Krishna's claim, the fact remains that Malayalis do commit suicide elsewhere than Kerala. But in this chapter I am not interested in spatial imaginaries of hope and suicide like this one for the strength of their empirical claims. Rather, I ask how they orient young people to the world around them. The spatial manner in which Krishna mapped hope and suicide was not unique among young people I met. Shaji, in his early twenties and in search of work in the Gulf when we were introduced, similarly insisted that Malayalis kill themselves only in Kerala. By leaving, young people like him found hope for the future.[3] Another young man foretold a grim fate on the day of his departure for a job in Dubai, announcing to me and a psychologist at his last group therapy meeting that if things did not work out in the Gulf, he would surely commit suicide. Chronically underemployed for the last several years with a number of failed businesses behind him, he said that if he couldn't make it in Dubai, he wouldn't make it anywhere. Fail in the Gulf, and nothing would remain.[4]

Imaginaries such as these dialogically configure "Kerala" against "non-Kerala" in the uneven distribution of life and suicide, hope and hopelessness, possibility and stagnation. Among both the elite and the nonelite men and women in the capital city who shared with me their designs for the future, spatial representations featured prominently in their aspirations, disappointments, and self-perceptions. More than just a way of seeing the world, these representations tied Kerala to stagnation and "elsewhere" to possibility in ways that informed their everyday endeavors and projects of worth. They provided the coordinates by which young people like Krishna and Shaji located themselves socially, morally, and psychically in relation to their peers, families, and communities and to a larger notion of global modernity. As they did for the young man who feared for his failure in the Gulf, they can mark the critical limit to a livable life.

Clinical approaches to suicide have privileged questions of time over space, particularly in their focus on hopelessness as a marker of suicidal ideation and a predictor of suicide.[5] In this chapter, I seek to recuperate, alongside the temporal, the spatial dimensions of phenomenological experiences of possibility and entrapment that are the larger terrain of suicide. Rather than presume universal terms by which hope and hopelessness are experienced, I contend that to understand something of prospective affect and its fallout first demands recognition of the distinct experiential modes by which individuals and communities define and live possibility and stagnation.[6] For those who shared with me their aspirational struggles, space was a key register through which the present and future were configured and perceived as buoyantly open, tentative, or fully stuck. In particular, it was through migratory possibility that young people experienced their life chances and painful exclusions.

Transnational migration shapes diverse realms of everyday life in Kerala. Beginning in the 1970s, the state witnessed a phenomenal migration expansion of the nonelite to the Persian Gulf states. The hike in oil prices led to an upsurge in construction activities and infrastructure building in the Gulf, creating a seemingly insatiable demand for an international and flexible workforce that has drawn in millions of contract laborers from such countries as Pakistan, India, Sri Lanka, and the Philippines. The mostly Muslim migrants that first left Kerala for the Gulf paved the way for the wider participation of Hindus and Christians. Although migrants are predominantly male, female nurses and now an increasing number of female domestic workers form a significant, but underrecognized, dimension of this migration.[7] The migration of high-skilled professionals from Thiruvananthapuram has also expanded significantly in recent years, setting a different bar for highly educated, upper-status youth who aspire to permanent settlement or long-term residence in places like the United Kingdom, the United States, and Canada. Among elites, parenting and educational investments are channeled toward children's future competitiveness on the global job market. Together with liberalizing economic reforms, migration has made for an expanding circulation of ideas, goods, money, and people, shifting the aspirational horizons of those able to move, as well as those who cannot. Through mass-media images, stories recounted among friends and neighbors, and public displays of wealth by returning migrants, young people see and hear of success among those able to gain social opportunity and wealth through migration overseas.

While shaped by structures of hope and aspiration at the crossroads of transnational migration, development, and liberalization, young people's dreams of migration also develop from the specific vantage point of their social position. Krishna, for example, lived intimately with migration through the circular movement of his two cousins who migrated periodically between Kerala and Abu Dhabi as construction laborers and were ultimately able to marry and build multistoried homes for their families. A young Ezhava man, Krishna longed for migration in ways that were shaped by his cousins' success and by a broader mobility ideal embraced by the Ezhava community. As was the case for other nonelite young men I met, the Gulf dictated Krishna's aspirations to mobility and his path to establishing a household. Access to social and cultural capital, family and community histories of migration, and aspects of social position like class, caste, and gender shape the imagined projection of self across space and time.[8]

Dreams of migration featured prominently in the aspirational struggles of both young men and women I spoke with. For some, these dreams were the only way to bring into focus a future for themselves, let alone a future adequate to their expectations. This feeling was particularly acute for the involuntarily immobile, those who had been "left behind" in the many senses of the term: physically abandoned by their outward-bound peers, stalled financially in precarious jobs, arrested temporally in transitioning through the life stages, and cast to the edges of global modernity. In light of the key role migration plays in aspirational horizons among young people in Thiruvananthapuram, attending to how the world looks and feels to those left behind is critical. In view of the question of suicide, the feeling of being left behind is critical, too, if we are to understand something of how young people experience possibility and hopelessness and how they define what makes for a livable life.

### TRAPPED

Abraham and I first met back in 2000 during my first trip to Kerala.[9] At the time, he was nearing the end of his bachelor's degree program in literature at Mahatma Gandhi University, in Kottayam. The twenty-one-year-old introduced himself as an aspiring journalist and film-maker. Over time, we would come to share our ongoing projects with each other—Abraham, his short stories and paintings, and I, my budding research ideas and charcoal drawings. Abraham grew up in a modest Latin Catholic home located several miles outside Kollam, an hour's train ride north of Thiruvananthapuram. His father was an agricultural laborer, and his mother was a cleaner at a local hospital; Abraham was the eldest of three children.

The two of us would remain in touch as Abraham graduated and moved to the capital city in search of work. Sporadic e-mails sent from Internet cafés reported that he was moving along in a string of temporary jobs, most of them freelance writing and photography gigs with small leftist newspapers and magazines. I wouldn't see him again until 2005. Abraham was living in a small rented house in Chackai, on the western fringe of the city, with several other friends, their numbers in chronic flux as jobs came and went. The afternoon I stopped by with a friend to visit, I found the house depressingly barren. Only a few mattresses on the concrete floor, a scattering of cooking vessels, plates, and spoons in the kitchen, and a pile of newspapers in the corner told of inhabitants. Although securing a steady job had turned out to be far more difficult than he had expected, Abraham decided against returning to his native Kollam. He would stick it out in the city, he told me, until he secured a stable job as a journalist. In the months following, he would update me on his spells of temporary employment as he periodically shifted from one job to another around the city.

Then one night in 2007 Abraham called. The late hour of the call concerned me. He had been out drinking with his friends, something that always dropped him into melancholic depths. I could hear the alcohol thick in his voice. About two months before, Abraham had quit a relatively stable job at a magazine for reasons still unclear to me. Since then, he'd been scraping by with a few freelancing assignments here and there. He confessed to feeling guilty for having nothing to supplement his recently widowed mother's modest earnings that had to support his younger siblings. Unable to afford the monthly rent at the house where he had earlier been staying, he spent his nights crashing with friends around the city. But their generosity was wearing thin. When I asked him why he had left this last job, Abraham's only explanation would be the echoing refrain of our conversations: "I just need to get out of Kerala."

Abraham made a strained effort to sound upbeat. He was being considered for a new job as a graphic designer for a tabloid, and if it worked out he would be leaving in two weeks' time for Ernakulam, a bustling city located north of Thiruvananthapuram in the central region of the state. While it was not far enough from here, said Abraham, it was a start. "Where will you live?" I asked. With friends for a few days, here and there, he replied. His voice dropped to a near whisper. Confessing his inability to speak openly about his frustrations with his friends, Abraham began to itemize his disappointments, grabbing at fistfuls of sadness as he spoke. I could hear my friend struggling to hold back tears. "I know I have talent, I have a gift, but then the circumstances around me are mediocre. Just mediocre," he vented. "The problem is that there are no opportunities for me here." I listened quietly as he denounced the conditions around him, his voice trembling in anger as he blamed the Kerala government for failing to make use of the talents of its young people. Pausing, he asked me pointedly why he, born in Kerala but just as intelligent as I, could not get a scholarship to travel around the world and spend time talking with people as I had. "Such a nice life you have," said Abraham. In a place like Kerala, where good jobs were hard to come by and the untapped resources of educated youth were squandered, it was little wonder, he said, why so many Malayalis his age—talented, intelligent, and brimming with expectation—turn to suicide.[10]

Migration from the viewpoint of those like Abraham—those "left behind"—has attracted minimal scholarly attention.[11] Privileging mobile subjects neglects the ways the intensification and expansion of movement for some have made involuntary immobility the experience for more and more individuals who now stake imagined futures other than where they are.[12] This privileging also fails to capture feelings of missed opportunity and entrapment among those who actively struggle to migrate against dim or impossible prospects and whose immobility comes into painful relief against the movement of others.

Attending to how the world looks and feels to those left behind offers a more comprehensive view of what we understand to be "migration" and whom we recognize as its participants. Within the classical migration literature, those who stay behind appear in the main as sending communities or as those receiving remittances, that is, as either the anchors through which migrants stay connected to homelands or the beneficiaries of the movement of others. The more recent turn to transnational frameworks has recognized that even those who do not migrate actively participate in the imaginaries and global flows facilitated by new media technologies and the widening circulation of ideas and people.[13] We also know that nonmigrants produce elaborate rumors and stories about the conditions related to the departure of migrants and the reasons behind their leaving, and they shape their own identities in the telling.[14] But experiences of involuntary immobility are also far more complex than can be revealed in relationships exclusively defined through the movement of others. More than being the mere absence of movement, immobility is productive of its own psychic, social, and moral realities in ways that shape the practical coordinates and commitments of daily life. Remaining behind can carry with it disappointments and frustrations, including those rooted in perceptions of missed possibility.[15] Intimate living among the bodies, stories, and lives of successful migrants offers motivating but cruel reminders of the life chances that have passed over those who cannot move. Experiences of involuntary immobility therefore complicate any simple story of globalization as one of either exclusion or inclusion, highlighting instead the ways those left behind are simultaneously positioned within and outside the aspirations and projects of global modernity.[16]

To Abraham, being left behind felt a certain way. Like other educated young people, he spoke of and imagined migration, not in the cultural and citizenship terms of belonging, but rather in the terms of *becoming.* In rendering Kerala a space of bleak futures and "elsewhere" the site of possibility, Abraham envisioned migration as the primary, if not only, route to becoming who he imagined he could be and was indeed meant to be. Migration was thus far more than longing; it was a necessary condition for Abraham to realize the person he felt to be latent within him. Through the lens of elsewhere, he experienced a kind of bifocality, the ability to see both his better self vividly projected across time and space and his lesser self stuck in present immobility. This made for a particular kind of stagnation in which Abraham experienced his life and himself as diminished versions of what *could* be. This feeling surfaced in our interactions. As he did that night on the phone, and on other occasions, Abraham wondered aloud why he couldn't spend his time as happily and freely as I did—moving about the world "just to talk to people." In drawing our lives together this way, he asserted his contemporaneousness with the anthropologist, a fact anthropology long denied its subjects of study.[17] Asserting his presence in the same projects of modernity, Abraham staked a rightful claim to the desires that had brought me around the world to him. The difference was that, unlike me, Abraham was stuck.

For Abraham, migration *from* Kerala more than migration *to* a specified elsewhere was the necessary condition to an adequate future, perhaps any future at all. Immobility in this case was marked less by a longing for a particular destination than a desire for "anywhere but here," a desire that hinged on the necessity of departure. This is a crucial point: what defined Abraham's sense of entrapment was his need to "get out of Kerala." It would have been enough, he said, to leave the state but stay in India. To see life's chances everywhere other than where one is makes for an experience of longing and also of being stifled. This was a condition young men and women described to me through feelings of frustration, loneliness, and exile at home. A few captured this experience through vivid embodied metaphor, as one young woman did when she described Kerala as an "allergy." How are experiences of immobility shaped by the desperate need to escape the place in which one may likely forever remain? What happens to perceptions of "home" when home is not where one belongs but is instead felt to be an allergy—abrasive and harmful to one's very constitution?

A few months after that late-night phone call, Abraham returned to Thiruvananthapuram. Over coffee, he explained his most recent disappearance. He had gotten the job in Ernakulam, but this, too, turned out to be temporary. Recounting how much he had enjoyed living in that big and bustling city, Abraham said it was unfortunate that they couldn't make his position permanent. Even then, my friend was upbeat, energized by his latest plan. He had decided to apply to film school in Pune, in the Indian state of Maharashtra. For young people with fresh vision like his, Abraham explained to me excitedly, this was where careers were launched. I agreed to help him put together his portfolio and apply for scholarships. This would be his big break, he assured me. This would be his ticket out.[18]

## LEAVING IS THE ONLY WAY TO LIVE

Dreams of migration and the ability to project an imagined self across space and time are shaped by aspects of social position, access to cultural and social resources, and family and community histories of mobility. If Abraham felt enabled by his college degree and longed for migration as the route to fully actualize his destiny as an aspiring journalist and filmmaker, twenty-nine-year-old Sabu had little choice but to look to migration as the way out of an impoverished life. An only child who lost both parents before he was ten, Sabu was forced to end his studies after completing the sixth standard. When we first met, the soft-spoken Sabu was working full-time behind the counter at a bakery. At the time, he was living in a two-room rented house with several other young men, making barely enough to cover monthly expenses. The Syrian Christian family who owned the bakery and had hired Sabu years ago knew of his situation. They gave him bonus pay when the holidays came around and provided him lunch during his shifts. Their generosity, he told me, helped to make ends meet. Even then, he was struggling.

With no better job prospects available to him in the city given his limited qualifications, Sabu had been searching for work in the Gulf for nearly two years now. There, he reasoned, he could make and save several times more than what he was earning doing the same work in Kerala. While life in the Gulf scared him, Sabu confessed, he had no choice. An aging bachelor by his account, he had to leave if he wished to get married, he explained. He was living from paycheck to paycheck, with no parents and no immediate kin to arrange for his marriage. Only through migration could Sabu overcome his social and financial deficits as a potential bridegroom upon return. Calling on friends working in Dubai and Bahrain, he was desperate to mobilize any contacts he had in the hopes that someone might help to find him work. Nothing had come through yet.

For Sabu, leaving Kerala was not seen as the route to self-actualization as it was for Abraham. Rather, it was a practical strategy to maximize earning potential. Sabu's struggles to get by must be understood not only as the result of his family circumstances but also in the larger context of economic changes wrought by Gulf migration. While Gulf migration has helped migrant households attain higher levels of income, the inflow of remittances has also pushed up land and food prices and the cost of health services, education, and transport in Kerala, with particularly adverse effects on nonmigrant families among poor and fixed-income groups.[19] Sabu captured this dilemma and its sole solution with poignant irony: "I have to leave to be able to live here."[20]

If, said Sabu, he found a job in the Gulf and things did not end badly ("So many stories in the paper of Malayalis dying in the Gulf"), he might finally have the chance to get married and have a family. Gulf migration, both deeply desired and deeply feared, would give movement once again to a life stuck as a perpetual bachelor: vertical transition through the life stages demanded horizontal movement overseas. He didn't want to live a fancy life, Sabu added, smiling shyly. It would be enough to marry a simple girl and have a small plot of land. But as each year in the bakery passed, he felt his chance slipping away. A low-status, low-caste Pulaya (SC) man trapped in economic uncertainty, with limited education and no immediate kin to help buffer his vulnerability, Sabu looked to the Gulf rather than to an open and boundless "elsewhere" as his only path to economic stability and marriage. Paired alongside Abraham's longings, Sabu's struggles to reach the Gulf begin to illustrate how social location and access to resources differently shape young people's spatial strategies.

Through migratory possibility, Sabu planned his progression through the life stages toward the locally recognized ideal of the masculine householder.[21] Others I met looked to migration to fulfill gendered obligations to the natal household. Twenty-five-year-old Altaf retrospectively narrated his motivations for going to the Gulf in terms of economic imperative, family obligation, the practical pull of migratory networks, and community identity. "Migration to the Gulf is what we

Muslims do," he told me the afternoon we met over coffee. A common friend had introduced us during Altaf's first visit home from Riyadh, Saudi Arabia. He was in the middle of his two-week holiday from his job working as an electrical engineer. When I asked Altaf why he had decided to go to the Gulf upon completing his degree, his response was straightforward. "Why the Gulf? Earlier I had been planning to start a business here in Kerala, so basically I needed to gather up some money. So that was the only reason for going," he explained to me in English. Altaf, a bachelor, mentioned the marriages of his two younger sisters. His father, who ran a small rice shop, could not afford two weddings on his limited income alone. Altaf's financial calculus was clear: "If you go to the Gulf, you will get high pay. You can earn money quickly. If you stay here, your pay will be much less for the same work. So for that reason and that reason only, I went to the Gulf." With two uncles already working in Riyadh, Altaf's path to the Gulf had been laid down long before he had completed his degree. "I have family there who brought me over. I'm a Muslim, no? For most Muslims, after schooling, usually for some years we will be in the Gulf to earn some money. That's why I went." For Altaf, migration enabled him to fulfill family obligations as a brother, son, and emerging patriarch and to embody what he configured as a fuller Muslim identity through his connections to the Gulf.[22]

Although he looked forward to returning to Riyadh and said he enjoyed his work there, Altaf missed his family, his sisters especially. Smiling, he told me how his mother had prepared all his favorite foods. He had come home too skinny, she said when she first embraced him. Altaf's friends were happy to see him, too. He was relieved, he confessed, that things still felt the same between them. Indeed, throughout our hour-long chat Altaf's phone buzzed constantly with incoming text messages. With just a week left before his return, I was grateful that Altaf had chosen to spend some of that time speaking with me. Gulping down the last of his tea, Altaf bid me good-bye, dashing out the door to meet up with friends. The days, he said as he left the tip, were flying by too fast.[23]

## "CHOOSING" UNCERTAINTY

For those without immediate or long-term prospects for migration, immobility does more than just trap, constrain, deny, and disempower. Young people actively respond to predicaments of uncertainty.[24] In

Thiruvananthapuram, many creatively produced situations of involuntary immobility as political and moral states. Through spatial representations and strategies, some young people staked claims of entitlement and deservedness. They asserted their talents and the better life they felt was rightfully theirs while denouncing the stagnant conditions around them.

Believing his opportunities to be subpar to his talents, my friend Abraham, the aspiring filmmaker and journalist, collaborated in the production of his precarious employment as a way of enacting his desires—and deservedness—of something better. Taking up a string of temporary jobs to bide time on the way to his dream of salaried employment as a journalist, Abraham deliberately held out for the distant horizons and job opportunities "elsewhere" that he believed commensurate to his talents and abilities. His capacity to hold out hinged on his social positioning and access to resources. While empowered by his college degree and animated by a sense of deservedness, Abraham also knew he was on borrowed time. After his father passed away and his mother found herself struggling to support Abraham's younger siblings on her meager pay as a cleaner at a hospital, he faced increasing pressure to contribute to the household. His longings to migrate were thus characterized by vulnerability and marked time, critically limited by his lower class and social location in the broader world of acute unemployment in Kerala.[25] His pursuits were also limited by Abraham's lack of the habitus that attunes higher-status graduates to the sphere of employment as social competition. As the first in his family to pursue college studies, Abraham entered the job market brandishing a degree but without the internalized sense of self-confidence, intuition, and communication skills those from urban middle-class (and usually upper-caste) families are most likely to possess. These are elements of cultural capital that have been shown at times to trump the importance of educational qualifications in the pursuit of salaried employment in India.[26]

Like Abraham, Dinesh embraced uncertainty rather than taking a job subpar to his qualifications. In doing so, he asserted both the failure of the Kerala government to provide hope for its young people and his entitlement to something better. When we met, the thirty-eight-year-old doctoral student in psychology explained to me in English how he refused to accept any job that was either inadequate or irrelevant to his training. Having been underemployed for over ten years after completing his master's degree in psychology, Dinesh decided to return to school for his doctorate rather than continue with dismal job prospects.[27] But with his dissertation defense and graduation around the corner, he had no firm plans for the future. When I asked what he saw for himself over the next five years, he told me, "I haven't made any decisions about that." From an upper-status Nayar family, the unmarried Dinesh was living at home with his parents in a middle-class neighborhood in the city. He had applied to clinical and research jobs in Kerala and in the United States. Nothing had come through yet. In the meantime, Dinesh told me, one of his younger cousins had been offered a job as an IT specialist in London. At twenty-three, she had just completed her master's degree in computer engineering. It was clear that the newfound mobility of this younger cousin—a cousin whom Dinesh repeatedly qualified as "less educated"—was a source of deep frustration. In the world of merit, Dinesh believed himself more deserving. Even then, a younger cousin's migration now shaped his sphere of possibility and his envious longing for departure.

While waiting for better prospects to come along, Dinesh said he would continue at the counseling center and suicide hotline where he had been working the last seven years. While the pay was minimal, he refused, he told me again, to take a job that did not utilize his hard-earned doctorate in psychology. In the meantime, he had also enrolled in one of the city's proliferating private coaching courses that promote "personality development" and "life skills," hoping that it might give him the competitive edge in future job interviews. Accepting prolonged economic uncertainty—the bachelor and only child admitted he was fortunate to have the safety net of living with his parents—Dinesh explained that his lack of clarity about the future was symptomatic of a broader uncertainty among educated youth in Kerala. "Our futures are uncertain, you know?" he said. Blaming the Kerala government for failing to provide job opportunities for educated young people like himself, Dinesh told me, "Even now, I am still unemployed. In general, we young people in Kerala have little hope." With a faint smile, he commented on the irony of his life: in seeking to help the unemployed, depressed, and suicidal, his education had landed him in much the same place as his clients.[28]

Unemployment in Kerala bears most pressingly on educated, unmarried youth like Dinesh and Abraham.[29] But the insights of the skeptic are useful to consider: manual jobs, for instance, are replete there but attract so few that migrant labor must be recruited from neighboring states and from as far away as Bihar.[30] By these accounts, complaints about unemployment in Kerala are misleading, for it is not that jobs do not exist but rather that youth today refuse to do the kind of work available to them. Some older-generation Malayalis told me that young people today choose to be under- and unemployed and, moreover, deserve their predicament. In a sense, many like Abraham and Dinesh do "choose" precariousness. They choose it, that is, as a way of enacting desires for and entitlement to that which they feel they deserve. At least for a time, they may collaborate in the production of their own social and economic uncertainty, refusing inadequate jobs in the hopes that better prospects will come along.

Under- and unemployed youth in Kerala, as in other regions of India, are experiencing uncertain periods of "waiting" that characterize prolonged transitions into adulthood.[31] Craig Jeffrey observes that while unemployed young men in northern India describe themselves as doing aimless forms of *timepass*, waiting enables them to acquire skills, engage in new cultural styles, and to mobilize politically.[32] Young people, Jeffrey argues, creatively respond to conditions of uncertainty, advance their goals, and maintain their identities as people in transition. For those like Abraham and Dinesh who actively respond to their circumstances, space and time in waiting are tightly bundled. Migratory imaginings enable young people in Thiruvananthapuram to project across time and space the progression of self otherwise denied them in the present. Dreams of migratory possibility therefore offer an important, albeit temporary, strategy to ease the problems of time.[33] In the face of economic uncertainty, they enable young people to envision a means for becoming through space, even if physical movement is elusive.

With hopes but no immediate chance to leave, young people produce their condition of immobility as embodied forms of moral commentary about the local developmental state, about themselves, and about mobile others.[34] In holding out for something better, Abraham spoke back to a hegemonic story of developmentalism, accusing the Kerala government for squandering the educational assets and talent of its young people. Some also stake personal claims of deservedness by delegitimizing the movement of others seen to be less worthy, as Dinesh did. Recognizing the ways young people produce their entrapment as a moral condition and assess what they deserve and are willing to wait for presents alternative inroads into experiences that have been too easily dismissed as youth laziness or aimlessness. Young people bring different capacities and resources to sustain these assertions and performances. Even for those like Dinesh, whose parents were able and willing to support him, choosing uncertainty is viable only for a time.

## EXILE AT HOME AND PRACTICES OF NOT BELONGING

By constructing his entrapment as a moral and political state, Abraham enacted what Michael Brown has called the "performativity" of space.[35] Expanding on the work of Foucault, Brown looks at the ways the gay "closet" operates as a spatial practice of knowledge/power. He suggests that space shapes identities and bodies through metaphorical and material discourses of constraint and release. Liberation—and thus by extension its dialectical counterpart, entrapment—is produced and enacted as a moral condition through everyday practice. In addition to passing up inadequate employment opportunities to hold out for something better, young people like Abraham draw on their physical surroundings to performatively dramatize their stagnation. Asserting one's lack of belongingness in Kerala, for instance, is a common way to index both migratory desire and cosmopolitan orientation. Using the urban spaces at their disposal to act out their feelings of entrapment, young people simultaneously assert their desire to belong "elsewhere" and the feelings of exile that define moral, social, and psychic existence in Kerala.

Neethu's eighteenth birthday was a memorable one. On that day, her parents granted her childhood wish: after years of turning down invitations, they finally agreed to allow her to visit her uncle, aunt, and cousins in Sharjah. Having never traveled alone, let alone out of the country, Neethu was both anxious and excited at the prospect of flying all the way to the Gulf by herself. In the month before her departure, she and I rehearsed the labyrinth of immigration, customs, and baggage stops she would have to navigate at the airport. Neethu, her mother, and I went shopping for new luggage that we would later pack with sweets and small gifts. Those weeks, Neethu talked incessantly about the trip, imagining all the things she would see and do in the Gulf. One evening in particular, Neethu's mother, Manju, and I listened to the teenager spiral off into fantasies of settling in Sharjah or Dubai. In a matter of minutes, she had revised her plans for her future, imagining that she would marry a Gulf migrant, vacation in the snowy mountaintops of Switzerland, and eventually settle in London or the United States. After that, she would bring over her parents, Neethu said, glancing at her mother out of the corner of her eye. Manju listened in bemused disbelief, shooting me looks as Neethu's forays around the world unfolded. Once Neethu was done, Manju carefully and gently managed her daughter's excitement, reminding her that this was just a two-week holiday. Neethu would not be moving to the Gulf or anywhere else for that matter. Moreover, since it was Harish Uncle who was paying Neethu's airfare and providing her room and board—the airfare alone was far out of the family's financial reach—in all likelihood, said her mother, Neethu would never get another chance to go abroad again.

Manju's management of her daughter's migratory desires that afternoon has a backstory. For several years now, Harish Uncle had been trying to convince Manju's husband to join his family in the Gulf, offering to leverage his professional contacts to find an opening for his brother. On other occasions Manju and I had discussed extensively why she and her husband had no interest in leaving Kerala, despite Harish Uncle's generous offers. Manju, who strongly identifies as an upper-caste Nayar, once explained that mostly lower-caste and lower-status people go to the Gulf "because they are willing to suffer a hard life to make money." Even though Harish Uncle and his family lived comfortably—he was a family physician, said Manju—they still endured difficulties in their treatment as strangers in the Gulf. These were aspects of Gulf life that Neethu did not understand, she told me. With good work at home as a bank manager, Manju's husband preferred to stay in Kerala. That decision carried with it another expectation on the part of Manju and her husband: that their daughter would remain in Kerala after marriage to look after them. Neethu's expansive dreams of settling abroad did not square with her mother's ideas about the reciprocities of care between children and parents. What for Neethu was a pleasure junket became a potential threat that weighed on Manju's mind, raising anxieties that Neethu's desires for the future might change after two weeks in the Gulf. This, Manju told me, was precisely why she and her husband had been so reluctant to let Neethu go, turning down invitations year after year.

In the days after Neethu's return, I stopped by the house to welcome her back. Several aunts, uncles, and cousins had also dropped by, and I found everyone seated around tea and sweets in the living room. Neethu, who had always spoken only in Malayalam with me, was now dropping fragments of English sentences here and there as she began regaling us with stories about her trip. This was something she had been doing since the car ride home from the airport, Manju announced to us with an amused grin—this, she continued pointedly, even though Neethu hadn't had any need for English while in Sharjah, her interactions limited to cousins, aunts, and uncles. Skipping past her mother's comment, Neethu went on about her trip, growing effusive about "clean and modern Sharjah!" Returning home, said Neethu, had been very difficult. "I have been so unhappy!" she told me. "When I walked into the house, I grew so angry with everything, so small and dirty, not like Harish Uncle's house." Manju, in the meantime, was shooting me looks. "It is impossible for me to adjust to things here now. When I got off the plane, it was so hot. Right now it is winter in Sharjah, so it is comfortable," continued Neethu to her audience. She explained how frustrated she had been on the car ride back from the airport. "When I was riding in the car, can you imagine? I was bumping up and down, up and down, because the roads here are so terrible. Not like the roads in Sharjah, so straight and flat! And everything here is so dusty, dusty everywhere. I have had a cold every day since I returned because of the dust in the air!" Neethu would complain for weeks about her symptoms, pressing her hand against her sinuses while waving the other in front of her eyes.[36]

Neethu's difficulties in "adjusting" materialized in her persistent cold and sensitivity to the heat and dust. They also emphasized her new perceptions of her home as small and dirty compared with Sharjah's bright, aseptic modernity. But beyond these responses, there was also a certain pride in Neethu's assertions that she no longer fit with her old way of life. In emphasizing the many difficulties of her return, she signaled for those around her a shift in sensibility and disposition, one that now oriented her to life overseas. Neethu would actively index this new cosmopolitan and modern sensibility as she commended the "sophisticated Arab people" of the Gulf and disparaged the "petty, jealous" ways of Malayalis. As I found one afternoon when I accompanied her to a pharmacy and a stranger pushed her way in front of Neethu to pay, her everyday interactions provided fodder for her to stage this new sensibility ("See how selfish Malayalis here are?"). Responding to the environment around her and acting out a newfound perspective onto a regional identity that she tied to the physical location of Kerala, Neethu produced a claim and a feeling of not belonging. She evidenced for herself and others a cosmopolitan outlook that oriented her to the Gulf as a beacon of modernity and the good life, even if she may never reach there again.

Vijay also used the city's urban spaces to express his desires for being elsewhere. Having completed his college degree in commerce the year before, Vijay was working part-time at a private bank when we met. A self-described dreamer, the twenty-two-year-old found it difficult to commit to any particular pursuit. Everything, he told me, stimulated his imagination. How could he pursue just one job for the rest of his life? While Vijay did not express desires for any particular career path, he spoke excitedly about migrating abroad to the United States, or Canada, or to London. Dreams of elsewhere were inspired by the books he spent most of his free time reading and from his encounters in the urban spaces around him. These days, he told me, he liked walking the grounds of the Napier Museum. The manicured lawns, central walking path, and flowering gardens were a popular oasis in the city. They also attracted many *madamas* and *saips*, white women and white men, in the morning and evening hours for jogging and leisurely walks. Vijay said in recent weeks he had been going there daily to strike up conversations with foreigners. His encounters became extensions of the lives of those he had read about in books: "When I meet a foreigner, I'll imagine, 'This is Heathcliff or Edgar,' or 'He must live near Jonathan' or near to some of the other characters I've read about." Speaking with foreigners, said Vijay, was fun and eye opening. He spoke freely with them about his opinions and ideas about topics ranging from politics to culture, and "even about sex," in a manner he felt he could not speak with Malayali friends and family. "If I told them the things I say to foreigners," Vijay said, his eyes growing wide, "they'd tell me I'm a bad person *(cheettha manushyan)*." With prospects for overseas migration remote, Vijay enacted a cosmopolitan and progressive sensibility through his gravitation toward foreigners in the city, simultaneously constructing Malayalis as stifling to his expansive ways of thinking.[37]

Precisely because human mobility in its myriad forms has featured centrally across the disciplines, there is a need, writes Arturo Escobar, "for a corrective theory that neutralizes this erasure of place, the asymmetry that arises from giving far too much importance to 'the global' and far too little value to 'place.'"[38] Involuntary mobility is one lens through which we can interrogate practices of place making from the perspective of those who long to be elsewhere. Both Neethu and Vijay actively produced Kerala as place as they enacted their desires for elsewhere within the urban spaces and through their daily interactions with the people around them. The city landscape and its residents offered resources at their disposal through which they creatively staged and dramatized their condition of exile at home.

## ATTAINING "MALAYALI-NESS"

We earlier saw the ways in which educated young people hoped for the fulfillment of latent potentials and talents in the movement out of Kerala. For Abraham, the aspiring filmmaker and journalist, that movement promised the actualization of the person he was meant to be. Such ideas may appear to resonate with neoliberal discourses of self-realization that identify "the calculus of the market within the very heart of the subject."[39] In positioning transnational migration as the route to the enterprising, talented, and fully actualized individual one is meant to be, these elite narratives of migration position the global market as the key to attaining a genuine selfhood. At the same time, however, we must not subsume these experiences under universalizing models of neoliberal subject formation. Among young people in the capital city, ideas and narratives of actualization through migration are shaped in distinct ways by regional imaginaries of migration and development, as well as by personal and community histories of social mobility.

Regional notions of the past inform the legitimacy of desires for mobility in the present.[40] Some elite youth I met scripted their personal aspirations to migrate within a larger, development-identified "Malayali" identity they claimed for themselves. It was Jacob who articulated in the most memorable terms how a more fully Malayali self could be achieved, ironically, only by leaving Kerala. On a Sunday afternoon while others slumbered through the heat with a postlunch siesta, I hopped into an autorickshaw to meet with Jacob at one of the upscale cafés that have cropped up around the city's greener, affluent neighborhoods in recent years. During the weekends, these places brim with Thiruvananthapuram's upper middle class. Hindi music videos blare from television screens, competing with the conversation that hums all around, while smartly dressed young men and women text on the latest mobile phones.

From a wealthy Syrian Christian family, Jacob had recently completed his MBA degree in London when we first met and was looking for a job in Canada or the United States. He spoke frequently about his difficulties coming back to Kerala after spending two years abroad doing his postgraduate work. While happy to see friends and family, he was itching to leave once more. It would become such a common theme in our conversations that I could not help but read his jittery disposition and the way he compulsively bounced his legs while sitting as signs of his readiness for departure. The Sunday afternoon we met for coffee, Jacob spoke to me in fluid English, explaining that now that he had been to the United Kingdom, he understood the key difference between Malayalis in Kerala and those abroad. The intelligent, sophisticated, and entrepreneurial Malayalis he met in the United Kingdom had impressed him deeply. Although among the many Indians he had met abroad, the north Indians thought themselves superior to south Indians, the Malayalis were always the most self-motivated, confident, and driven. Both Malayali men and women were this way, he added, seething about the north Indians' sense of superiority. Explaining to me that Malayalis "have always" migrated, he situated contemporary migration within a "long history of Malayalis moving around the globe." The Malayali within Kerala, Jacob continued, is lazy and unmotivated. But the moment he has a chance to leave, he becomes someone entirely different—someone creative, hard working, and resourceful. "A Malayali can do anything better than anyone else in the world, as long as he is outside Kerala," he asserted seriously. Then with a laugh: "A Malayali could learn Chinese more fluently than a Chinese person, provided he's anywhere but Kerala!"[41]

Jacob's quip might initially appear unremarkable in light of the region's long history of migration and transoceanic contact. Mobility and movement have been central tropes in a constructed regional and cultural identity. Malayalis in Kerala and in the diaspora refer to a "Malayali" proclivity for migration, one linked to a vibrant history of cultural exchange and trade relations between the Malabar coast and other regions of the world, from Persia, to Italy, to China beginning as early as 3000 B.C.[42] This tale, into which contemporary migration is written as just one small chapter, has made for a popular trope of the Malayali as intrepid traveler. Anecdotes about the peripatetic nature of Malayalis were recounted to me with both pride and hyperbolic humor and were referenced to explain the vise-like grip Gulf migration has on young people today, an obsession known colloquially in English as the "Gulf craze" or the "Gulf syndrome." A Malayali truism goes: wherever you might travel, including every far-flung corner of the world, you will always find an enterprising Malayali. This claim has even acquired interplanetary dimensions in the rewriting of Neil Armstrong's first steps on the moon. In an anecdote told to me too many times to count, Armstrong bounces across the lunar landscape only to discover that an enterprising Malayali—running a teashop and reading a newspaper—has already claimed the place. People draw on the figure of the nomad to evidence different attributes of a migration-identified "Malayaliness." Some say that the migratory nature of Malayalis demonstrates their cosmopolitan outlook; others, their drive to succeed; and still others, their resourceful and creative ability to thrive just about anywhere in the world. These discourses inflect the specific import of migration to the aspirational projects of young people, particularly for those like

Jacob, who wrote his personal desire for settlement abroad into a larger Malayali tale of transoceanic movement.

But Jacob's comments bear closer scrutiny for the particular way they tie migration to the actualization of another aspect of "Malayaliness." Replicating an elite discourse of Kerala developmentalism, Jacob claimed that migration is not only the realization of a nomadic identity; it also unleashes a Malayali exceptionalism that lies dormant in Kerala. In other locations, Jacob saw the opportunities and conditions that optimize the abilities and talents of "the people"—conditions, he made abundantly clear, that do not exist in Kerala. Jacob hitched his personal desires to settle abroad to a larger project of realizing an exceptionalism that is the Malayali's destiny—an exceptionalism embodied by the confident, self-motivated, driven men and women who had impressed Jacob during his two years in London. This is an elite configuration of regional identity, one Jacob could claim from his high status and social location as a young man from a wealthy Syrian Christian family who was educated abroad and who strongly identified with a dominant, development-centered idea of Malayali exceptionalism.

Framing one's personal trajectory of migration as the realization of a collective fate was a theme that emerged in my conversations with young men in particular. Twenty-four-year-old Prabhu, who like Jacob touted the success of Malayalis overseas, similarly configured his own longing to find employment abroad in the terms of actualizing a development-identified Malayali identity. Having completed his master's in computer applications (MCA), Prabhu was working for a software company in Technopark, Thiruvananthapuram's IT business center, when we met. Prabhu called upon an elite discourse of Malayali exceptionalism to explain success overseas, a discourse he laid claim to as a well-educated, middle-class Ezhava. "That's the special thing about Malayalis. We have intelligence. We have brains! Brains!" he proclaimed, banging his hands on the table in emphasis. "So what does that mean?" I asked him. "It means that in any country a Malayali reaches, he will make money, settle, and have a good standard of living there," said Prabhu. As with many of these narratives about untapped Malayali potential, Prabhu's observations highlight a central dissonance in the imagining of Kerala as place. Prabhu drew on a dominant development narrative to make a claim for the exceptional brains of Malayalis today. Yet, at the same time, he saw migration of the individual out of Kerala as the path to realizing a development-defined regional Malayali identity. Spatial mobility resolves the contradictions of the postcolonial present. The tension between access to education as promoted by the local developmental state and high rates of unemployment can be resolved, paradoxically, only by leaving Kerala. Using the claim of "brains!" to highlight the mismatch between education and employment in the state, Prabhu retooled a development achievement as the passport to success overseas.[43]

Sangeetha also framed her desires to leave Kerala in terms of realizing a constructed identity she associated with the region, an identity that was explicitly gendered and inflected by her social location. A self-identified feminist from an upper-status Nayar family, thirty-year-old Sangeetha was working as a magazine editor when we met. She was looking for a career change and had just finished applying to law programs, all of which were located outside Kerala. I always enjoyed my conversations with outgoing and charismatic Sangeetha, conversations that ran the gamut of politics, films, fashion, and food as well as many other things. A frequent topic of conversation for us was physical mobility for young women in the city, a topic about which we had shared frustrations. Sangeetha constantly chaffed against the gendered norms she felt pressing upon her. ("Why can't they make kurtas with pockets" she liked to ask, "as if women have no need to carry anything around?") In her professional and personal life, Sangeetha's frustration with life in Kerala took shape in the embodied everyday, in things as mundane as the daily inconveniences of pocketless kurtas, to limitations in travel around the city after dark, to the rising violence against women across public and private spaces. As a middle-class, working woman, Sangeetha spoke openly about feeling oppressed in Thiruvananthapuram, unable to walk freely on her own on the street in the evening hours, unable to trust the police, unable to stand on a bus without worrying about being touched.

She once mentioned to me the irony of having to leave Kerala to become the figure of the progressive Malayali woman so well known to the rest of the world. While Sangeetha herself talked about how this idealized and hegemonic figure was deeply problematic—one she said was conjured up by foreigners—on occasion, she also drew on it to argue the problems of her own everyday existence *in* Kerala. "Kerala is first in a lot of things," she grimly joked, "high in women's literacy and education, but even higher in violence against women and suicide."[44] In contrasting her own stifled movement across the urban landscape with the trope of the empowered Malayali woman which in other registers she denounced, Sangeetha highlighted how patriarchal violence and classed norms of respectability shaped her experience of entrapment. Sangeetha's embodied experiences of locality as physical immobility, social constriction, and vulnerability to violence shaped her desires to leave Kerala as the route to realize an idea of Malayali Womanhood she saw to be both false and compelling.

Feelings of stagnation and possibility, hope and hopelessness, are shaped by the particular social locations from which individuals long for spatial movement. If many of these stories thus far have focused on migratory longing and quests for becoming, Aakash's story opens us up to a different perspective on migration. It offers a productive counterpoint to experiences of immobility among elites: if some among the immobile oriented themselves toward boundless, open horizons elsewhere, Aakash's story points to the hardships, inequalities, and limits in labor migration. This story also helps to complicate the reductive categories of "Gulf migrant" and "Gulf family" that we have encountered in various guises thus far in this book, including in the discourse of mental health experts. In the clinic, we saw that concerns about suicide and migration are linked in part to concerns about "failed migration"— the failure of return migrants to achieve locally recognized social and economic markers expected of them.[45] But as we will see, "failed migration" and life's critical limits do not always map neatly onto one another. Instead, they take shape within complex economies of labor, reciprocity, and care that stretch across space and time.

### BROKEN PROMISES

I held the cracked plastic photo album gently in my hands. Preeti turned the pages. Many of the photos now stuck to the inside of their sleeves, their colors bleeding from the humidity of rainy seasons past. "The one standing here—that's him," she said, pointing to a photo of a tall man wearing sunglasses and leaning casually against the front hood of a luxury car. "This is the car he drove in Saudi."

On a rainy afternoon, I met Preeti in her home, a small rented house off the road to Vettucaud, at the outer edges of the city, which she and her two small children shared with another widow and her infant. On the cot where she and the children usually slept, thirty-six-year-old Preeti told me the story of her husband Aakash's suicide ten years before. "My story," she said, closing the photo album, "begins with our marriage." The eldest of five children, Aakash was barely a teenager when his father passed away. With the family struggling to make ends meet, Aakash dropped out of school at fourteen to take up a job as a porter at a furniture shop.

After Preeti and Aakash were married, Aakash's mother approached him with a proposition. "My husband was the eldest son in his family, with three sisters and one brother younger to him," Preeti explained to me. "His mother told him that if he could get his three sisters married, she would give him the family home." Knowing that the job Aakash had then as an autorickshaw driver would never pull in the money needed for the dowry and marriage costs for all three sisters, they decided that Aakash should try for a job in the Gulf. "So we sold my gold ornaments to get the money to buy a visa to Persia," said Preeti. Preeti was five months pregnant with their first child when Aakash left for Saudi Arabia. There, he worked as the personal driver for a Saudi family. Preeti spent those years living with her mother-in-law, suffering what she described as daily abuses and her mother-in-law's controlling ways. Everything Aakash remitted home went directly to his mother, who saved what she could and set aside the minimum for the needs of the household, monitoring in Preeti's description "every little drop of oil, piece of soap, every one rupee." To this day, Preeti does not know how much her husband made during his time abroad. At one point, Preeti's suffering became so unbearable that she left the house for her natal home, threatening divorce. Upon Aakash's encouragement, conveyed through phone calls and letters, Preeti eventually returned several weeks later to the house—the house, Aakash reminded his wife in consolation, that would soon be theirs.

But some promises would not be kept. Aakash returned six years later to his wife and the son he had never met, having earned enough for his three sisters to be married. "His mother had told him, 'Son, if you manage to marry off your three sisters, I will give you the land and family home.' That's why, when his visa expired, he came back, saying he would get the land and house," said Preeti. "But his mother didn't give us anything." In fact, within months of Aakash's return, his mother demanded they vacate the home and find somewhere else to live. "What to do? We didn't think his mother would cheat us this way," said Preeti sorrowfully. "He came back from Saudi, happily thinking that at least we would get the property." Instead, Aakash's mother insisted he return to Saudi and find a way to support his own family. "When he came back, she cheated us," Preeti repeated, weeping now. "She had transferred the property rights to Aakash's younger brother."

During the months they managed to stay in the house against worsening pressure from Aakash's mother to leave, the young couple struggled to discern the options before them. In the midst of those dark days was a single light: Preeti and Aakash's second child, a baby girl, was born. But the lengthening shadow of family betrayal cast a pall over even this happiness. Indeed, Preeti told me that after the delivery, Aakash became increasingly desperate. "I used to tell him we can take a house loan and live elsewhere," she said of her efforts to encourage her husband to start anew. "Your mother is telling us to leave this house, so let's take a loan and live elsewhere." But Aakash had different plans in mind. "When we would talk about our difficulties, he would say, 'We'll kill ourselves. Both of us, the two children—we four should drink poison and die together.'" When she refused again and again to concede to Aakash's plan, he finally relented. At the time, Preeti was hopeful that her husband's submission meant he was moving past his mother's betrayal and thinking of the future. But reflecting back on those grim days, she reminded herself of other creeping signs of her husband's declining state: his heavy drinking since his return and his increasingly mercurial moods. Venturing further into untouched memories, Preeti recalled how during those months she suffered the anger that Aakash was unable to direct at his mother. Some nights when he came home drunk and out of control, if dinner was not to his liking Aakash would throw his plate of uneaten rice at her. Many of those nights, Preeti said, she endured his beatings.

Preeti said she remembered the day Aakash died like it was yesterday. That morning, Aakash and his mother had had a particularly heated argument. Later that evening, Aakash ordered Preeti to take the children into the backyard by the well for a bath. "When I came back into the house, I noticed the whisky bottles he kept in the front room were gone," Preeti recounted, her voice trembling. Something, she sensed, was wrong. Without thinking, she crossed the house to her mother-in-law's bedroom. "He had hanged himself after drinking. In her room. It was in his mother's room that he hanged himself," she said, weeping. "He didn't do it in our room. He did it in the room where his mother sleeps." It was just two weeks after the birth of his daughter.

For Aakash and his family, hope was projected across time, space, and selves. Leaving Kerala offered escape from the financial paralysis that had brought the reproduction of the family to a grinding halt. Through his enhanced earning potential in the Gulf, Aakash reinstated what Lawrence Cohen, in his adaptation of Gayle Rubin's phrase, has called the "traffic in women": the transfer of married women out of the natal home. In this way, Aakash gave movement once again to a "family experienced as stuck."[46] Through the chain of reciprocities set in motion by his mother, Aakash had counted on the promise that in providing for his sisters' marriages, he would secure the stability and future of his own marital household. Gulf migration was the foundation for this plan, allowing for the continuation of family cosmologies. Hope for the future fulfillment of these reciprocities shaped commitments and suffering in the present. Aakash endured years of separation from his young wife and the son he would not meet for six years for the sake of long-term gain for the family. Preeti suffered her mother-in-law's daily abuses, bartering her peace of mind for the promise of a better future for her children. But if this story tells us something about the spatial strategies of families like Aakash's—going to the Gulf was *the* only way he saw to ensure the reproduction of natal and marital households—it also speaks in tragic terms of how these strategies can fail, even when migration is "successful." By local standards, Aakash was not a failed migrant. Able to fulfill his obligations to his mother and three sisters, he returned home with sufficient wealth to float the family to smoother waters. But his story does more than point to how ideas of "failed" and "successful" migration oversimplify experience; it also suggests the importance of thinking through space as "social relations 'stretched out.'"[47] It highlights the ways that long-term commitments to the reproductive family, critically limited by poverty and inequality, shape spatial strategies, exposing at times hope's fatal limits.

In Preeti's mind, Aakash had failed as a father and a husband, betting everything on his mother's flimsy promise at the expense of Preeti and the children. Even now, Preeti told me, she gets angry with herself for not compelling her husband to keep something aside as security. "Back then, I used to tell him that even though we expected to have the house in the end, we should buy at least just two cents of land. We should buy something." But Aakash's faith in his mother never wavered. "'What have I gone to the Gulf for? My mother will give it to us,' he'd say. When I would tell him again to set something aside for us, he would beat me. It was only later when he returned and she cheated us that he thought, 'If I had only listened to what my wife had said.'" Opening once more the photo album resting on her lap, Preeti pointed to a picture of Aakash posing casually under a tree, his left arm draped on a branch above. "I got a husband just as I wished for, fair and handsome," Preeti told me. "But what was he able to do? He couldn't provide anything while he was alive."

Preeti was now supporting her two children by working in the kitchen of a college cafeteria. She still felt tremendous guilt for not having convinced her husband to save something. Perhaps if he had, his mother would not have been able to take advantage of them this way. Soon after Aakash's death, said Preeti, she had thought of suicide. At the invitation of a friend, she started attending a local Pentecostal church. That helped to ease her sadness. She had also started receiving some assistance, including help with her children's school fees, from a local nonprofit Christian organization run by an American woman. While regrets and sadness about the past were always there, Preeti told me, placing her hand over chest, seeing her children each morning helped her to continue on. Thumbing through the photo album in silence, I asked Preeti how looking at the pictures made her feel. "Often when I become sad, I will burn some of the photos. Burn them. Truly I have," said Preeti. "When I feel sad, feel tension, when I don't feel like seeing these pictures at all," she said. "I burn them." And then, gazing at one of the few photos taken after Aakash's return, Preeti paused, quietly tracing her finger around the figure of her husband. "After a person dies, people will put his picture in a large frame, hang garlands on it, and light incense. But we shouldn't do that. We can't do that." "Why?" I asked. "When an elderly person dies, it is good to do this. They have lived a complete life. But in this case, for a young man like this, it will be unlucky," Preeti said. "He died young. He went without fulfilling his hopes."[48]

### A SPACE OF DEATH

One morning in 2006 I came across this obituary in the pages of the newspaper *Mathrubhumi*.

DIED IN DUBAI

*Poovar:* Malayali died in Dubai. The deceased, 54 year old Vijayan, had begun to construct a new home. Family received the news. Nine months ago he went to Dubai. There he had lost his passport and papers. Even though he was waiting on a request for duplicates, he was arrested by the police one week ago. Wife: Priyamvada. Children: Bindu, Indu.[49]

"Malayali died in Dubai." In its oddly impersonal and generic announcement of the demise of a Malayali abroad, the obituary pronounces death in the Gulf as a remarkably unremarkable event. In its silences, it also generates a host of speculations. Many lead down paths to backstories of possible employer or police abuse, suicide, or foul play. Had Vijayan truly "lost" his passport and papers, or had his employer confiscated them as a technique of control?[50] What had happened to him during police custody just one week before his death? In its stark economy of words, this obituary raises more questions than it begins to answer. In the void of all that is unspoken about lost papers, arrest by the police, and death, one is left with the remnants (or beginnings) of a story of violence in the Gulf that is increasingly visible in Kerala public life. It is a story that lifts a corner of the veil over rising suicide, death, and disappearance among India's contract laborers.

Stories of mysterious death, the repatriation of bodies, labor exploitation, and of missing migrants configure "the Gulf" in very different terms from those with which Krishna opened this chapter. They point to the dark underbelly of overseas labor migration. Contrary to Krishna's dialectic imaginary of Kerala as a space of hopelessness and the Gulf as a space of limitless possibility, accounts that circulate in the personal tragedies of families, in news media, and in popular cinema now depict the latter as a place of violence, abuse, exploitation, and death.[51] I end this chapter with these thoughts to point to the shifting and ambivalent nature of spatial imaginings and also to suggest that contradictory imaginaries of "the Gulf" coexist across registers. Obituaries like the one above gesture to violence and death and sit uneasily alongside migratory dreams of hope and possibility. Even then, young people like Abraham, Krishna, Neethu, and Sabu cast their die with the chance to leave—to be anywhere but here. The observations of one Gulf migrant are telling. "Even God has left Kerala," he told me, "so we are leaving, too."

# 6

# Fit for the Future

"Malayali children today," observed one psychologist, "are like touch-me-not flowers: one touch and they fade away." Capping off his troubling observations about child suicide in the state, the psychologist's comment reflected a prominent concern shared by mental health professionals, parents, educators, and state officials alike. Spoiled by their parents and sheltered from hardship, Malayali children today, by such accounts, lack the tensile strength and emotional durability to survive life's ordinary challenges. These days, the psychologist grimly remarked, even a mild scolding can drive a child to suicide.[1]

Media accounts would suggest these concerns are not misplaced. One newspaper article itemizes several stories of child suicide:

> Eleven-year-old Saumya of Mamalassery committed suicide by hanging herself using her mother's sari for the simple reason that she was scolded for quarreling with her younger sister. In yet another incident, 14-year-old Neethu of Kottayam committed suicide by consuming poison as she was not allowed to watch TV. Similarly, a 24-year-old youth in the harbour city of Kochi committed suicide by consuming an excessive dose of sleeping pills because his parents refused to buy a car for him. Of course, his well-to-do parents followed in his steps when they ended their lives by hanging moments after their son was found dead.[2]

Another article reports on adolescent suicide in a similar vein, observing, "Just the other day one adolescent committed suicide because he was prevented from watching the World Cup." The author declares, "Life has become cheap for the children."[3]

The figure of the emotionally frail, suicidal child for whom life has become cheap featured centrally in the tales of social decay that I heard in the capital city. In public discourse, child suicide appears to be a social pathology of the middle class: when refused cars and television time, Malayali children self-destruct. Whether committed as stubborn protest, uncontrolled reflex, or emotional capitulation, children's self-destruction is said to evidence what one psychologist described in English as an epidemic problem of "low frustration thresholds."[4] But if the figure of the fragile, impulsive child is most visible in these accounts, these fears are less about the problematic child as an atomized subject than they are about a particular experience of crisis in middle-class parenting in contemporary Kerala. Blame is laid at the feet of parents, whose emotionally and materially indulgent practices in the home are said to produce boys and girls who wilt, like delicate flowers, in the face of mild stimuli. Anxieties about the suicidal child are therefore anxieties about the parenting practices and the home that engineer such a child.

This chapter explores expert and everyday efforts to reform parenting among elites in the capital city in response to child suicide. It examines the kinds of futures that are imagined and launched from this crisis-ridden point of departure.[5] Throughout this book, I have argued that suicide shapes ways of living and of living with one another. This is powerfully evidenced at the site of child rearing, where the micropractices within parenting and personal action are tied to the making of collective futures. As we will see, parents in the capital city are called upon to reform themselves and their parenting techniques as a means of producing healthier generations for the future. Child suicide demands new ways of living, for parents and children alike.

In Thiruvananthapuram, fears of child suicide have acquired a social life of their own. They transect multiple domains of concern, including children's psychological health and social development, consumption as parental investment, the goals of educational reform, and the failures of the nuclear family. With particular clarity they also reveal shifting ideas of potential danger, nurturance, value, and parental responsibility in these anxious times. Fears of child suicide bring into crisis "the project of building quality into the child."[6] In the media accounts above, children's material needs are amply provided for, yet these very provisions foster the desires for immediate gratification, which in turn precipitates self-destruction. Ideas of "quality" child rearing that link consumption to investment in human capital appear wildly inverted in child suicide: here, material provisions produce not quality children with the value-adding resources to thrive in life but rather undisciplined and frail suicidal subjects. Among elites in the capital city, suicide has unhinged definitions of what constitutes "good" parenting.

The call to address child suicide has been a visible and urgent one. It has flown prominently under the banner of suicide prevention in the state, in a manner vastly disproportionate to reported numbers. In 2011, for instance, the Kerala State Mental Health Authority found that 1 percent of total reported suicides in the state were committed by children fourteen years of age and younger.[7] Even then, as an issue of public concern and a category of intervention, child suicide has mobilized state officials, mental health experts, educators, and parents alike toward an array of reform efforts. As has been argued of suicide more generally throughout this book, child suicide must be understood not on the strength of numbers alone but also as a social and moral reality that inflects contemporary political, social, and kin life.

Why has child suicide captured attention in ways that numbers alone cannot explain? What is at the heart of the fear of it? In public discourse, child suicide evokes more than the loss of the unrealized individual; it evokes familiar and haunting anxieties about the fitness of the population at large. Population quality has long featured as a core governmental concern in regional and national development agendas in India, with children's poor health taken to be a marker of backwardness and weak civilian preparedness.[8] Seen to herald a new rise of frail, ineffectual, and unviable citizen-subjects, contemporary child suicide reanimates questions about the strength, productivity, and readiness of children as assets to region and nation. In doing so, it does not simply reprise the same fears of the past but rather reorients and reframes these concerns in light of Kerala's liberalizing and globalizing present. Concerns about child suicide, we shall see, are ultimately concerns about readiness in the face of an increasingly uncertain global future.

### POPULATION QUALITY AND THE "RETURN" OF WEAK CHILDREN

The sun was setting as John and I strolled along Shanghumugham Beach outside the city. I had last seen my friend three years before, under the sad circumstances of his grandmother's death. This reunion was a far happier one. En route to visit his family in Allapuzha for a two-week holiday from his job at a travel agency in London (or rather, East London, as he was keen to distinguish, "for I might as well be living in a different city altogether"), John had stopped over in Thiruvananthapuram for a few days' visit. Catching up on life events and family news, we watched as children on the beach weaved in and out of the gathering clusters of sunset watchers, their cries of delight ringing through the evening air as wave after wave chased against their bare legs.

We sat down on the beach and dug our toes into the sand. John asked how research was going. I recounted in broad sweeps the highs and lows of the last few months. My friend offered words of encouragement. "We need to know more about this problem," he contended, "especially with so much suicide among children these days." Curious, I asked John how he explained this troubling phenomenon. John, recently turned twenty-four, was quick to blame certain developments among "the new generation." I followed his gaze out to the water's edge. "My grandfather would say that earlier, if you dropped a hundred children into the ocean, ninety-nine of them would swim back, and only one would drown. But these days," said John, "if you threw in a hundred kids, ninety-nine of them would drown. Nobody knows how to swim." With his Malayalam scattered with English idioms of popular psychology, John noted that the children of his grandfather's generation were able to fend for themselves. "But nowadays we are becoming more and more *dependent* on our parents. We get everything from them. We are essentially *spoon-fed*." Although Malayali children today possess "booksmarts," they lack the practical skills to survive. Mathematics and chemistry, said John, are of no use to the child who cannot save himself from drowning.[9]

John's observations were part of a broader commentary he shared with me that evening about what he described as the twofold problem driving child suicide: the danger of excessive parental protectionism on the one hand and the overdue need for educational reform on the other. At home, John explained, parents coddle to such an extreme that children never learn what it means to work hard or to struggle to achieve. At school, children memorize facts to succeed at their exams but fail to acquire "practical knowledge" to survive in the real world.[10] By John's account, Malayali children today have lost the ability to live. The dangers of these developments exceed the single child. In reckoning in numerical terms this dramatic decline in survival skills—a drop from ninety-nine to just one child able to return to shore—John framed the problem on the scale of society: that is, as a crisis of population quality. A failed "swim test" ominously foretells the rise of a generation of weak citizen-subjects that threatens the political and economic security of region and nation.

In pointing to a lack of practical knowledge among Malayali children today, John emphasized the dangers of parental "overpampering," an English term I heard frequently among the educated elite. A physician and father of two described how parenting today has devolved into indulgent coddling, where the average Malayali child is "raised as a kind of superman whose ego is built up to the maximum and who feels overpowerful." In engineering out all distress from the child's experience, he told me, parents "build up the child to believe he can do anything he wants and be anything he wants but then throw him into a world that has so many problems and challenges." It is little wonder, said the physician with displeasure, that children raised this way shatter like brittle glass when the world does not bend to their will.[11] In a newspaper article written in English, the psychiatrist Praveen Lal reflects in similar terms on children's inability to handle frustration as the basis for child suicide: "The level of tolerance in children in the younger generation is abysmally poor. Children can neither take 'no' for an answer nor are they mentally robust enough to take the emotional upheavals of life in their stride." Dr. Lal sees this as a problem endemic to nuclear families, in which "children are pampered by their parents more than they used to be earlier. No wonder they get frustrated easily." He observes, "While playing games at home, parents choose to get defeated by the child. But the same child often loses games at school and is unable to handle failure."[12] The epidemic weakness of children is a joining thread across the concerns articulated here: if the children John described fail at the practical skill of survival, the children discussed above fail at the ordinary trials of social interaction.

While weak children are seen here to be a recent development, the fear of that condition is itself not new. Population quality has long been a key governmental concern in regional and national development agendas. These agendas have promoted the reduction of births as the path to greater human longevity and productivity and, ultimately, to development.[13] The national development-focused push toward the small family took on distinct regional contours in Kerala. J. Devika has traced legislative and social efforts to reform the family institution in the making of healthier and stronger children for a modern Kerala, a process driven by a complex of ideas, institutions, and practices.[14] Demographic anxieties converged with concerns to produce modern citizen-subjects for whom "liberation" from the large family was considered fundamental. Efforts to modernize the family were also fueled by colonial and postcolonial struggles to end matrilineal kinship arrangements, once a significant presence in the region.[15]

In 1867, the native missionary Reverend George Mathen of the Church Missionary Society (CMS) wrote a scathing report against matrilineal households. Because inheritance in these households followed the female line, reformers like Mathen saw fathers in these arrangements as having no incentive to properly care for their children. By contrast, wrote Mathen, "if patriliny were the rule, fathers would have had concern for the care and wellbeing of their offspring, and would not abandon the mothers of their children. Because of this difference, the mothers too would not reject the husbands of their youth, and seek after other men."[16] Missionaries and native elites sought therefore to "civilize" matrilineal arrangements said to lack the longevity, investment, and stability associated with monogamous marital bonds. They believed that the putatively anchoring presence of the father as provider and mother as homemaker would improve children's health and thus improve the health of the population at large. "Children born to couples living in mutual fidelity are found to be strong and healthy," noted Mathen, "but the offspring of those who lead a loose and stray life are mostly weak and sickly."[17] "Gentile" forms of patrifocal domesticity and the provisioning of resources to fewer children as the "natural" responsibility of parents were promoted against the presumed neglect of children born to matrilineal households.

As legislative interventions and economic transformations in the late nineteenth and early twentieth centuries rendered unviable earlier modes of domestic life and inheritance, the small, conjugal, patrifocal family deemed necessary to progressive society and healthy children acquired moral and practical purchase. By the 1950s, new ideologies of responsible parenting would gain widespread acceptance among the educated elite.[18] As described by J. Devika, parenting as a "craftlike activity" positioned children as the "raw material" through which parents would produce capable, self-regulating individuals and realize their own developmental potentials as parents.[19] The ideological injunction to endow fewer children with higher-quality resources thus made imperative both reproductive restraint and the enduring stability of conjugal living associated with patrifocal arrangements. Children as human capital demanded intensified forms of investment that promised to pay dividends for society at large.

The development of the small patrifocal family, its dichotomous gender roles, and the funneling of resources toward fewer children therefore aligned with ideas of "quality" parenting in the pursuit of making strong, capable, and productive individuals fit to lead region and nation.[20] During the post-Independence period, Kerala emerged as an exceptional success in this regard. By the 1970s, the widespread acceptance of the Family Planning Campaign in Kerala was read by demographers, development scholars, and the popular press as a sign of the people's commitment to improving the health of the population and to an ethos of development more broadly.[21] For those looking on with optimism, this demographic revolution would become a key facet of the Kerala model discourse, garnering the region worldwide attention.[22]

But contemporary fears about child suicide have cast a dark pall over this demographic success and crowning achievement of Kerala modernity. Concerns about the rise of a psychologically frail generation have rekindled long-standing governmental questions about population quality, heralding the uncanny "return" of weak children. Yet these fears are reoriented and reframed in the liberalizing present. If reform efforts through the nineteenth and twentieth centuries sought to prepare children to be assets for a nascent nation-state on the path to development, in the liberalizing present definitions of "population quality" and "child fitness" have shifted. As will be discussed later in this chapter, children must now be prepared for elite visions of an increasingly globally oriented future, in ways that stratify the population in the production of middle-classness. Fears of child suicide also provoke critical commentaries on horizons past. Through the lens of child suicide and its crisis-ridden narratives, the small modern family that had earlier been promoted as the pathway to human longevity and better futures appears a failed promise. Many in Thiruvananthapuram now cite its structural failures, openly challenging the idea of the small family long advocated as an unproblematic social good by social reformers and development scholars. For dystopic critics in particular, the small modern family has morphed into something else entirely: the "social machine" producing suicidal life.[23]

## BROILER CHILDREN AND THE LOSS OF THE WORLD IN MINIATURE

Kulippicchu kulippicchu kuttiye kaanaathaayi. (The baby bathed
again and again will disappear.)
—Malayalam proverb

As the language and concerns of child socialization and psychological development find their way into Kerala public discourse, disenchantment with a class-specific form of the nuclear family is now widely expressed by voices across medical and religious domains, media, literature, and cinema. Dr. Kurien's was one such voice. Echoing concerns about weak and ineffectual Malayali children, Dr. Kurien blamed children's shrinking life worlds. A senior clinical psychologist with decades of experience in child and adolescent mental health, Dr. Kurien said that these days, Malayali children "only see the inside of their home, school, and tuition center." Sequestered from the world, they never learn "to face the difficulties of life." Elaborating on the consequences of this development, the psychologist drew an unlikely parallel between Malayali children and chickens.

Unlike free-range chickens that roam about and forage for food, broiler chickens are raised in sheds and provided feed. "With a broiler chicken," said Dr. Kurien, speaking in English, "if you put it outside it can't live on its own because you are giving it chicken feed. It can't stand in the sun because it's always inside." These days, boys and girls in Kerala are raised as "broiler children," quipped the psychologist. Just as with a broiler chicken whose environment is carefully controlled, "if you tend to take the child from your house doorstep to the tuition center, to the school and then back to the tuition center, and then back home, they don't have the opportunity to learn the skills of living." Physically sheltered from the world and emotionally sheltered from hardship, broiler children fail to develop the ability to weather even ordinary difficulties. "That is why I say," Dr. Kurien concluded, "children in Kerala are learning their school lessons, but not learning to live a life."[24]

Dr. Kurien's figuring of the nuclear family and its broiler children is a classed one. It is characterized by parents' intense channeling of resources and energies toward educational success. In crafting scholastic achievers, however, parents deprive children of the meaningful experiences and social interactions critical to the development of "coping skills and practical knowledge," by Dr. Kurien's account. In positioning rote book learning as obsolete and rigorous socialization as the goal, Dr. Kurien pushed for parents to cultivate in their children the new embodied capacities associated with the global expansion of educational-developmental psychology.[25] As we will see, in Kerala these include the psychologized capacities for courage *(dhairyam)* and confidence *(aathmaviswaasam)* necessary, in Dr. Kurien's words, "to face the difficulties of life," qualities that are increasingly valued among Thiruvananthapuram's elites.

In this time of suicide, experts believe that building confidence and courage in children is imperative, in part as compensation for what they see to be the structural inadequacies of the nuclear family form. Sajan, a doctoral student in psychology, accounted for contemporary suicide by contrasting the anemic interactions of the nuclear family with the robust socialities of the joint family. Speaking in Malayalam but drawing heavily on English terms of popular psychology, Sajan suggested that in the joint family, the child "was used to frustration, because that was a larger family with more members." By his description, "One person may be a very *possessive* person; one may be very *submissive*, so this child in the joint family lived with many different types of people. But now we have the nuclear family, where there isn't this much *exposure*. It's just one sibling, and the parents are hardly ever there." Underscoring the importance of socialization to children's psychological development, Sajan said, "There needs to be tiny, tiny frustrations within the family. We need practice to face these things. When we go out into wider society, we go out there without that kind of *exposure*." He concluded, "The family should be his society in miniature. The joint family was a small version of the world, wasn't it? We have lost that."[26]

Sajan's comments illustrate an elite discourse I heard often that constructs a traditional joint family/modern nuclear family binary as the backdrop for moral plays about social decay in the present. By reading a language of child socialization and psychological education into the past, Sajan celebrated the joint family as a microcosm of life itself—"a small version of the world." As a kind of training ground for society, with its mixed personalities and competing demands the joint family gave children opportunities to develop the frustration tolerance and adjustability needed for the larger world beyond. While the joint family was a tangled web of give and take, in Sajan's view the nuclear family revolves around a single axis oriented from parent to child. If demographic and development discourses have endorsed the small family as the key to healthy futures, Sajan faulted it for producing maladjusted and suicidal children.

Others offered similar diagnoses on the anatomical flaws of the nuclear family. In the words of Sister Theresa, a trained counselor and yoga instructor, "Earlier, there were many children in the family, so they might fight with each other; there would be a lack of things, and you would not be getting everything that you wanted." By contrast, in the nuclear family, she explained, "There are only one or two children, and the parents are giving them everything. No one says 'no' to the children. They can't take it! Just to watch TV, two children might fight with each other, and neither is giving up for the other." Today, Sister Theresa warned, "you cannot say 'no' to the children."[27] Nostalgia for an idealized, traditional Keralan life presents the rates and rhythms of individual fulfillment in the joint family household as protracted, unpredictable, and dispersed in ways that balanced children's satisfaction against those of their siblings as well as those of grandparents, aunts, and uncles. By contrast, in the nuclear family immediate gratification obviates the need to share. As a result, children never learn to adjust to others or to weather frustration.

Sister Theresa's reference to poorly shared TV time suggests that concerns for the structural deficits of the nuclear family acquire distinct contours in the liberalizing present, particularly with regard to anxieties about consumption. For the concern is not only that the nuclear family lacks "quality" interactions but also that it is now saturated with the compensatory indulgences of consumer goods. Sheela, a lecturer in sociology and mother of two, drew out for me the repercussions of consumption in the context of nuclear family living and the intensified parent-child relationship. Plotting a chain of destruction that begins with immediate gratification and ends with children's depression and suicide, Sheela faulted Malayali parents today for raising spoiled children with no willpower to survive. Speaking in Malayalam, she observed:

> By *willpower* I mean that children don't have the ability to face problems because of the way they are raised. [In a mocking tone] "Do you want candy? Do you want a car? Do you want a bike?" Like that, parents are buying everything for their children. So then after awhile, they run out of money. When they can't buy anything anymore, the children go into a major *depression* and then they kill themselves. Whereas with *willpower,* whatever happens, we will have the ability [to face problems]. If these children had more *willpower,* they could face things better.[28]

This description of children driven to death when the family coffers run dry hinges not on simple disappointment but, rather, on the failure to satiate a primal urge akin to hunger. Unnecessary things showered on the child turn into indispensable needs, without which the child literally cannot live.

Sheela's fears identify a particular experience of time in parenting. Ruled by the tyranny of children's insatiable desires, the middle-class nuclear family appears as the site where temporalities have dramatically contracted. Resources are funneled into fleeting parent-child interactions rather than distributed across the long-term kin reciprocities associated with joint family living. Material gratification is immediate, and any negative response to the child's wants—denial, punishment, or even a mild scolding—may trigger suicide in the child as an emotional reflex. The quickening cadences of consumption in the nuclear family produce life out of control. This anxiety surfaces in media accounts of parents who, unable to sustain rocketing consumer demands, go into severe debt and take their children with them in family murder-suicides.

Contemporary concerns about the dangers of consumption in middle-class child rearing reveal fissures in the ideologies of responsible parenting that gained wide acceptance among the educated elite by the mid-twentieth century in Kerala. As the small patrifocal family gained ground in the region, consumption increasingly aligned with notions of quality child rearing. By the 1960s, material investment in fewer children had come to be seen as a marker of the progressive, modern family and fundamental to a decent existence, "less like over-indulgence and more like the road to the genteel life."[29] But if the small family came to be widely embraced across social groups on the premise that fewer children with better resources made for healthier, stronger futures, the contemporary threat of child suicide suggests that consumption in the liberalizing present has grown wildly out of control, tipping the scales from healthful to fatal. Consumption and parenting have been thrown into new relation: the forms of investment once promoted as the key to strong futures now appear to be the engine driving the production of weak, suicidal children. What, then, defines "good" parenting in this time of suicide, consumption, and nuclear family living?

### CUTTING THE STRINGS

Azhakulla chakkayil chulayilla. (There is no fleshy fruit in the pretty jackfruit.)
—Malayalam proverb

Fears of impulsive and self-destructive children suggest that parental investment has taken a lethal turn in Kerala's liberalizing present. The pendulum, some might say, has returned with force to the side of "bad" parenting. There is an element of tragic irony in these developments as reported by reformers and social commentators, for it is not for lack of concern that parents are said to produce fragile children. Rather, parents seem to be caring too much in the "wrong" ways.

In an issue of *Vanitha* (Woman), a popular Kerala women's magazine whose glossy pages target a middle-class readership, an article seeks to raise awareness about the harm parents may unwittingly be doing to their own children. The article's title page includes a large photo collage of a young boy in school uniform, his angled limbs hanging from strings manipulated from above by a monstrously oversized pair of hands. The title of the piece drives home the metaphor: "School Is Opening: From Here on Out, the Puppetry Begins."[30] The author, psychologist Dr. Krishnan Gireesh, invites his audience of middle-class mothers to critical self-reflection: "Let's evaluate ourselves. It's the start of the academic year. Studies, tuition, quiz competitions, youth festival . . . By the pulling of the strings of expectation, parents are turning children into marionettes." He asks, "Are you among them?" In this portrait of overbearing parents and their marionette children, the child is merely an extension of his parents, as the web of strings makes literal. Animated by the will and desires of others, the Malayali child is otherwise lifeless, a worker drone to parental expectation and regimented schedules.

In an article in *Grihalakshmi* (Homemaker), another popular women's magazine, Dr. Gita makes explicit the provenance of depression and suicide among Malayali children, faulting authoritarian parental pressure.[31] "Every child has different abilities. The suppression of those inner aims *(aantharika lakshyangal)* leads to their ruin," warns Dr. Gita. "If [children] have particular aims for themselves, they should study according to them. Do not control them excessively. When parents pressure children who do not wish to become doctors or engineers, they must remember one thing: they will compromise their children's mental health." Family life as depicted here has gone awry: parents drive their own children to mental breakdown and death by suppressing "inner aims." As proof of the catastrophic effects of parental pressure, Dr. Gita cites the spike in suicides and distressed phone calls to suicide hotlines following the annual release of the SSLC exam results—a month grimly dubbed Kerala's "suicide season" by one hotline counselor I knew.

In the accounts above, forms of intensive parenting that emerged as the hallmark of the small modern family now appear as unrefined and oppressive practice, less the making of better-quality children than the selfish imposition of parental desires. Dr. Gireesh, author of the article on child marionettes, writes, "Parents' worries for their children's future are creating tense environments in most homes. Without knowing their children's abilities and capacities, in the name of 'status' and 'protecting' their children's future parents are creating pressures that are having negative effects on their children." The irony in the psychologist's tone is not lost on the reader. The tragic twist lies in the good intentions of parents themselves: in seeking to protect their children, parents instead deliver them to poor mental health and suicide.

Popular forms of parenting advice have been identified as a key terrain in understanding how children's emotional lives are elaborated and governed in the new contexts of market capitalism.[32] They also reveal a trend in the global expansion of educational-developmental psychology, wherein "the child's interior is the next frontier."[33] Enjoining parents to improve themselves, Dr. Gireesh advises his audience to abandon parental pressure now marked as backward, totalitarian, outdated, and potentially fatal. Rather than goading children into bringing home perfect grades or becoming doctors and engineers, he proposes instead that parents cultivate their children's individual potentials. Such advice implies vastly different ideas about parental authority and knowledge. Parental protectionism envisions children's futures as the domain of parents to be engineered, safeguarded, and secured by parents themselves. Parents pull the strings that steer their marionette children toward prescribed goals. This presumes the omniscience of mother and father: they know what is best for the child. By contrast, the reformed parenting proposed by Dr. Gita and Dr. Gireesh configures a different type of child-subject in relationship to parental knowledge. Here, the child-subject's potential lies deep within, unfolding from psychic depths rather than being pregiven in the knowledge of parents, to be defended and secured for the future. The uniqueness of the child *(kuttiyude athulyatha)* is apparent in the present only as an inchoate and latent potential that parents are now held responsible to nurture.

New ideas of responsible parenting redefine child neglect. Dr. Sumita, a professor of sociology, criticized delinquent parents with no regard for their children's personality development *(vyakthithwa vikasanam)*. "They treat their children like dolls. They decorate them with nice clothes, make them fat like a foreigner with chubby cheeks and light skin, all of these things," observed Dr. Sumita. "Parents give more importance to external beauty *(baahya saundaryam)*. They have no interest in the development of children's personality *(vyakthithwam)*. They just want to display them, like something kept in a showcase." Malayali children, she continued, "are looked after by their parents—in their education, in their food, in their dress, but not in their personality. Parents don't understand what the child actually needs." In Kerala's liberalizing present, the interiority of the child has emerged in elite discourses as a new site for elaboration and thus of potential neglect, one that lies fallow when parents address physical and biological needs alone. Like Dr. Gita who enjoined parents to affirm their children's inner aims, Dr. Sumita's concerns for personality development point to the elaboration of a new domain in children's subjectivities. In shifting energies and resources from physical needs to the cultivation of an interiorized subject, reformed parenting in light of suicide opens up new opportunities, interactions, and possibilities. As we shall see, it does so in ways tied to the making of middle-classness and to the production of elite visions of a global future.

## PLAYGROUNDS, QUALITY TIME, AND OBJECT LESSONS

Arayil aadiye, arangatthu aadaavuu. (Only after practice in the house
should one dance on the stage.)
—Malayalam proverb

Crisis-ridden narratives of child suicide authorize a broad regime of institutional and everyday interventions in an attempt to redress the shortcomings and excesses perceived in relation to the nuclear family and in light of the anxious future. Mental health experts, educators, parents, and their children were not short on ideas of how to boost immunity to suicide and preparedness for the future. Some of these strategies, like Pramod's, were modest yet visionary, revealing social priorities and guiding horizons. "Build playgrounds," Pramod told me, "a lot of playgrounds."[34] According to Pramod, a lawyer in his thirties, retrieving the childhood lost to the tightening vise of scholastic achievement would stem suicide in the population at large. Playgrounds could reorganize children's spatial and social landscapes, teach the lessons of adjusting to others, and reclaim a developmental period in childhood that is increasingly colonized by parents' advancing efforts at preparedness.

Others endeavored to prevent suicide through the means immediately available to them. As part of his mission to combat child suicide, Father Simon promoted larger families in his parish area. "Five children for each family is my goal!" he exclaimed one afternoon. Even if the joint household could not be reinstated given the practical realities of modern life, Father Simon was confident that bigger nuclear families offered a reasonable surrogate. He happily boasted to me that the families in his parish area were now mostly three- or four-child families, thanks to his one-to-one encouragement of married couples. He joked that during premarriage counseling, he warns everyone, "I will only take your confession if you promise to have five children!"[35]

Most strategies for the prevention of child suicide focus intensively on the reform of the parent-child relationship in the context of middle-class nuclear family living. These include activities that experts suggest can be readily installed in the home. In an article in the women's magazine *Vanitha,* psychologist Dr. Justin Padamadan offers an instructive primer on the top ten things that parents can do to improve children's social and psychological development.[36] Among them are practical tips on how to engage children in conversation about their day at shared evening meals ("Asking them about their grades does not count"). Also provided are detailed suggestions for games that can be played in the home to enhance self-confidence, such as performance-based games that encourage shy children to learn to speak in front of others. Dr. Padamadan also enjoins parents to improve themselves through forms of what Arlie Hochschild calls "emotion work," prompting them to express love more openly and freely to their children through words and physical gestures.[37] Through such strategies, the home becomes a space governed by new kinds of disciplinary experience, modes of perception, and intervention, as well as by new possibilities for optimizing life.[38]

As a central lens through which child suicide comes into view as a classed pathology, consumption is targeted as an important site for reform but also for possibility. The accelerating cadences of material consumption in the middle-class nuclear family, as we have seen, have been widely blamed for producing insatiable, impulsive, and suicidal children. Concerns that children have been made impulsive by desires for immediate gratification motivate suicide prevention strategies that seek to recalibrate temporalities and promote anti-impulsive endurance. Child psychologist Dr. Mary suggested pragmatic ways to slow down children's demands for consumer items. "What we should advise parents is not to overindulge," she told me in English one afternoon in between clients. "Let the children be deprived of whatever they cannot have." To restructure children's impulsive ways, Dr. Mary advised, "They should learn to wait, which will make them more tolerant." This language of tolerance proposes a hydraulic model of the self in which hardiness against explosive, self-destructive tendencies may be steadily improved over the long term through carefully calibrated doses of denial and postponement. Parents can thus inculcate in children "skills of tolerance," and tolerance, Dr. Mary noted, "is going to be anti-suicidal, isn't it? When you can tolerate so many things, it means you need not contemplate suicide at all." Children, she concluded, "must know to wait for their wants. Don't deprive them of a need but a want. They can wait for a want."[39]

Dr. Sushma, another child psychologist, offered concrete examples of how lessons in delayed gratification might be built into everyday interactions between mother and child: "Give them exercises wherein they have to postpone their gratification. Maybe the mother and child can play: 'You asked me for something, and I'm going to make you wait. Wait.' Such types of exercises can be practiced." Exercises in what Dr. Sushma called "suicide inoculation training" teach children to defer their desire for and even willingly refuse everyday consumer items: a new toy or the seemingly innocuous second piece of chocolate. Dr. Sushma provided another illustration of such an exercise for me. "Let's say my sandal breaks, and I just don't have time today to go out and buy myself a pair of sandals, so I use my old ones. So you tell that to your child: 'See? I wanted a new pair, but since I don't have time, I'm using these. I'm using the one that is broken, and I didn't buy a new pair immediately.'"[40] Dr. Sushma described how such a demonstration by the mother can encourage the child to do the same when in that circumstance and perhaps to even playfully compete to hold out longer for a replacement purchase.

These didactic exercises are thus deeply relational. The mother's ability to control her own impulses to buy a new pair of shoes is pedagogically instructive to the child, who learns and aspires to do the same. To uphold the rules of the game, the mother herself must show restraint. ("How can we tell our children not to have a chocolate," one mother put it, "if we ourselves cannot say 'no'?") Premised less on simple deprivation than on a cultivated discretion, such games do not presume the consummate skill of the authority; instead, they thrive on the limitless possibilities for the self-development of all participants. Waiting is neither the suspension nor the absence of social life but, rather, a creative enterprise and an artful mode of self-making. Cast in the terms of a game, waiting is meant to be fun—a friendly competition between mother and child over who might defer desires the longest. It is the pretense of playing a game sequestered from reality and governed by its own set of rules and penalties that makes the discomfort of these activities sufferable. Dr. Sushma says parents should tell their children, "Just tolerate it, because it's part of the game! It's all in the game; you don't have to feel upset."[41] These games suggest that experts and authorities make, manage, and discipline temporality at the level of quotidian practice, where "practice is not *in* time but *makes* time."[42] Malayali children learn to wait as a skillful, life-avowing, and anti-suicidal way of being.

Although consumer purchases for the sake of indulgence or churlish materialism were frowned upon, experts like Dr. Sushma and Dr. Mary did not prescribe in their place a brute austerity. On the contrary, they encouraged parents to channel their resources in new ways. Rather than squandering resources in arenas of consumption now marked as overindulgent, backward, and the cause of "spoiled" children, parents are enjoined to invest in new modes of consumption that are seen in contrast to be refined and healthful and that target the cultivation of children's inner lives. In the capital city, the commodification of educational-developmental psychology in the form of a growing universe of goods and services has emerged as a widely valued form of elite parental consumer investment. In this way, saving children from suicide has been tied to the cultural production of middle-classness. Moreover, in seeking out self-help books and personality development camps for their children, parents are consuming in new ways that not only promise to make their children more resilient against suicide; they simultaneously prepare them to become future workers for the global job market. For increasingly so, the capacities that define ideas of child fitness in a time of suicide align in powerful ways with the skills and competencies for intensified competition, entrepreneurial capitalism, and transnational border crossing. In Kerala's liberalizing present, to be anti-suicidal is to be as flexible as flexible capitalism demands.

### COURAGE AND CONFIDENCE FOR A GLOBAL FUTURE

In July 2006, the Kerala State Resource Center and the Indian Association of Clinical Psychologists jointly sponsored a workshop titled Interventions in Suicidal Behavior. Over the course of the day-long program, mental health professionals, community members, and state officials blamed rising suicide on an epidemic lack of courage (dhairyam) and self-confidence (aathmaviswaasam) among Malayali children today. Others spoke of a rampant inferiority complex *(apakarshathaa bodham)*. By many accounts, parental overprotection was to blame. To illustrate this dilemma and its broader implications, several participants drew on a shared example: the failure of Malayali children to command spoken English.

Speaking from her twenty years of experience as a counselor at colleges and universities across Kerala, one psychologist opined in English, "Our children have very low self-esteem and low coping skills. They are oversensitive, particularly when compared to Indian children in other states, like Bihar and Maharashtra." Casting the problem in the terms of a regional pathology, she said, "We have no self-esteem. A Malayali child can only speak one or two sentences in front of a class in English before he stops for fear of making a mistake." On the other hand, she added, "a Bihari child, even if laughed at, will keep on talking." In the speech that followed, a member of the Kerala State Resource Center slipped seamlessly from the topic of poor confidence and suicide to poor confidence and failure in the global labor market. Describing how a confidence deficit has led to suicide among Malayali children, he then told a fictional anecdote of a young woman who, though qualified to secure a job in the United States, lacks the fortitude to hail a cab in English when she arrives at the airport. Throughout the day-long program, failed language acquisition joined concerns about timid and suicidal children with concerns about ineffective global workers for the future.[43]

Anecdotes relating suicide to the failure to master spoken English abounded during fieldwork. At times, this link could be literal. On several occasions I was told, for example, that a child who errs when forced to speak English in the classroom and is laughed at by peers will turn to suicide out of humiliation. Failures to command English were also caricatured more generally in the figure of the child who, while adept at reading, writing, and comprehending English, cannot carry a conversation beyond the basic social graces. This is a problem rooted, people said, in both the fear of making a mistake and in the shortcomings of language acquisition as technical study rather than lived interaction.

The links people drew between suicide and poor English acquisition suggest some of the ways a long-standing governmental concern for population quality in development discourse is reformulated in India's liberalizing present. If fluent English is a marker of the technocratic elite in India, verbal impotence has become emblematic in Kerala of the timid child with irrelevant skills to "survive." This is not only a fear about the literal survival of children prone to suicide; it is also an elite fear that Malayalis lack the competitive edge to survive in the global job market. Efforts to bolster children's anti-suicidal immunities thus converge with efforts to rear future workers with the confidence, resilience, and adjustability demanded of flexible labor.[44] In Thiruvananthapuram, this is powerfully evident in the growing regime of consumer products, goods, and services now offered to the elite in the arena of educational-developmental psychology. Parents in the capital city have taken up these new projects with enthusiasm, and with every passing year, more and more summer camps and extracurricular programs promise to bolster children's confidence, develop their personalities, help them acquire what in psychological discourse is known as "life skills," and expand their social and emotional competencies. At a three-week camp for children that integrated personality development and yoga, I observed a guest speaker for the day, a retired army officer, command a room of boys and girls to internalize the tips for effective communication through the acronym SOFTEN: *S* for "smile," *O* for "open stance," *F* for "friendliness," *T* for "touch," *E* for "eye contact," and finally, *N* for "nodding." To put these tips into practice, squirming children and shy teens were drawn up to a dais in front of the group to give impromptu presentations in English about their career aspirations.[45]

Summer programs like this one are intended to supplement the shortcomings of conventional school education, as much as they are to compensate for the socialization processes presumed to be lacking in the home. They reflect a pursuit of the extracurricular that has become a facet of global middle-class life, one shaped in Thiruvananthapuram by efforts to protect children from suicide and poor mental health as much as to cultivate the kind of polish that will ensure future success.[46] For upwardly mobile new elites in particular, this means endowing children with forms of embodied cultural capital that will gain them the competitive edge: the internalized sense of self-confidence, intuition, and communication skills that higher-status, upper-caste families are most likely to already possess in some form. In this way, defensive parenting as suicide prevention underscores the heterogeneous nature of the middle-class social field in Kerala, a field that is widening but is also deeply stratified by differential access to social, cultural, and economic capital.

Efforts to cultivate the tensile psychologies and inner lives of children are not the exclusive domain of mental health professionals and parents alone. Adolescents and young adults, too, shared fears that their childhoods had created psychological deficits they had to actively work to overcome in the present. Migration emerged in many narratives as the single most effective means to do so. Twenty-five-year-old Balu told me "Singapore life changed me." Over lunch one afternoon, he recounted his experiences during his one-year training internship at a four-star hotel restaurant. Balu explained in Malayalam, "Here [in Kerala], everything is supplied by my parents; everything is done by my parents. And that makes me *spoiled.*" Living at home, said Balu, "You become too *dependent* on your parents, and then you don't know how to live away from them." For Balu, moving to Singapore was, however, not without its risks. "When you are suddenly taken away from your parents, that sudden departure . . . the umbilical cord gets cut off and that is actually a really big shock for you. That's actually a big reason for suicide." Balu considered himself lucky in this respect. "Singapore ended up a very good *learning experience* for me," he said, reflecting on his eventual adjustment to life on his own. "But for a person who might take that kind of change negatively, it could impact them negatively."[47] Although Balu recounted a story of success and personal growth, he also recognized an inherent gamble in the decision to "cut the cord." Balu's narrative of his time abroad suggests the complex ways he looked to the development of aptitudes on the global labor market as a means to correct perceived psychological shortcomings. It is a risky process that, as Balu describes it, paradoxically courts suicide for the sake of overcoming suicide's possibility. In speaking of the perils of parental overindulgence as well as how one's psychological underdevelopment might be overcome, Balu's reflections highlight the ways youth assess and navigate the dangers and promises of transnational migration and global capitalism in relation to ideas about psychological growth, suicide, and parental nurturance.

Mathew also spoke of his time while earning his master's degree abroad as a needed opportunity for personality development. Speaking of the nuclear family, the twenty-three-year-old observed, "Parents' first reaction is to protect, to protect their child. But what they don't understand is that by protecting the child, they are actually destroying him. It's just like kissing him to death!" Mathew exclaimed, laughing. "You keep kissing, kissing, kissing, and if you don't give him oxygen, he'll be smothered!" He drew on the example of his cousin: "In my cousin's case, there is just too much force. Whenever he goes out, they are calling him on his mobile: 'Where are you, where are you? You have to come back by seven o'clock.' These kinds of things actually kill a person!" Commenting on his cousin's problems adjusting after marriage, Mathew observed, "Whatever he wants to do, someone else has to do it for him. He has no *independence.*" While his own separation from his family had been tremendously difficult, said Mathew, his cousin's postmarital problems served as a motivating lesson on the necessity of independence.[48]

Lalitha, too, spoke about her job abroad as a "chosen" hardship necessitated by her childhood. I met her and her mother at their home during Lalitha's two-week holiday from her job at a tourism bureau outside London. The articulate young woman explained to me in English how "there is no better opportunity for personality development than immersing oneself in a foreign context." Concerned that she had been raised "emotionally soft," Lalitha talked about how leaving the state for neighboring Karnataka for college studies had helped her become more mature but "still not fully confident." Interestingly, it was her mother who had encouraged her to pursue work abroad. Lalitha's mother chimed in from the kitchen, explaining how since Lalitha was a teenager, she had wanted her daughter to become "more independent and mature." In characterizing how she was raised, Lalitha compared herself with her best friend, Renu. "Renu is strong because whatever problems she met in her childhood, no one was there to support her. She's stronger. She is so strong. When problems come up, she won't feel tensed. She won't cry. She'll manage it. But when some small trouble would come for me, I'd be crying, crying, crying!" Lalitha said, laughing. "I'd cry the entire day! But when Renu had problems, she would handle them. She knows what life is. Renu bears it well, because that is how she was raised." Speaking of her time away from home, Lalitha observed, "Because I hadn't dealt with problems before, it gave me experience. Before, I wouldn't go out of the house that much without my mother. Now at least I can do that much." For Lalitha, leaving home was "like medicine": bitter and unpleasant to take in the moment but healthful in the long term.[49]

Balu, Mathew, and Lalitha spoke of their time abroad, not in terms of the technical skills or professional experience acquired. Rather, they used the "soft skills" language of *independence, growth, learning experience,* and *personality development.* This is a language that Bonnie Urciuoli calls "skills discourse."[50] Urciuoli has noted the fetishization of terms like *teamwork, communication,* and *leadership*—expertise that is collectively termed "soft skills"—in the context of the Internet-based sale and consumption of management-training services for corporate labor. The valuing of soft skills over the technical skills once associated with industry jobs and professions is central to Foucauldian technologies of the corporate-worker self. This shift in preference involves the transformation of the worker into a set of transferrable "skills" that are ambiguous in nature and reflects the forms of embodied capital, behavioral expectations, and self-relation required for flexible labor. For those like Balu, who comes from a lower-class Ezhava family and is the first to attend college, these are the embodied capacities he needs to develop to successfully navigate the social field of employment. They are also the elements of cultural capital that higher-status young adults like Mathew and Lalitha, whose families have seen significant transnational migration among the educated, are likely to already possess in some form. Nevertheless, all three young people looked to migration as the opportunity to acquire the "skills" to face life with resilience, confidence, and poise—an opportunity they perceived as missing from their childhood and adolescence. Fears of suicide can be terrifying and debilitating, but they can also be enabling, encouraging new prospects and projects for self-development among youth.

When taken together, strategies to boost immunity to suicide reflect competing orientations to aspects of the liberalizing present: while they vilify the perils of immediate gratification and churlish materialism, they promote other "healthful" forms of consumption. They also position transnational migration and the global labor market as the path to a well-adjusted, suicide-free future. But routes to confidence and psychological adulthood are not without their risks. Balu's observation of the dangers of cutting the cord illustrate tensions felt by young people as they seek out opportunities for anti-suicidal development as an enterprise fraught, ironically, with the very possibility of suicide.

## PARENT TRAP

How do parents navigate this terrain of child suicide in ordinary life? What have their responses been to reform efforts? Among those I spoke with in Thiruvananthapuram, parents of the elite, and mothers in particular, expressed fears for their children's psychological development. In similar terms to those of mental health experts, parents remarked how Malayali children today, admittedly including their own, never develop the ability to face life with the courage, willpower, and confidence that come with handling difficult situations and making decisions independently. Their concerns shaped interactions and planning in the home. Some expressed reluctance to scold or discipline, worried that their child might threaten suicide in retaliation or frustration. Others, like Lalitha's mother, who encouraged her daughter to leave for London to make her more independent, proactively strategized children's life options to compensate for perceived parental shortcomings.

Many found the practical interventions promoted by psychologists difficult to install in the home. Consider, for example, the inoculation methods by which parents are encouraged to teach children to wait for consumer goods. Bindu, a working mother, caricatured the ease with which spoiling children can get out of hand. "The child says, 'I want that! I want a chocolate!' The parents think, 'We have money. I'll buy it and give it to my child.' As this increases, bit by bit, and the demands get bigger, it gets out of control. Now they [the children] think it is their right: 'I want that now!'" Bindu went on to describe how she kept her six-year-old daughter's desires under control through techniques of postponement. "Sometimes when we go to the store, she'll say, 'I want that book, I want that other book.' If I decide to buy a book for her today, she'll get it only on Wednesday. I will only buy it for her on Wednesday. And only one book. Nothing more." The management of children's desires requires the skillful balance of denial against discretionary gratification, a process that disciplines Bindu's reluctance to say "no" as much as it does her daughter's compulsions. But as Bindu recounted, denial does not always elicit the anticipated response from her child: "[If] you don't put the TV on, if you say, 'Don't turn on the TV,' [my daughter will say] 'Then I'll kill myself!'"[51] Parents do not take these threats lightly, familiar as they are with media stories and rumors of children's threats resulting in fatal tragedy through acts that, perhaps intended only "to scare," went terribly wrong. Feared, I was told, are the three words on the tip of children's tongues: "I'll show you!" (Njaan kaannicchu tharaam). While the problem of insatiable children has resonance beyond Kerala, the threat of death renders the stakes of this problem in unique terms.

As Bindu's reflections suggest, suicide inoculation training can have the paradoxical and unintended effect of transforming everyday interactions into zones of what Pradeep Jeganathan calls "anticipated violence." Parallel to the ways checkpoints in Sri Lanka map a cartography of foretold violence in urban space, as Jeganathan observes, suicide inoculation training "delineates and focuses attention on the target," thereby announcing "in no uncertain terms: 'This is a target.'"[52] While seeking to tame the possibility of suicide, strategic denial in the home intensifies anxiety around disciplinary sites. The suicide threat demonstrates the excesses of a domain so saturated with modes of perception and dangers that the child may upend forms of discipline by deploying that which is most feared, the very utterance for which the child's wants are denied: "I will kill myself." The "art" involved in the art of parenting rests here on the delicate balance of eliciting just enough frustration toward its gradual eradication without tipping the scales so far as to draw out the feared threat. As it was for Bindu, this could be a frighteningly elusive balance to find.

Parents I spoke with also expressed difficulty in reconciling desires to support their children's psychological health with concerns for the continuity of long-term reciprocities. While they were sympathetic to the idea of restraining material provision in the family, some saw this to be in conflict with their own security in advancing age. Providing all that a child desires now might help to ensure reciprocities in later years. In this way, immediate gratification as parental investment converges with hopes for "good" family life in the form of mature children caring for the elderly. At the level of everyday life, parenting reflects uneven relationships to suicide risk management, relationships that conflict at times with other affective commitments and temporal orientations within the family.

This ambivalence is also apparent in parents' struggles to balance competing ideas of parental responsibility, nurturance, love, and risk in everyday life. One morning at a personality development summer camp for children, I met with Dr. Sharmila, a psychologist and television personality who appears regularly on daytime programming as an expert on mental health and family issues. She had invited me to meet her at her son's class so that I might get a sense of "more progressive programming for children" in the city. By midmorning, I found myself in Thiruvananthapuram's affluent suburbs in a newly refurbished heritage building, a quiet respite nestled away from the busy streets. As I watched the children unfold their yoga mats on the floor, I had one of my first glimpses of summer programming for the elite. For an hour, the young female yoga instructor guided the children patiently but firmly through basic stretches, poses, and breathing exercises, all in English. Morning yoga would be followed by the day's guest speaker: a retired university professor who would speak to the children on the topic of "personality development and spirituality." Perfectly coiffed in a carefully starched cotton sari, Dr. Sharmila invited me to stand with her in the doorway to chat as the children went through their stretches. Our conversation would unfold entirely in English.

While an advocate for the reform of parenting, Dr. Sharmila offered critical reflections on "parenting today" that reveal the polarizing pulls of the multiple positions she inhabits as practicing psychologist, public figure, wife, and mother. Articulate and poised, she began by talking about the need for new programming in the classroom, since nowadays, said Dr. Sharmila, children rely on teachers for the emotional and psychological development they fail to receive at home. Child rearing, in this sense, has been outsourced. "There is no longer any parent-child relationship," announced Dr. Sharmila, "only the teacher-child relationship." Breaking from this register of social critique, the mother of two then began to reflect on her personal circumstances. In a confessional tone, she conceded that the lack of a parent-child relationship was due in large part to women working outside the home. After all, said the psychologist with a tinge of irony, wasn't this the reason why her young son was here at the summer camp for the few weeks before the start of the school year? She gestured at her six-year-old son bending himself into downward dog pose. "I'm at the hospital most mornings during the week," said Dr. Sharmila, "so this is a good alternative to him sitting idly at home."

Reverting to her professional register and earlier commentary on "Malayali parenting," Dr. Sharmila criticized mothers who "live only for their children's grades" for creating unhealthy patterns in the home.[53] So deeply do mothers involve themselves in their children's grades and studies that a poor mark can drive both mother and child to suicide, she told me. In the next moment, her tone softened as she sympathized with parents' concerns for academic success. Many parents of her generation had firsthand experiences with economic and employment insecurity. It is understandable, she said, that parents project these worries onto their children. "Parents naturally have concerns for their children's future," she said. "Children have to be able to compete if their lives are to be protected." While critical of parental "overinvolvement," Dr. Sharmila also sympathized with the deeply felt need among parents to defensively protect their children in an age of uncertainty.

Critical of her peers in one moment, Dr. Sharmila situated herself among them in the next. Switching to the first-person plural voice, she placed herself among the mothers she had just criticized, speaking in defense of the camp of "bad" parents. "We are cast as the devils," she lamented. "It's unfair that teachers demonize parents, charging us with neglecting children at home and not providing enough assistance with their schoolwork." While she conceded that the poor reputation of parents in the eyes of educators is linked to real problems in the home, this reputation is not entirely justified. She took herself as an example. "With some mothers working, children are not getting the quality time with their parents," she noted. Yet working mothers such as she were making a concerted effort to find that time. Dr. Sharmila shared her own personal struggles to make quality time for her children and how they often failed despite the best of intentions. Coming home from work at 6:00 or 7:00 P.M., she said, working mothers feel they have to compensate for the lack of time with their children by "yelling, beating, and screaming at their children to study more." Then she noted, "Meanwhile, the fathers are waiting outside the house, maybe at a tea stall down the street, waiting for the house to calm down and be able to return." Practical constraints and the division of household labor preclude even "good" mothers from finding time with their children. The guilt that results, observed Dr. Sharmila, creates a vicious cycle. Mothers like herself, she admitted, dote on children with material goods as a surrogate for time spent together. From her perspective as a psychologist, Dr. Sharmila's promoted the need for quality interaction that involves neither totalitarian parenting nor compensatory material indulgence. Yet her daily struggles as a working mother suggested to Dr. Sharmila that such time is a near impossibility given the gendered demands of middle-class nuclear family life.

Confessing her desire to be the better mother she felt she ought to be, Dr. Sharmila turned to another woman just to the other side of the hallway. Dr. Sharmila praised her friend effusively. "She is the role model for all mothers," she exclaimed to me. "Top on her priority list, at the very top you will see, 'my children, my children, my children!'"[54] Dr. Sharmila's view of her own child rearing as alternately "good" and "bad" and alternately part of and yet outside the developments in parenting that she criticized suggests the conflicts and challenges she faces as she navigates risk, responsibility, nurturance, and the ideological and practical demands of everyday life in an era of child suicide.

### GROWN IN THE FIRE

Theeyil kurutthathu veyilatthu vaadilla. (That which grows in the fire will not wilt in the sun.)
—Malayalam proverb

This book opened with perceptions and experiences of the contemporary as a time of betrayal, contradiction, and decline in Kerala's capital city. Today, the claims of a once hegemonic Kerala model are being actively dismantled; at the same time, liberal economic reforms and transnational migration foment moral and social anxieties about guiding trajectories for the future. As past horizons of collective struggle threaten to recede into obsolescence and contemporary socioeconomic processes reorient the developmental state, children and child rearing serve as critical sites for anxieties and contested imaginings of possible futures.

Fears about the rise of a frail and suicidal generation of Malayalis have rekindled long-standing governmental concerns for population quality. But these concerns are also configured in new ways in the liberalizing present. They generate questions about not only whether the children of today will be capable and productive enough to lead region and nation but also whether they will have the competitive edge to thrive in an increasingly globalized world. Emerging discourses focused on children's subjectivities and psychological capacities have gained popular purchase among elites and are channeling parental energies and resources toward new ideas of quality child rearing. By reforming themselves, parents not only seek to prevent child suicide; they also aim to prepare children to face uncertain times. But although these efforts claim to promote the improved fitness of "the people" in a time of suicide, in fact, this is a deeply classed endeavor. For as we have seen, in the capital city suicide prevention has emerged as a key site in the cultural production and elaboration of middle-classness. It is children of the elite whose lives are to be protected and enhanced in the pursuit of class-specific visions of a globally oriented "collective" future.

In a time when state welfare provisions are retracting and losses are one's own to manage, increasingly individuals and families are appointed the sole responsibility for securing their lives against suicide. By and large in their efforts at suicide prevention, elite parents and mental health experts have not called upon the state to build better futures for coming generations. If many in the capital city have openly faulted the developmental state for failing to deliver on the past promises of the Kerala model, they have turned to themselves and their families to forge ways of better living for the future. In a manner characteristic of liberal solutions to social problems, efforts to promote resilience in living and immunity to the threat of suicide are unwavering in their message: it is ultimately the individual alone who must learn to endure this time of suicide with balance, to be grown in the fire so as not to wilt in the sun. In the face of increasing uncertainty and waning social support systems, suicide prevention has been circumscribed to the domain of elite parenting in the home. Possibilities for imagining alternative futures are domesticated in many senses of the term.

# Afterword

When I last visited Manju in Thiruvananthapuram, nearly two years had passed since we had seen one another. Greeting me at the doorway of her home, Manju embraced me, then laughed and asked if I still recognized her in spite of the few pounds she had put on. Much had changed in the intervening years. In 2008, Manju and her husband had taken several loans to renovate and expand their home and had since started renting out the upstairs apartment to bring in extra income. I nearly missed the house on my way over, not having recognized the imposing two-level concrete edifice that stood where their modest single-level home used to be. Their twenty-three-year-old daughter, Neethu, had also completed her college degree in history. She was now working long hours as a customer service representative for a company in Technopark. With the house renovations finally completed and their loans paid off, it was time to get Neethu married.

Like other middle-class families in the city, Manju and her husband had mobilized a variety of resources to find their daughter an appropriate match. That afternoon over steaming cups of milky tea, I learned of how they had spoken with extended family to identify young men of interest around the city. Manju had also opened accounts with two marriage bureaus. Many of these bureaus have gone online to offer clients the convenience of browsing the profiles and photos of thousands of prospective grooms and brides, a service that Manju and her husband took advantage of from the comfort of their newly purchased laptop and home Internet connection. Walking me through one of these websites, Manju demonstrated how to set the filters for religion, caste, profession, and country of residence. She clicked on her message inbox to share pictures of the prospective grooms whose parents had contacted her expressing interest in the profile she had created for Neethu: one of an engineer in Allapuzha and another of an IT professional in Thiruvananthapuram. Proudly demonstrating her new fluency with computer technology, Manju explained how she had conducted a wider Internet search on each of the young men, mining additional photos and biographical pieces from company profiles and Facebook pages. The fruits of Manju's careful labor had been organized in a desktop file for Neethu to peruse.

Yet such things seemed to matter little to her daughter these days. The problem, said my friend, was a young man named Ranjit. It was because of Ranjit that the process—"all of this," gestured Manju at the laptop screen—had come to a grinding halt. When the young man had first contacted them online through a marriage bureau several months back, Manju and her husband had been optimistic. From Thiruvananthapuram and nearing the completion of his master's degree in business in Canada, Ranjit had a solid education, a promising career ahead, was also a Hindu of the Nayar caste, and appeared to come from a "good family." At the time, Ranjit was deciding between jobs in Canada and Kerala but had told Neethu's parents that he was leaning toward return. On first appearance, the young man seemed to fulfill all of the qualities Manju and her husband had hoped for in a prospective groom for their daughter. But when Ranjit and Neethu began Internet chatting on Facebook—and a few weeks later, video chatting by Skype—Manju began to worry, not only about the boy's character, but also about what such a match might mean for Neethu's future. Bypassing the parental coordination of the conditions and terms of their encounters, as Manju and her husband were accustomed, the young couple spent hours online each day talking with each other. These days, said Manju, her daughter spoke of Ranjit as "my future husband."

On paper, Manju said, the young man looked perfect. This, she told me, was the only reason why they didn't put a stop to what was unfolding right under their noses. "What worries you?" I asked. Neethu had always aspired to settle abroad, Manju reminded me. Since adolescence, Neethu had fantasized about marrying a Gulf migrant, living in Muscat, vacationing in Switzerland, and retiring in the United States. Migration through marriage had long been critical to the futures she imagined for herself, as we saw in chapter 5. When Manju had first asked her daughter what qualities were most important to her in a spouse, Neethu had responded plainly that she had just one requirement: that he have solid prospects for settling abroad. The desire to migrate, said Manju, had made Neethu blind to anything else.

Manju felt profoundly conflicted. Perhaps Ranjit was the perfect match for their daughter that he seemed to be; perhaps it was all too good to be true. If Neethu did marry Ranjit and they decided to settle in Canada, thought Manju aloud, allowing herself a moment to imagine the possibility, what would her daughter do if he turned out to be a bad man? Manju held my gaze: "You know the suffering that women go through here if their husbands turn out to be of bad character. What if she goes there to Canada and this man tortures her?" Reasoning aloud, she said, "At least if such things happen here in Kerala, family would be here to intervene. Neethu would have family to help her—her parents, cousins, aunts, and uncles." Her voice dropped, "But there, she would have no one."

Manju's fears were spiraling now. With limited English, Neethu would be completely reliant on her husband. Isolated and alone, with no friends or family. What if it were even worse, and Ranjit prohibited her from using the phone or leaving the house? If Neethu went to Canada, said Manju, her eyes growing wide, no one could know of her suffering. She would have no choice but to bear it alone. Manju, who had once discouraged her daughter's dreams of migrating to the Gulf, now conceded that at least the Gulf was closer than Canada. At least there she would have family to watch over her. And like most Malayali children, she continued, Neethu had never faced any difficulties or hardships growing up. "You know how such children are nowadays. Neethu doesn't understand what *real life* is. How could she ever endure such torture alone?" If ever such troubles were to befall Neethu after marriage, Manju reasoned, her daughter would surely kill herself. She shook her head. No, absolutely not. There was no way she could ever let her daughter marry that man, she told herself over and over again, as if repetition might bring conviction.

From her kitchen in Thiruvananthapuram, Manju divined from past parenting practices the future suicide of her daughter in Canada. Her grim prophecies connected child rearing to gendered violence to suicide in a manner that tied together pasts, futures, and selves. They also joined together multiple domains of desire, fear, and value in Kerala's liberalizing present. Aspirations for upward mobility through migration, the excitement of young love made possible by the Internet, and a mother's desire that her daughter achieve the good life were weighed against fears of troubled domesticities and concerns about the shortcomings of protective parenting in a global world.

During the weeks of my visit, suicide was a powerful presence in this household. It haunted Manju's struggles to decide whether to end the relationship against the desires of her strong-willed daughter or to hope for the best. It also surfaced as the disquietude on Manju's face when Neethu's mobile phone would ring and she would slip silently from the room; in the mounting pressure from Manju's elder brother that she end the relationship lest she wish suffering upon her daughter; in the squabbles between Manju and her husband as their opinions on the matter parted ways; and in my conversations with Neethu, who took it upon herself to defend her evolving relationship against her mother's fears. Life under the shadow of suicide illustrates the concern at the heart of this book: more than terminating life alone, suicide produces new ways of living and of living with one another.

In foretelling the possibility and the proximate cause of her daughter's suicide, Manju projected death across time and space. She did so in ways that highlight for us new challenges in the anthropological study of suicide in our times. Mobility and the rapid growth of communication technologies are expanding and reshaping the virtual and actual worlds in which people dream, dwell, work, and love.[1] As experiences of space, time, and possibility transform dramatically, so, too, do people's relationships to ideas of a livable life. This is not to assume that these transformations are the result of a ready-made global force affecting local places, experienced by all people or communities to the same extent and in the same way.[2] To understand how suicide is layered into the everyday, an anthropology of suicide considers how people experience time and space differently and unevenly from specific vantage points. These vantage points are shaped by cultural and historical imaginaries of space and place, by personal and collective histories of struggle and mobility, and by people's social location and access to resources. Like others encountered in this book, Neethu, for example, aspired in ways structured at the crossroads of development, migration, liberalization, and global change. She is both facilitated and hindered at these crossroads in her pursuit of love and marriage overseas. While Neethu is educated and driven by stories of migrant success, gendered family expectation and her lower position within the larger field of white-collar employment limit her prospects for migration to her candidacy as a "bride who travels."[3] Manju's risk calculation of her daughter's choices is also shaped by her own social location. For this concerned mother, fear of abusive husbands—a fear one always has when one's daughter gets married, she noted—appeared more manageable in the Gulf than in faraway Canada. Through a spatial imaginary shaped by cultural and personal linkages to the Gulf region, Manju's dread focused not on the likelihood of domestic violence itself so much as on its remote occurrence, signified in a manner beyond literal distance. Understanding how individuals and communities differently perceive and strive for a livable life across time and space is key if we are to understand something of the particular ways those like Neethu and Manju discern possibility and encounter life's critical limits.

Aspirational horizons are more than abstraction. They are the practical coordinates by which people locate themselves in the world, orient themselves to specific futures, and thus engage—and sometimes lose the capacity to engage—the present. Neethu's pursuit of love abroad as the path to the good life is shaped too by the resources available to her. She is enabled by communication technologies within easy reach and by the greater economic freedom she has recently discovered with a salary in the burgeoning IT sector, a salary that rivals her father's. During the weeks of my visit, Neethu maneuvered around her parents to carve out room in cyberspace, where she might, as she explained to me one morning, "really get to know" her future husband. Yet she also confessed reservations. While confident one moment that the extended courtship had allowed her time and interactions that her parents never had when they first met, Neethu wondered in the next whether one could truly get to know a person through the Internet. Filled with both hope and uncertainty, she committed to walking the path to a life with Ranjit, carried forth by the inertia of their interactions. In doing so, she provoked her mother's fears of the suicide that gathers on the horizon like an oncoming storm.

What makes life worth living? If this book has hovered around a question seemingly fundamental to the human condition, it alights on the conclusion that what makes life livable is neither timeless nor universal. Descending from the heights of philosophical detachment, these chapters have plunged us instead into the particular histories, local moralities, everyday resources, and perceptions of time and space that shape the distinct aspirational horizons against which individuals and communities orient themselves, strive, and sometimes desperately fail.

This descent has made significant demands. It has challenged us to ask by what presumptions suicide in a developed part of the developing world might appear imprudent and wasteful. Recognizing how individuals and communities differently aspire and bear loss leads us to confront our own judgments about the conditions and circumstances under which life "should" be worth living and for whom. It has also pressed us to interrogate the uneasiness we may feel when some barter their safety, bodies, and lives for a chance at something different, in ways that contravene our liberal notions of the "good," responsible, life-avowing subject. Ultimately, it has enjoined us to understand the distinct experiential terms and historical conditions in which young people like Neethu dream, strive, and suffer drowning disappointment and betrayal. Suicide asks much of us, the living.

These challenges appear all the more pressing at a time when representations of suicide in the mass media have emerged as an important facet of our contemporary experience. Highly publicized spectacular events of self-violence have become part of our everyday political and moral landscape: the immolations that catalyzed the so-called Jasmine Revolution in Tunisia; the surge of suicides among China's Foxconn factory workers earlier that year; the unfolding suicide epidemic among the U.S. military; the ongoing hunger strikes of Guantánamo Bay detainees. The presence of cameras, social media, and satellite television has rapidly expanded the means and possibilities for spectacular death to attract a global audience of witnesses. Self-violence has become a platform to command world attention. Increasingly so, it also serves as a central optic through which those of us watching now judge parents, cultures, societies, religions, corporations, and governments. What does it mean for publicized self-violence to play a role in how we access, understand, and judge the lives and worlds of others?

The visibility of highly publicized self-violence in daily life raises the question of how such events become meaningful in public imaginaries. Histories in the governance of life and death shape our assumptions about how death "should go" for certain people and populations and our confusion, outrage, or ambivalence when suicide disrupts these assumptions. These are the different histories by which suicide in the developing world engenders moral offense or is simply inscrutable; military suicide confounds and confuses meanings of death in times of war; the hunger strike of suspected terrorists evokes antipathy for many; and the public immolations of Arab youth in the ostensible name of democracy and freedom engender the admiration of media pundits against the background of suicide terrorism.[4] An anthropology of suicide endeavors to ask how and why willful death is taken up as a project of worth—indeed, as it may be for individuals, families, and communities, a way to live.[5] But it also recognizes the histories and relations of power through which we sort out and stratify the value of individuals and populations through the act of suicide itself. Tied up in this concern is how certain deaths come to be seen as more grievable than others.[6]

In a time when we generate understandings of others through their publicized self-destruction, history, meaning, and power remain key concerns in the anthropological study of suicide. Yet our modes of attention must also be supple enough to recognize the reverse side of the spectacular: the ways death is layered into ordinary life. Ethnography is powerful in this regard, allowing us to reckon with how people live with suicide in its innumerable forms. For some in this book, suicide insinuated itself into life as pursuant guilt, disquieting possibility, ambiguous threat, passing joke, and unsettled spirit. Some accumulated death to enhance the lives of others or to make life livable, if only for a time. Others accumulated death to exist differently. Kin are learning to live in new ways with one another in the hopes of securing better futures, and some are doing so out of a necessity of a different kind: because life in the wake of losing a loved one is simply not life as it was before.

In the long shadow of fear and uncertainty that suicide casts in Kerala, living is no longer as it was, including for Manju and Neethu. As mother and daughter struggle to discern hopeful futures with suicide as an ever-present possibility, they direct resources, love, and lives in light of risk and desire. Manju's divination of her daughter's death has taken on a momentum of its own. Like the gravitational pull of a collapsing star, Manju's fears draw Neethu ever closer to a core uncertainty. These fears have come to orient how Neethu now perceives herself and her future. For although she continues to pursue a life with Ranjit, Neethu has come to believe in the truth of her mother's divinations and of the chance of her own self-destruction. She knows, she tells me, that her mother is right: never could she endure such suffering alone, if ever it were to befall her. Suicide would be the ultimate price. Armed and vulnerable with this prophetic knowledge, Neethu pursues the path before her to love and life overseas. She does so with eyes wide open.

# Notes

**INTRODUCTION**

1. Field notes, Thiruvananthapuram, India, October 2005.

2. Kerala's suicide rate began to rise significantly in the mid-1990s. It rose to a high of 30.8 per 100,000 in 2003 but has seen some decline in recent years, to 25.3 in 2011 (as compared with the all-India average of 11.4 for that year). See www.ksmha.org for more government statistics. See also Halliburton 1998.

3. While *family suicide* is a commonly used term, following mental health activists in Kerala I prefer the term *family murder-suicide* to describe the mixed agency among kin involved in these death pacts.

4. Farmer 1992:6.

5. www.ksmha.org.

6. There are significant differences in reported suicide rates among Kerala's districts. The suicide rate is consistently low in Malappuram District, whose population is predominantly Muslim, which reported a rate of 9.8 in 2010. The rate of increase in suicide has been the highest in Thiruvananthapuram District, which reported an average suicide rate of 38.8 over the period of 2000–2010. Family murder-suicide is also the highest in Thiruvananthapuram District. See www.ksmha.org.

7. "Lesbian suicides" and "farmer suicides," for instance, are two examples of highly visible and well-publicized categories of suicide that have circulated widely in the Kerala media and in public discourse. See Münster 2012 on "farmers' suicides" as a category of state enumeration and intervention in Wayanad District. See Deepa 2005 and Mokkil 2009 on the politics of the visibility of "lesbian suicides" in the Kerala public sphere.

8. The bulk of this research was conducted over a twenty-four-month period between 2005 and 2007, with shorter periods in 2002, 2003, 2004, and 2009.

9. Liberalization reforms began in the late 1980s under Rajiv Gandhi's government, which removed some of the controls, restrictions, and high taxes under the Nehruvian planned economy. It was in 1991 that the government of Narasimha Rao and the then finance minister Manmohan Singh installed comprehensive economic reforms. These included the opening of public sector institutions such as education, banking, airlines, and electric power to private sector and foreign investment; deregulation of the Indian financial system; and a loosening of restrictions on monopolies.

10. In deciding to focus on Thiruvananthapuram's widening middle-class social field, including experiences of upward mobility among formerly underrepresented groups, it should be clear that I do not purport to present a comprehensive study of suicide patterns in the state overall or even in the capital city. Rather, I draw on the strengths of ethnographic methodologies to explore in depth one dimension of how contemporary suicide has been popularly understood and experienced in Thiruvananthapuram.

11. On development as affective experience in India, see Pandian 2009. See also Ferguson 1999.

12. On suicide and neoliberal transformations, see Livingston 2009; Mohanty 2005; Parry 2012; and Staples 2012.

13. See, for example, Biehl 2005; Bourgois and Schonberg 2009; Garcia 2010; Han 2012; Klaits 2010; Livingston 2012; Scheper-Hughes 1992; and Stevenson 2012.

14. Foucault 1983, 1997.

15. Scheper-Hughes 1992:xii.

16. Critical of universalizing constructions of "the suffering stranger"(Butt 2002; see also Kleinman and Kleinman 1996; and Malkki 1996), medical anthropologists have responded with a move to historicize and contextualize experiences of suffering. Approaches to "social suffering" (Kleinman et al. 1997), "structural violence" (Farmer 1996, 2004), and "the violence of everyday life" (Scheper-Hughes 1992) shift the locus from questions of individual pathology to the political and economic processes, institutional structures, and relations of power that shape suffering and to the human responses to social problems.

17. Agamben 1998.

18. Redfield 2013.

19. Consider an editorial by the journalist Lonappan Ouseppachan, in which he argues, "The Malayali, for all his awareness, political consciousness, and literacy, is stuck in a mental trap of his own making. He is educated, so believes he deserves a white-collar job. When he can't find it easily, he is pissed off. He wants a government job if he can't become an engineer or doctor. His problems are those of the middle class person who wants everything on his terms. He deserves his current situation, and will get out of it himself when desperate enough. Give the Malayali no sympathy. He deserves none." http://singapore .kaumudiglobal.com/news.php?newsid+1871, accessed October 15, 2007.

20. Gupta 1998:11. For radical critiques of the universalist telos of development discourse, see Escobar 1995; Ferguson 1994; and Parajuli 1991. See also Pigg 1992. For a review of post-structuralist approaches to development discourse, see Agarwal 1996.

21. The dominant narrative of Kerala's exceptionalism also foregrounds the state as having gone through a unique development experience in the nation. Nehruvian developmentalism, based on heavy industries and technological progress, was widely accepted post-Independence as the path to realizing the secular modern nation. In the context of a national imaginary that prioritized economic production, Kerala's stagnant industrial growth initially positioned it as a backward region. The narrative of Kerala's exceptionalism argues, however, that Kerala ultimately achieved the development telos, not through the route of industrialization, but rather through its distinct forms of public action (Devika 2008:256).

22. R. Jeffrey 1992:ix.

23. Parayil 2000:vii.

24. This acclaimed status had been linked to the figure of a seemingly unmarked, empowered Malayali Woman, indexed most prominently by the educated and migratory (Christian) nurse and by the matrilineal (Nayar) woman who captured anthropological imaginations. In the dominant narrative of Kerala's exceptionalism, this status has been linked to demographic successes and women's educational achievement in the state. For examples in the scholarly literature of the high status attributed to women in Kerala, see, among others, Drèze and Sen 1997; and R. Jeffrey 1992.

25. See, for example, Alexander 1995; Franke and Chasin 1994; R. Jeffrey 1992; and Ratcliffe 1978.

26. April 15, 2009, *New York Times,* http://travel.nytimes.com/frommers/travel/guides/asia/india/kerala/frm_kerala_3479010001.html, accessed March 11, 2013.

27. For a radical critique of the Kerala model discourse, see Devika 2008, 2009, and 2010.

28. See Halliburton 1998. "Paradox" has been a popular narrative framing in discussions of the Kerala model's achievements and disappointments more broadly. For a critical analysis of how this device has been used in the Kerala literature, see Sreekumar 2007.

29. The progressiveness of the Malayali was often claimed in opposition to the Bihari, the latter commonly taken by my interlocutors as the archetypal "backward" Indian villager. This is striking in light of the observation widely made that in the development imaginary, in at least one respect Kerala and Bihar appear to share a degree of kinship. Tharamangalam (1998:28) comments that the two states are increasingly linked in their failure to evidence economic expansion: "In the scramble for attracting investments in the post-liberalization period, Kerala is yoked with Bihar, a state that has become synonymous with persistent failures on the development front."

30. This construction of Kerala as "poverty-free" masks economic vulnerability within the region. It obscures, for example, the mass starvation deaths among adivasi families that led to a *jathra* (political procession) organized by activists to Thiruvananthapuram in 2001 and the larger movement for adivasi rights in Kerala. On the movement for adivasi rights led by C. K. Janu, see Bijoy and Raman 2003; and Raman 2002.

31. In India, where attempted suicide also remains illegal under the Indian Penal Code, suicide registers in multiple ways this failed obligation to region

and nation to stay alive. Under Section 309 of the Indian Penal Code, attempted suicide is an offense punishable by a one-year imprisonment, a fine, or both. At the time of writing, the Union Health Ministry has been pushing to decriminalize suicide, with several states consenting to the Law Commission's recommendation for removal of the criminal provision from the code. www.thehindu .com/news/national/attempt-to-suicide-to-be-decriminalised/article2477158 .ece, accessed August 27, 2013.

32. Roy 2007.

33. On how development discourse in postcolonial India draws upon colonial registers of difference, see Bose 1997; Chakrabarty 2000; and Ludden 1992.

34. I draw here on Stevenson's (2012) analysis of how this colonial desire operates in the context of state responses to Inuit suicide in the Canadian Arctic.

35. The word *hartal* is largely used interchangeably with *bandh,* a Hindi word that literally means "closed" and that refers more specifically to a general strike usually called by a political party, during which schools, shops, colleges, workplaces, and public and often private modes of transportation are shut down during daylight hours (Lukose 2005b:510).

36. Rose 2007.

37. Mbembe 2003:11

38. Murray 2006. See also Asad 2007; Enns 2004; and Linos 2010.

39. See, for example, Andriolo 2006; and Feldman 1991.

40. Such readings of suicide are rooted in a construction of the liberal subject as a repository of intentionality, consciousness, and will. On the construction of the liberal subject in suicide studies and its gendered underpinnings, see Canetto 1992; Canetto and Lester 1998; and Jaworski 2003.

41. Not even the suicide note—taken as the truest evidence of intent— can fully determine authorship or meaning in the act, since even this form of testament can be discredited for any number of reasons.

42. On the locally respectable, classed ideal of the contained female body in Kerala, see Lukose 2009.

43. For an examination of the historical development and the gendered and generational practices that shape the masculinist "political public" in Kerala, see Lukose 2005b.

44. This narrative underscored the fact that Rajani had jumped from a building that housed the office of the commissioner for entrance examinations.

45. This subject position of dalits as passive victims has been stridently refused by radical dalit political struggles that have gained force in Kerala in the past decade. See Devika 2013.

46. The ambiguities around the definition of Rajani's death as suicide or murder resonate with Veena Das's observations concerning the legal management of practices of *sati,* or widow burning. Das writes, "The ambiguity of legislation does not quite know whether to treat the woman with respect to whom sati is committed as victim or criminal" (Das 1995:113). While on the one hand sati is interpretable as an illegal act of suicide punishable according to the Indian Penal Code, the issue of the widow's "coercion" onto her dead husband's funeral pyre

simultaneously raises the culpability of those who force, tacitly consent to, or permit such acts to occur and are therefore punishable under the law. As Das and others have argued (see, for example, Mani 1998), both subject positions must be understood as ideological constructions that have served as sites to stage conflicts and debates surrounding national subjectivity.

47. Among those who stood accused of murder were Chief Minister A. K. Antony, the minister for the Welfare of Scheduled and Backward Communities M. A. Kuttapan, and the education minister Nalakath Soopy. Also named were the loan officer of the Indian Overseas Bank who declined Rajani's educational loan and the superintendent of Thiruvananthapuram General Hospital, accused of destroying criminal evidence. *The Hindu* 2004b.

48. Field notes, Thiruvananthapuram, India, August 2004.

49. Ezhavas are presently considered one of the "other backward classes" (OBC), in government parlance.

50. C. Osella and F. Osella 2006; F. Osella and C. Osella 2000b. This prevailing mood of progress is captured by A. Aiyappan, himself an Ezhava who became a prominent social anthropologist. His 1965 monograph, *Social Revolution in a Kerala Village,* outlines the Ezhava community's continuing progress in the post-Independence period.

51. C. Osella and F. Osella 2006.

52. George and Kumar 1999; Salim 2004.

53. Although such scholarships subsidize tuition expenses for students like Rajani, they do not account for maintenance costs for such things as books and hostel fees. This contributes to Kerala's high drop-out rates at the bachelor's degree level in arts and sciences colleges, estimated to be nearly 30 percent by the third year (George and Kumar 1999:7), and to the low enrollment rates of "scheduled caste"/"scheduled tribe" students in government-run and -aided private institutions, whose annual reservations quotas are seldom filled (Salim 2004:15). (See n. 54 regarding these governmental terms.)

54. Reservations policies earmark a percentage of government jobs for lower-caste groups and were expanded in the Mandal Commission Report of 1980. They target, in governmental parlance, scheduled caste (SC), scheduled tribes (ST), other backward classes (OBC), and other underrepresented communities in an effort to promote enhanced social and educational opportunities for these groups.

55. Rajani's father repeatedly referred to his daughter's intelligence and devout work ethic in interviews following her suicide. In one interview, he told the press, "She used to burn the midnight oil. Having cleared the Plus Two course with distinction, she had her sights set on an MBBS (a medical degree). She finally settled for engineering, as it would entail less financial burden on the family. Since we could not afford to send her to a coaching institute, she relied on used books procured from other students and cleared the entrance examination" (*The Hindu* 2004a).

56. Field notes, Thiruvananthapuram, India, August 2004.

57. Drawing on the work of Julia Kristeva, J. Devika (2013:2) argues that regardless of whether the test was carried out or not, the demand placed in Rajani's case to prove eligibility of welfare through sexual purity illustrates the

powerful mode of abjection through which low-caste groups are marginalized in public discourse in Kerala. See also Devika 2009.

58. I draw a parallel here to the ways Mani (1998) argues that the sati served as the "ground" for ideological and political debates in colonial and native elite concerns for the practice of widow burning in colonial India, saying far more about these actors and their agendas than anything of the experiences of the sati herself.

59. Deshpande 2006; George and Kumar 1999; Salim 2004; Sancho 2012.

60. Mathew 1997; Zachariah and Rajan 2005. As has been documented in India and elsewhere, unemployment and underemployment increasingly threaten even the most advantaged sections of the youth population. See, for example, Jeffrey et al. 2008; Mains 2012; and Parry 2005.

61. The unemployment rate in the state neared 40 percent among those with secondary schooling in 2003. Among degree holders the unemployment rate overall was 36 percent, while minimal unemployment was reported among those with below-primary-level education (Zachariah and Rajan 2005:25).

62. Jeffrey and McDowell 2004; C. Jeffrey 2010.

63. On local norms of masculine householder status in Kerala, see F. Osella and C. Osella 1999.

64. On mass media, advertising, and consumption in India, see Fernandes 2000; Mankekar 1999; Mazzarella 2003; and Rajagopal 1999.

65. See Fuller and Narasimhan 2007; and S. Radhakrishnan 2011.

66. Donner and De Neve 2011. As opposed to approaches that take the "middle class" to be a sociological category or empirical condition, my approach is grounded in the work of anthropologists and others who have explored the everyday ways through which middle-classness in postliberalization India is produced as contested cultural practice inflected by gender, caste, and community. These approaches recognize that the everyday production of middle-classness as cultural practice involves moral, ideological, and material struggles and contestations and is marked by unequal access to forms of social, cultural, and economic capital. These approaches also problematize the category of the "middle class" as a unified, idealized, and singular body, one that works ideologically to conceal the cultural dominance of certain sections of the middle class and the stark inequalities within it. See, for example, Lukose 2009; Mankekar 1999; Mazzarella 2003; and F. Osella and C. Osella 2000b; see also Liechty 2003 on middle-classness in Nepal. For an overview of the literature on the study and conceptualization of the middle class in India, see Donner and De Neve 2011.

67. See Lukose 2009; and F. Osella and C. Osella 1999, 2000a, 2000b.

68. I draw here on Bourdieu 1984.

69. On how ethical life in contemporary south India is shaped by longer histories of virtue, see Pandian 2009. On ethical life as lived practice in South Asia, see Pandian and Ali 2010.

70. Conjectures have been made to account for this lacuna within anthropology. Hippler (1969:1075) suggests that the discipline's inadequate theorizing of human psychology kept anthropology analytically ill equipped to enter the domain of suicide studies.

71. For a review of the anthropological literature on suicide, see Macdonald 2007; and Staples and Widger 2012.

72. See Staples and Widger 2012 on suicide and ethnography. Following the events of September 11, 2001, and in light of the suicide bombings in areas of ethnic and nationalistic violence, anthropological attention to suicide has grown as scholars seek to complicate mainstream discourses on terrorism. See Allen 2002; Asad 2007; Hage 2003b; and Linos 2010.

73. The conceptualization of suicide as a marker of social cohesion is the legacy of sociologist Émile Durkheim's ([1897] 1951) classic study. In his typology of suicide, Durkheim recognized that some suicides arise from the opposite extreme of poor social cohesion, or anomie. In the case of what he terms "altruistic suicide," it is overintegration of the individual personality into society rather than excessive individuation that, Durkheim argues, leads to suicide. It should be noted, however, that I am not turning to Durkheim's notion of altruistic suicide—a trope that has been problematically applied to sati in the Indian context—but am in fact departing from sociological understandings of suicide as a straightforward marker of social cohesion more generally.

74. Comaroff 2007:203.

75. During preliminary fieldwork I utilized an open-ended ethnographic approach that Spradley (1979, 1980) calls "grand tour observations," wherein open-ended, general observations produce broad categories of information. This allowed me to remain observant of the diverse sites and practices where suicide became meaningful. On this basis, I then devised methodologies and selected sites for the extended fieldwork conducted between 2005 and 2007. During this period, fieldwork included: ten months of participant observation at two hospitals (one government-funded, one privately funded); participant observation as a trainee in suicide prevention training workshops and as an invited presenter at public educational programs; interviews with psychologists, psychiatrists, social workers, and family counselors; interviews with suicide attempters and family survivors; interviews with police officers and lawyers; interviews with parents and educators; oral histories and interviews with young adults; archival research at the Kerala State Crime Records Bureau and the Kerala State Archives; and analysis of magazines, newspapers, books, films, and television and radio programs. I conducted interviews with over 150 individuals from 2002 to 2009, with the majority interviewed on multiple occasions.

76. Mol 2002:6.

77. In 2011, the Kerala State Mental Health Authority found that 1 percent of total reported suicides in the state were committed by children fourteen years of age and younger. This represents a slight increase from an average of fewer than 1 percent during the time I was conducting fieldwork. See www.ksmha .org, accessed August 31, 2013.

78. Durkheim (1938) famously suggested that social facts regulate human social action and act as constraints over individual behavior and action. Suicide rates are markers of social facts, argued Durkheim ([1897] 1951), in that suicide is not just personal but also a societal characteristic. By examining suicide rates across time and place, Durkheim's approach promised to make possible the study of the behavior of entire societies rather than just that of particular individuals. For a critique, see Douglas 1967.

79. Mental health professionals and other higher-status, educated professionals, for example, often chose to speak in English in their formal interviews, but spoke with me and their patients in Malayalam in the clinical setting.

80. This scene is notable for the idea that suicide can be rendered knowable through increasingly technoscientific methods of investigation, a trend reflected in recent suicide studies that seek to develop rigorous predictive tools to calculate an individual's suicide risk at any given moment. See Tingley 2013, for example, on research conducted by a suicide "Columbo."

81. Nancy Scheper-Hughes (1995:417) exemplifies this project when she calls for an anthropology that is "politically and morally engaged," at the forefront of which will be a "new cadre of 'barefoot anthropologists'"—the "alarmists and shock troopers" to produce "politically complicated and morally demanding texts and images capable of sinking through the layers of acceptance, complicity, and bad faith that allow the suffering and the deaths to continue without even the pained cry of recognition of Conrad's evil protagonist, Kurtz: 'The horror! The horror!'"

82. Herzfeld 2001.

83. Das 2000, 2007.

84. Das 2000:221.

85. In some instances, families sought me out. See, for instance, Ajith's story in chapter 3.

86. On recognition of the limits of ethnographic knowledge, see Garcia 2010; and Stevenson 2009.

87. Scheper-Hughes 1992.

CHAPTER 1

1. Field notes, Thiruvananthapuram, India, December 2005.

2. The linking of suicide to collective historical experience has been documented in the narrative explanations of suicide epidemics among other communities. See, for example, Dabbagh 2005; Kral et al. 2011; O'Nell 1996; and Wexler 2006.

3. I draw on Gupta (1998), who proposes an analytic for the postcolonial condition that recognizes its conjunctural nature. See also Lukose 2009.

4. See Lukose 2009 for more on the discourse of the consuming, globally oriented "new generation" in Kerala.

5. See Redfield 2013 for a discussion of how this distinction operates in humanitarian work.

6. On the recent "happiness turn" in policy and governance frameworks, see Ahmed 2007. The use of happiness as a metric now extends to economists and even some governments, who see it as a measurable and governable asset.

7. Devika 2007:4.

8. The key event marking this divide is widely taken to be the presidential address delivered by E. M. S. Namboothiripad at a 1994 international congress held in Thiruvananthapuram (Tharamangalam 1998:24; Isaac and Tharakan 1995). In his speech, the founding leader of the Communist Party of India-Marxist (CPI [M]) and first chief minister of Kerala warned against letting "the

praise that scholars shower on Kerala for its achievements divert attention from the intense economic crisis that we face. We are behind other states of India in respect of economic growth, and a solution to this crisis brooks no delay. We can ignore our backwardness in respect of employment and production only at our own peril" (Isaac and Tharakan 1995:1994).

9. On the "inherent weaknesses" of the Kerala model, see Tharamangalam 1998. Some scholars in this camp have mobilized these arguments to justify the retraction of the state's commitment to social development, suggesting that the very welfare policies that once distinguished the Kerala model no longer appear sustainable in an era of decelerated economic growth.

10. For a critical analysis of how the concept of paradox has been used within the Kerala literature, see Sreekumar 2007.

11. This "new" Kerala model seeks to advance a shift away from the "old" model's central focus on redistributive policies by building synergies between civil society, local government bodies, and the state government. The new model's emphasis on participatory, community-based sustainable development is best exemplified by the People's Campaign, launched in 1996, which mobilized over three million people toward "bottom-up" development planning for all of the state's 1,052 villages and urban neighborhoods. See Isaac and Franke 2002; and Véron 2001.

12. Some scholars have debated a possible turnaround in Kerala's economic growth. Kannan 2005 has suggested that Kerala has shown a "virtuous" cycle of capital growth since the mid-1980s. See Oomen 2007 for a summary of these debates.

13. See, for example, Devika 2007, 2010, 2013; Kodoth and Eapen 2005 Lindberg 2005; and Mitra and Singh 2007.

14. Tharamangalam 1998:24.

15. Devika 2007:7; see also Sreekumar 2009.

16. George 2006.

17. "Aikya Keralam," or "United Kerala," was the name of a popular movement that agitated for the consolidation of all Malayalam-speaking regions into the single state of Kerala.

18. Devika 2010.

19. On radical dalit assertions in the Kerala public sphere, see Devika 2013. On mobilization among adivasi communities in Kerala, see Bijoy and Raman 2003; Raman 2002; and Steur 2009.

20. It has now been widely argued that development in Kerala occurred at the expense of dalit, adivasi, and coastal communities. See, for example, Sreekumar and Parayil (2006:220), who describe adivasi communities as the "worst hit victims of Kerala's 'development,'" and J. Kurien (2000:194), who notes that fishing communities have emerged as "outliers" of the Kerala model's "central tendency." While this discourse acknowledges inequalities in the region, others have pointed out that it problematically configures these communities as victims awaiting the intervention of the state and of elites rather than as political reformers in their own right. See Devika 2013; and Steur 2009.

21. Compare to Ferguson's (1999) ethnography of decline in the Zambian Copper Belt.

22. On migration and unemployment in Kerala, see Zachariah and Rajan 2005, 2007; and Zachariah et al. 2003.

23. Lukose 2009:57. Donner and De Neve (2011:9) point out that the valorization of consumption is also replicated in much scholarly work that takes consumption as the sole lens for examining India's middle-class subjects.

24. See, for example, Breckenride 1995; Donner 2011; Lukose 2009; Mankekar 1999; and Mazzarella 2003.

25. At the same time, this stance is neither stable nor unitary. Sangari (2003) points out that the Hindu right, rather than promoting strictly anti-consumerist or Gandhian notions of austerity, takes a "schizophrenic" stance that pulls its ideological commitments toward both neoliberal economic policies favored by its middle-class vote bank and toward the Hindu right's assertions of cultural nationalism.

26. The location of the Malabar coast on the southwest region of the Indian peninsula, at the nexus of Indian Ocean trade routes between the Middle East and Southeast Asia, made it the epicenter of a long history of trade and intercultural contact. A growing colonial plantation economy in Southeast Asia and what is now Sri Lanka also pulled migrant labor from the Malabar coast region beginning in the nineteenth century. See Sooryamoorthy 1997.

27. Field notes, Thiruvananthapuram, India, November 2005.

28. Lukose 2009:7

29. Contrary to this popular discourse of youth disengagement, scholars have documented radical forms of political engagement among youth in postcolonial India, particularly among the underemployed. See C. Jeffrey 2010; and Lukose 2005b.

30. Lukose 2005a:915.

31. On how local histories shape ethical virtues of self-making in postcolonial south India, see Pandian 2009.

32. Along with Nambudiris (Malayali Brahmins) and Tamil Brahmins, Nayars are considered upper-caste (savarnna) Hindus.

33. Field notes, Thiruvananthapuram, India, June 2007.

34. F. Osella and C. Osella 1999:991. Near the end of the nineteenth century in Kerala, the community of Syrian Christians owned significant land and was active in trade and commerce. Because of the advancements made by this community, Syrian Christians are classified in governmental parlance as a "forward caste."

35. Important to the emergence of Ezhavas as new elites was the strong anti-caste social reform movement led by the spiritual leader Sree Narayana Guru, a movement that became part of a broad set of transformations that have altered caste relations over the past century.

36. On social and economic mobility among the Ezhava community, see C. Osella and F. Osella 2006; and F. Osella and C. Osella 2000b.

37. I draw here on Bourdieu's (1984) notion of distinction.

38. Field notes, Thiruvananthapuram, India, March 2006.

39. Field notes, Thiruvananthapuram, India, February 2006.

40. Sangari and Vaid 1989.

41. See Banerjee 1991; Niranjana 1999; and Tarlo 1996.

42. Lukose 2009:13.

43. Chatterjee 1989.

44. This contrasts with the aspiring lower-caste, lower-class masculinity of *chethu* discussed in detail by Lukose (2009). While this masculinity is also marked by precariousness, Lukose points out that being *chethu* does not pose the same kind of potent moral threat that the consuming female subject poses.

45. Field notes, Thiruvananthapuram, India, April 2006.

46. Chatterjee (1989) has argued how concerns for the home as the privatized sphere to be protected against the materialism of the West have featured as a familiar theme in Indian cultural nationalist discourse since the nineteenth century. Cultural nationalist discourses have resurged in reformulated terms since the late 1980s under the influence of Hindutva ideologies.

47. Mukhopadhyay and Seymour (1994) use the term *patrifocal* to emphasize how structures and practices of the family are focused on the interests of men and boys, in ways that profoundly affect women's lives. The features of patrifocal families include patrifocal residence, patrilineal descent, and patrilineal inheritance and succession, all of which emphasize the centrality of men to the continuity and well-being of families. The relative marginality of females is reflected in the expectation that a woman will shift residence and affiliation to her husband's family after marriage.

48. Devika 2007. In the early twentieth century, a series of legislations introduced measures "recognizing" the conjugal family by defining relations of protection and dependence between husband and wife and between father and children. The Kerala Joint Hindu Family (Abolition) Act of 1976 eliminated the legal conception of joint family property among Hindus and has been followed by the ritual and material reorganization of marriage. On the social and legislative reform of families and property rights in the region, see also Arunima 2003; Eapen and Kodoth 2003; Kodoth 2001a, 2001b; and Saradamoni 1999.

49. The impulse to "modernize" matrilineal arrangements emerged in part from European missionaries' and native elites' moral indignation over the customary institution that framed sexual relations between men and women known as *sambandham* (literally, "relationship"). As landlords or trustees of temple lands, Nambudiris (Malayali Brahmins) controlled large areas of land that were rented to Nayar tenants. Under these conditions, Nambudiri men, of whom only the eldest son married within the caste, were able to use their dominant position to ensure sexual relations with Nayar tenant *taravads* (matrilineal house-land units). See Kodoth 2001a.

50. On discourses of the "bad" modern family in India, see Cohen 1998.

51. December 9, 2002, *The Hindu*, www.hindu.com/thehindu/mp/2002/12 /09/stories/2002120900310200.htm, accessed March 20, 2013.

52. I heard the term *Othello syndrome* used on occasion by mental health professionals in reference to fears of adultery in Gulf migrant households.

53. In 2007, Kerala reported thirty-nine cases of family murder-suicide, the highest for any Indian state or union territory, followed by Andhra Pradesh with thirty-four reported cases (National Crime Records Bureau, Government of India).

54. Devika 2007; see also Sreekumar 2009.

55. Devika 2007:12.

56. Eapen 1992; Gulati and Rajan 1991; Kumar 1992; Mitra and Singh 2007.

57. For analyses of how family structure, inheritance practices, gender ideology, and economic transformations have shaped the rising incidence of dowry and domestic violence and women's mental health in Kerala, see Eapen 2002; Kodoth and Eapen 2005; Mitra and Singh 2007; and Mukhodpadhyay et al. 2007.

58. Such acts have been depicted as a compassionate alternative to abandonment in Malayalam films like *Acchen Urangaattha Veedu* (2006) and *Parunthu* (2008).

59. On the development of the "home sciences" in colonial India, see Hancock 2001.

60. On experiences of "waiting" among north Indian youth, see C. Jeffrey 2010. See also Mains 2012.

61. Mathew 1997; Zachariah and Rajan 2005.

62. Field notes, Thiruvananthapuram, India, June 2004.

63. Field notes, Thiruvananthapuram, India, November 2006.

64. Sivaramakrishnan and Agarwal 2003.

65. On young men's narratives of the value of education in north India, see C. Jeffrey et al. 2004 and 2008.

66. Christians, by reason of religious allegiance, had early access to missionary schools and had become successful at finding employment and doing business with British companies (F. Osella and C. Osella 2000b:140). Christian schools became so popular that opening them became a profitable economic niche.

67. Kodoth and Eapen (2005:3280) make a similar observation that "women's education is being oriented in directions that either foster female domesticity or at least does not threaten to destabilize it. A relevant hypothesis here is that a secondary or general higher education is perceived to be in the interests of family, fostering 'informed' child care, health, and education." See also Mitra and Singh 2006.

68. Halliburton (2005) has noted the proliferation of psychological idioms including *tension* in Kerala.

69. Field notes, Thiruvananthapuram, India, August 2004.

70. Field notes, Thiruvananthapuram, India, June 2009.

71. Field notes, Thiruvananthapuram, India, July 2004.

CHAPTER 2

1. Field notes, Thiruvananthapuram, India, February 2006.

2. I draw on ten months of participant observation at two hospital sites with clinicians working within allopathic paradigms of mental health. While many of the same patients who frequented these sites also sought care for their conditions through other healing therapies, including Ayurveda, in light of the centrality of allopathic psychiatrists' and psychologists' voices in public discourse on suicide in Kerala, I chose to limit this portion of my research to allopathic psychiatric and psychological services. See Halliburton 2009 on the

ways patients choose and experience multiple therapies for the treatment of mental illness in Kerala.

3. I draw here on Pinto's (2011) examination of how north Indian psychiatrists "read" patient lives for signs of illness.

4. Foucault 1983, 1997.

5. Davis 2012. On psychiatry and epistemology, see Kirmayer 2001; Kleinman and Good 1985; Lakoff 2005; Luhrmann 2000; and Young 1995.

6. See Davis 2012; Fassin 2000; Fassin and Rechtman 2009; Kitanaka 2012; and Martin 2007.

7. I draw loosely here on Ahmed's (2004) notion of the "stickiness" of affect.

8. On transformational shifts in the discourse between clinicians and patients in the healthcare encounter, see Chua 2012; Katz and Alegría 2009; and Katz and Shotter 1996; and Lester 2009.

9. At Central Hospital, it was standard practice for clinicians to inquire after a new patient's community and, if relevant, caste background, along with age, marital status, education, and family living situation at the start of the intake interview. Clinicians sometimes surmised parts of this information from the patient's family surname, dress, or both. This information was formally documented as part of the patient file.

10. On the political-economic and social factors influencing the heavy use of allopathic psychopharmaceuticals in India, see Ecks 2005; Ecks and Basu 2009; and Nunley 1996.

11. Field notes, Thiruvananthapuram, India, February 2006.

12. On local norms of masculine and community achievement in the context of Gulf migration, see F. Osella and C. Osella 1999, 2000a.

13. Immigration laws restricting visa issuance, together with the economic calculus of maximizing remittances, mean that Gulf contract laborers migrate on a temporary basis without their families. Presumptions that Gulf employment involves illegal means to the acquisition of "black money" color local perceptions of Gulf migrant success. See, for example, the story of Baby Chacko recounted by F. Osella and C. Osella (2000a:124). On the gendered moralities that shape understandings of Malayali emigrant women in the Gulf, see Kodoth and Varghese 2012.

14. C. Osella and F. Osella (2008) argue that assumptions that the living arrangements of Gulf migrant families are static or always involve women "left behind" obscure the diverse range of household arrangements of these families, as well as the different resources and agential strategies they bring to bear in navigating transnational fields. See also Gulati 1993.

15. For an ethnography of work and living conditions among Indian contract laborers in Bahrain, see Gardner 2010. Gardner examines systemic forms of violence and inequality structured by the kafala (individual citizen-sponsorship) system. Vora (2011) points out that noncitizen elites and business owners are also integral to the maintenance of the kafala system and thus to the governance of nonelite migrant groups.

16. Academic literature and the media have acknowledged that suicides among nonelite migrant workers in the Gulf are inordinately high. Keane and McGeehan (2008) suggest that actual figures are significantly underreported as

a result of manipulation by private companies and the government. See also al-Maskari et al. 2011.

17. Sreedhar 1994:75.

18. Sreedhar 1994:76.

19. Sreedhar 1994:76–77.

20. Sreedhar 1994:52.

21. Although third-party observers shape relations of power and how conversational sequences are directed between clinicians and patients in the research setting, few have theorized these dynamics in detail (although see Rapp 2000). See Katz and Shotter 1996 on the possibilities for the observer to act as a "cultural go-between" who is dialogically responsive to conversational events in the clinic.

22. It is also worth mentioning that the local ethics review board that approved my research at Central Hospital did so on the condition that I have no direct verbal interaction with patients for concern that it might interfere with their treatment. As the interactions recounted here and as Buchbinder (2010:110) has suggested, while intended to protect patients, even presumptively noninteractional participant observation "may be susceptible to collusion in a sort of symbolic violence" in the clinical encounter.

23. Field notes, Thiruvananthapuram, India, March 2006.

24. On the concept of therapeutic emplotment, see Mattingly 1994.

25. See J. Kurien (2000) on coastal communities as "outliers" of development. Devika (2013:10) argues that this construction of dalits as oppressed and passive victims figures these communities as the "'acceptable' outcasts, upon whom the elite constantly exercise their pastoral authority."

26. Devika 2013. See also Steur 2009.

27. Lukose 2009; and F. Osella and C. Osella 2000b.

28. For ethnographies of how mental health professionals navigate their sense of therapeutic efficacy in institutional settings, see Brodwin 2013; and Rhodes 1991.

29. "BPL" is an economic benchmark and poverty threshold used by the Indian government to indicate economic disadvantage.

30. Spinners of coir rope form an all-female workforce and are among the lowest paid workers in Kerala. Coir rope is made from the extracted fibers of coconut husks. See Issac et al. 1992.

31. Nunley (1998) argues that limited staff and resources encourage the active involvement of family members in allopathic psychiatric treatment in India.

32. Field notes, Thiruvananthapuram, India, June 2006.

33. Pinto 2011.

34. On ideas of falling in love as being modern, independent, and developed among youth in rural Nepal, see Ahearn 2001; see also Dwyer 2000.

35. Field notes, Thiruvananthapuram, India, March 2006.

36. Chapter 4 of this book further discusses women's talk of suicide in the home.

37. Field notes, Thiruvananthapuram, India, January 2006.

38. Field notes, Thiruvananthapuram, India, November 2005.

39. Field notes, Thiruvananthapuram, India, December 2005.

CHAPTER 3

1. Field notes, Stanford, California, October 2008.

2. I draw here on Livingston's (2009) analysis of suicide commentaries as reflections on the "social dimensions of investment" in Botswana.

3. Das 2000, 2007.

4. Münster (2012) makes a similar argument with respect to the ways "farmers' suicides" operate as an overdetermined and highly politicized state category of enumeration and intervention in Wayanad District, a category that is linked, moreover, to a reified idea of the "agrarian crisis" in Kerala. See also Deepa 2005 and Mokkil 2009 on the politics of the visibility of the category of "lesbian suicides" in the Kerala public sphere.

5. Mol 2002:132.

6. Briggs 2007:326.

7. See Scott (1998) on how the modern state has imposed order on aspects of society to render them "legible" to control.

8. Hacking 1990.

9. Durkheim's ([1897] 1951) classic study of suicide is a preeminent example.

10. See Appadurai 1993; Cohn 1996; and Pandey 1990.

11. These categories in part include "bankruptcy or sudden change in economic status," "suspected/illicit relation," "barrenness or impotence," "death of a dear person," "drug abuse/addiction," "poverty," "failure in examination," "failure in social reputation," "unemployment," and "family problems," as well as two categories reserved for suicides of "other causes" and "causes not known." Notably, "insanity or mental illness" is its own category among the twenty-six. These categories vary only minimally across Indian states today. Updates to these categories have been made over time. "HIV/AIDS," for instance, is now included.

12. Nunley 1996.

13. Field notes, Thiruvananthapuram, India, January 2006.

14. Field notes, Thiruvananthapuram, India, July 2004.

15. Lakoff 2005; see also Kitanaka 2012.

16. As Widger (2012) suggests in the Sri Lankan context, these histories could also include the civilizational discourses through which individual and collective violence was conceptualized by the colonial state.

17. Rajani Anand's suicide was discussed in this book's introduction.

18. Field notes, Thiruvananthapuram, India, April 2006.

19. Hall 1980.

20. On the high social value of medical and engineering degrees in Kerala, see Wilson 2011.

21. Field notes, Thiruvananthapuram, India, April 2006.

22. Mol 2002:132.

23. See Marecek 1998; Spencer 1990; Waters 1999; and Widger 2009.

24. Dowry death was created as a new offense under section 304-B of the Indian Penal Code. Section 113-A was also added to the Indian Evidence Act to raise the presumption of the abetment of suicide on the part of the husband or his relatives if the wife commits suicide within the first seven years of marriage

when there is evidence that she has been subjected to cruelty. Section 174 of the Criminal Procedure Code was also amended to require authorities to conduct a postmortem investigation into every case involving the suicide or death of a woman within a period of seven years from her date of marriage. See Mohite and Chavan 1993.

25. Waters 1999.

26. Field notes, Thiruvananthapuram, India, March 2006.

27. I draw here on Briggs's (2005) notion of communicability.

28. Feldman-Savelsberg et al. 2000.

29. On discourses of the "bad" modern family with regard to elderly care in India, see Cohen 1998.

30. Field notes, Thiruvananthapuram, India, March 2006.

31. On ghosts as vital presences, see Kwon 2008; see also Ochoa 2010.

32. Among both mental health professionals and non-experts that I spoke with, equivalence between site, method, and motivation was explicitly gendered. Distinctions between the public sites of fatal male suicides and the domestic sites of women's acts of self-injury are informed by demographic patterns but are also taken as evidence of organic differences dividing male strength from female weakness.

33. Field notes, Thiruvananthapuram, India, September 2006.

34. The English word *line* is slang for a romantic relationship outside marriage.

35. Stevenson 2009:56.

36. Field notes, Thiruvananthapuram, India, September 2006.

37. Kleinman et al. 1997:ix.

38. Kleinman et al. 1997:xxv.

### CHAPTER 4

1. Called such because they "cut both ways" (Buckley 2012:252), blades have flourished in Kerala with the availability of Gulf remittances (Nair 1999:219–20). The absence of any security requirement makes these companies an attractive option to those who need large amounts of money fast. However, their high interest rates mean that loans spiral into vicious cycles of debt from which it is nearly impossible to escape. Defaulters are brought back into line by company *goondas,* hired musclemen who intimidate until payment is secured. In response to these repercussions or to avoid them, some borrowers choose suicide, as has been reported in the media. The risk associated with blade loans has been depicted in films like *Parunthu* (2008), which opens with the suicide of a family driven to desperation by the harassment of a blade mafia chief.

2. Field notes, Thiruvananthapuram, India, November 2005.

3. Cohen 2001.

4. Cohen 2001:25.

5. Borneman 1997:583.

6. See, for example, Devika 2007; Eapen and Kodoth 2003; Kodoth and Eapen 2005; and Sreekumar 2009.

7. Devika 2007:12.

8. Kodoth and Eapen 2005:3280.

9. Eapen 1992, 2004; Mitra and Singh 2006.

10. Scholars have argued that these trends highlight the need to examine nonconventional markers of well-being beyond "gender development," including property rights, political participation, gender-based violence against women, and mental health. For examples of such studies, see Kodoth and Eapen 2005; Mitra and Singh 2007; Mohamed et al. 2002; Mukhopadhyay 2007; and Panda and Agarwal 2005.

11. Canetto 1992; Canetto and Lester 1995.

12. Durkheim ([1897] 1951:166) attributed what he identified as the relative immunity of women to suicide to the conviction that women are "fundamentally traditionalist by nature" and that they "govern their conduct by fixed beliefs and have no great intellectual needs." He ascribed the low incidence of women's suicide mortality to the allegedly organic influences of gender, suggesting that as "a more instinctive creature than man, woman has only to follow her instincts to find calmness and peace" ([1897] 1951:272).

13. Hage (2003b) draws upon Bourdieu's (2000) notion of the social game to develop an anthropology of suicide bombing in the Palestinian context. In his *Pascalian Meditations,* Bourdieu suggests that social games compose the end-driven "chase" that society offers us and by which we propel ourselves forward, feeling objectively and subjectively endowed with a kind of social mission. Hage inverts Bourdieu's social games to consider the ways the accumulation of death produces forms of capital. "This is how Bourdieu describes the way society invites us to live," notes Hage. "In the case of Palestinian colonized society, it is also how it can invite us to die. The struggle to accumulate symbolic capital ('the chase') defines for Bourdieu the essence of how we make our lives worthy of living. But here we are faced with a particular 'chase': the accumulation of death as a mode of seeking a meaningful life. There emerges a paradoxical social category: suicidal capital" (Hage 2003b:80). I depart from Hage in my focus on how individuals accumulate death from within life itself.

14. On children and embodied value in marketized contexts, see Anagnost 2004, 2008; and Matza 2012.

15. Devika 2002a.

16. *Eve teasing* is a euphemism, used in the English form in India, to describe flirtatious or aggressive behavior toward women or girls.

17. Mukhopadhyay and Seymour 1994. These concerns have been dramatized in Malayalam films such as the popular feature *Pavithram* (Purity), in which the moral decline of young Cochu begins with her move from her home in the village to college life in the city and ends with her participation in a local beauty contest. See Lukose 2005a:927 for an analysis of *Pavithram* through the lens of clothing and gender, and which explores how sexualized economies of "modernity" and "tradition" are mapped across the urban-rural binary.

18. Kavitha's mother initially proposed her daughter study outside the state. Part of her logic, as she explained to me, was to encourage Kavitha's self-sufficiency.

19. Field notes, Thiruvananthapuram, India, May 2006.

20. Chatterjee 1989:630.

21. On how Indian law, citizenship, and the state define political rights and cultural identities through gendered categories, including the female "victim," see Rajan 2003. On the discourse of women's adjustability in South Asia, see Ring 2006; and Singh and Uberoi 1994.

22. Demonstrating how colonial discourses of sati operated as the site on which to stage conflicts and debates over definitions of Hindu tradition and the civilizing missions of colonialism, Mani (1998) argues that the ideological construction of the devoted wife coexisted ambivalently with other constructions. British "official" discourse produced around sati also constructed an alternate configuration of the Indian widow as a forced, unwilling victim. "Colonial officials systematically ignored such evidence of the widows as subjects with a will of their own. . . . The widow thus nowhere appears as a full subject. If she resisted, she was considered a victim of male barbarity. If she conceded, she was seen to be a victim of religion" (Mani 1998:117). See also Das 1995; and Rajan 1993.

23. Pinto 2011.

24. Field notes, Thiruvananthapuram, India, August 2008.

25. Field notes, Thiruvananthapuram, India, August 2008.

26. See C. Osella and F. Osella 2006.

27. Field notes, Thiruvananthapuram, India, June 2006.

28. Field notes, Thiruvananthapuram, India, August 2008.

29. Rosaldo 1982:223.

30. Field notes, Thiruvananthapuram, India, January 2008.

31. Field notes, Thiruvananthapuram, India, March 2007.

32. Field notes, Thiruvananthapuram, India, March 2007.

33. In 2001, approximately two-thirds and three-fourths of those enrolled in undergraduate and graduate courses, respectively, were female (Kodoth and Eapen 2005:3280). For examples of the discourse on the acclaimed status of Kerala women, see Drèze and Sen 1997; and R. Jeffrey 1992.

34. Kerala currently ranks in the highest group of Indian states in cruelty at home, with 35.7 percent of women in Thiruvananthapuram (in both rural and urban areas) reporting experience of at least one form of physical violence at least once in their married life, and 64.9 percent reporting experience of psychological violence (Panda 2003:43–44; Panda and Agarwal 2005). The disparity in the educational achievements of wives compared with their husbands appears to be particularly pronounced among Gulf migrant families. A study by Zachariah et al. (2003:113) suggests that despite the educational achievements of Gulf wives, 82 percent among those interviewed were most likely to remain housewives. This is particularly significant in comparison to the overall Kerala percentage of 60.9 who remained housewives.

35. Mitra and Singh 2007:1234.

36. Kodoth and Eapen 2005:3280; Mitra and Singh 2006.

37. The common encouragement for middle-class women to pursue a liberal arts education rather than a technical degree further demonstrates the expectation that they will be the primary caretakers of the home and not career women, whose professional obligations might detract from their duties as mothers and housewives. It also reflects growing middle-class social expectations that white-

collar work is the only acceptable means of women's employment, which in turn limits available options. This is in keeping with R. Kumar's (1992) suggestion that women keep aspirations for white-collar employment alive by continuing in the education stream longer.

38. Scholars concur that the matrilineal system of *marumakkathayam* that operated among the majority of families in Travancore, in which property was collectively owned by the members of a joint family, or taravad, ensured greater security for women, because kinship was traced on the female side and inheritance maintained along the female line. It was not possible for a person to stake individual claim to a share of the property, and children always stayed in their mother's taravad, even after marriage. Although inheritance followed the female line, and most land appears to have been registered under the names of females, it is agreed that in practice women did not control their property. As the head of the taravad, the *karanavan,* or eldest male of the joint family, maintained substantial control over all resources (Saradamoni 1999:71). Saradamoni (1999) points out that in suggesting that women had greater security over their lifetimes under the marumakkathayam system, this is not to say that women necessarily had greater autonomy or freedom in comparison to patrilineal systems. It would be unwarranted to conclude that women in joint families were more "empowered," as popular accounts that conflate "matrilineal" and "matriarchal," for example, might be inclined to do (Saradamoni 1999:68–71).

39. Dowry practices in Kerala involve direct payments to the groom's family that can be used in any way the family desires and are not maintained as the exclusive property of the bride (Billig 1992:197). Billig (1992) has suggested that the term *groomprice* be used over *dowry,* since the former signals how the form and function of payments by the bride's family has shifted toward its control by the husband's family, with women retaining little decision making over its use. On how dowry has gained widespread acceptance in the state with shifts in marriage practices and the growth of migrant remittances, see Billig 1992; Eapen and Kodoth 2003; Kodoth 2005, 2008; F. Osella and C. Osella 2000a; and den Uyl 2005.

40. Panda 2003 has shown that women's property ownership greatly mitigates against the possibility of physical and psychological violence and is the strongest predictor of a lack of violence among both urban and rural women in Kerala. See also Eapen 2004; Mitra and Singh 2007; and Panda and Agarwal 2005.

41. Pinto 2011.

42. Field notes, Thiruvananthapuram, India, March 2007.

43. The literature among scholars working in Sri Lanka is particularly rich in this regard. See de Alwis 2012; Marecek 1998; Marecek and Senadheera 2012; Spencer 1990; and Widger 2009, 2012; see also Billaud 2012; and Lee and Kleinman 2000.

44. Spencer 1990.

45. de Alwis 2012:48.

46. See, for example, Counts 1980; and Strathern 1975.

47. Spencer 1990:613.

48. Problematizing ideas of the individual "choice" to die, Ozawa-de Silva (2008) shows how Internet suicide pacts among young Japanese reflect the importance of relationality in Japanese conceptions of the self and in the process of suicide.

49. Berlant 2007:759.

50. On the discipline and containment of the perceived social contagion of disability within families in India and how disordered persons may be forcefully "hidden" in domestic space, see Das and Addlakha 2001; and Marrow and Luhrmann 2012.

51. Waters 1999.

52. Das and Addlakha 2001:512. On how legal domains shape women as subjects at the intersection of psychiatry and familial life, see Pinto 2012.

53. On care and vulnerability, see Garcia 2010; Han 2012; Klaits 2010; and Livingston 2012. But see also Ticktin 2011.

## CHAPTER 5

1. Field notes, Thiruvananthapuram, India, April 2007.

2. On suicide among Indian migrant workers in the Gulf, see al-Maskari et al. 2011; and Keane and McGeehan 2008.

3. Field notes, Thiruvananthapuram, India, December 2006.

4. Field notes, Thiruvananthapuram, India, February 2006.

5. One important illustration of this in the clinical literature is the Beck Hopelessness Scale, a twenty-item true-false self-report instrument designed to measure three major aspects of hopelessness: feelings about the future, loss of motivation, and expectations. The test is designed to measure the respondent's negative attitudes, or pessimism, about the future. It is widely used in clinical and research applications as an indicator of suicide risk in depressed people who have made suicide attempts. See Beck and Steer 1988.

6. On hope in the anthropological literature, see Crapanzano 1985, 2003; Hage 2003a; Miyazaki 2004; and Zigon 2009.

7. On the migration of female nurses from Kerala to the Gulf, see Percot 2006; and Percot and Rajan 2007. See Kodoth and Varghese 2012 on the need for scholarship and state policy in Kerala to recognize and address nonelite female migration to the Gulf.

8. On community and caste histories of migration and social mobility in Kerala, see P. Kurien 2002; and F. Osella and C. Osella 2000b.

9. Prior to the start of my fieldwork in 2002, I lived in Kerala for ten months during 2000 and 2001.

10. Field notes, Thiruvananthapuram, January 2007.

11. For exceptions, see Carling 2002; Chu 2010; and Ní Laoire 2001.

12. Carling 2002 argues that the term *involuntary immobility* is useful both as an empirical characterization increasingly relevant to nation-states that have traditionally seen significant emigration and as an analytic that raises important challenges to traditional migration theories.

13. Appadurai 1996; Schiller et al. 1992.

14. See Chu 2010; Melley 2011; and Reichman 2011.

15. Ní Laoire 2001.

16. Lukose 2009.

17. Fabian 1983; see also C. Osella and F. Osella 2006.

18. Field notes, Thiruvananthapuram, India, April 2007.

19. Prakash 1998.

20. Field notes, Thiruvananthapuram, India, May 2007.

21. On migration and masculinity in Kerala, see F. Osella and C. Osella 1999.

22. On business and labor practices among Muslim entrepreneurs migrating between Kerala and the Gulf, see F. Osella and C. Osella 2009.

23. Field notes, Thiruvananthapuram, India, December 2005.

24. C. Jeffrey 2010; Mains 2012.

25. Unlike Syrian Christian groups, which are classified in governmental language as a "forward caste" because of their experiences of economic and social mobility, as a community Latin Catholics in Kerala are categorized as "other backward class" (OBC), having seen less consistent social and educational advancement overall.

26. On the significance of these qualities in the Indian IT industry, see Fuller and Narasimhan 2007.

27. Experiences of "waiting" and of *timepass* (C. Jeffrey 2010) often take the form of pursuing further education. Youth and their families are increasingly drawn to strategic investment in formal school, extracurricular education, and parallel educational credentials, such as certification programs, to increase human capital and one's prospects on the job market.

28. Field notes, Thiruvananthapuram, India, August 2006.

29. Zachariah and Rajan 2005.

30. Scholars have noted the gap between the types of jobs available in Kerala and those desired by the educated middle class. Some have suggested that the survival of the state's economy depends upon the recruitment of migrant labor from neighboring states to fill jobs viewed as undesirable at home. Kerala has become an attractive destination for labor in-migrants as a result of the severe scarcity of manual laborers within the state and the prevailing high wage rate in comparison to other states. With the rise of construction projects in the state, fueled by migrant remittances from the Gulf, most of Kerala's in-migrant laborers work in the construction sector and are brought into the state through contractors or agents working in different parts of the country. See Prakash 1998; and Zachariah et al. 2003.

31. Jeffrey and McDowell 2004; C. Jeffrey 2010.

32. C. Jeffrey 2010.

33. Mains 2007; see also Lefebvre 1991.

34. On moral narratives as a key practice in the making of middle-class youth subjectivities in India, see Nisbett 2007.

35. Brown 2000.

36. Field notes, Thiruvananthapuram, India, December 2005.

37. Field notes, Thiruvananthapuram, India, June 2006.

38. Escobar 2008:7.

39. Anagnost 2004:202.

40. Chu 2010.
41. Field notes, Thiruvananthapuram, India, September 2006.
42. See Sooryamoorthy 1997.
43. Field notes, Thiruvananthapuram, India, July 2006.
44. Field notes, Thiruvananthapuram, India, January 2007.
45. See F. Osella and C. Osella 2000a.
46. Cohen 2001:24.
47. Massey 1994:2.
48. Field notes, Thiruvananthapuram, India, April 2007.
49. *Mathrubhumi* 2006.
50. In his ethnography among Indian contract workers in Bahrain, Gardner (2010) documents the largely accepted practice among employers of confiscating the passports of foreign workers.
51. Recent popular Malayalam films have represented migrant conditions in the Gulf. For example, the 2011 film *Khaddama* (Housemaid) depicts the plight of a young widow who goes to work as a domestic servant for a Saudi family. The local television program *Pravasalokham* (The World of Migrants), aired on Kairali TV, a channel floated by the Communist Party of India-Marxist, seeks to connect families with kin who have gone missing in the Gulf. For an analysis of historical shifts in representations and imaginaries of the Gulf within popular Malayalam cinema, see R. Radhakrishnan 2009. For a critical analysis of gendered representations of the victimization of domestic workers in the Gulf, see Kodoth and Varghese 2012.

## CHAPTER 6

1. Field notes, Thiruvananthapuram, India, September 2005.
2. *The Tribune,* 2001.
3. *The Hindu,* 2002.
4. Field notes, Thiruvananthapuram, India, December 2005.
5. On children, youth, and futures, see Anagnost 2008; Anagnost et al. 2013; Cole and Durham 2008; Cole 2010; and Mains 2012. See also Edelman 2004.
6. Anagnost 2004:192.
7. This percentage represents a slight increase from an average of less than 1 percent during the period I was conducting fieldwork. See www.ksmha.org, accessed August 31, 2013.
8. Gupta 2001.
9. Field notes, Thiruvananthapuram, India, October 2005.
10. John's comments resonate with a larger discourse within the public arena about the reform of classroom pedagogy in Kerala and in India more broadly. One rhetoric of reform argues that traditional methods of teaching and learning are prescriptive, based primarily on the one-way transmission of information rather than on interactive models, and on rote memorization and information dissemination rather than on the development of critical-thinking skills. On "textbook culture" in the Indian educational system, see K. Kumar 1988.
11. Field notes, Thiruvananthapuram, India, October 2006.
12. *The Tribune,* 2001.

13. On population quality and governmentality in India, see Gupta 2001; see also Dasgupta 1995.

14. Devika 2007.

15. There is some dispute over the extent to which matriliny was present in the formerly princely state of Tranvancore. R. Jeffrey (1992) has suggested that around half of the total population was matrilineal, while den Uyl (1995) and Saradamoni (1999) argue that the actual figure is greater. Saradamoni (1999) argues that although anthropologists and others have focused on upper-caste Nayar practices as the gold standard of matriliny (Fuller 1976; Gough 1959; Renjini 2000), matrilineal practices were not uniform or static in Travancore but demonstrated a flexibility and diversity across groups and over time.

16. Discontent with marumakkathayam grew in large part out of reformers' moral indignation over the customary institution (sambandham) that framed sexual access claimed and received by Nambudiri men to upper-caste Nayar women, as well as reciprocal marriages between Nayars. As Kodoth (2001a) explains, sambandham was facilitated by a system of landownership and tenancy. As landlords and trustees of temple lands, Nambudiris controlled large areas of land in south Malabar (where sambandham was most prevalent), which they rented to Nayar tenants. Under these conditions, Nambudiri men, of whom only the eldest son married within the caste, were able to use their dominant position to claim sexual relations with Nayar tenant taravads.

17. Cited in Devika 2002a:17. On how the domestic domain came to be instrumentalized during the colonial period as the "laboratory" in which family and society could be improved, see Hancock 2001.

18. Devika 2007.

19. Devika 2002a:11–13; see also R. Kumar 1992.

20. In spite of popular claims that family planning and the small family were readily and unproblematically embraced in the path to Kerala modernity, efforts to reform the region's diverse family practices were also initially met with concerns that small families would produce weak and selfish children (Devika 2002b:26).

21. For an analysis of the conjunction of historical shifts that enabled the widespread acceptance of the Family Planning Campaign in Kerala, see Devika 2002b. On how men and women negotiate sterilization as family planning in Kottayam, Kerala, see den Uly 1995.

22. On Kerala's demographic transition, see Krishnan 1976; and Ratcliffe 1978; see Bhat and Rajan 1990 for a revisited look.

23. Rose 1996.

24. Field notes, Thiruvananthapuram, India, October 2005.

25. For more on this expansion, with specific reference to postsocialist Russia, see Matza 2012.

26. Field notes, Thiruvananthapuram, India, January 2006.

27. Field notes, Thiruvananthapuram, India, December 2005.

28. Field notes, Thiruvananthapuram, India, February 2006.

29. Devika 2002a:48.

30. *Vanitha*, June 2006.

31. *Grihalakshmi*, February 2005.

32. See Kuan 2011.
33. Matza 2012:806.
34. Field notes, Thiruvananthapuram, India, March 2006.
35. Field notes, Thiruvananthapuram, India, January 2007.
36. *Vanitha,* June 2012.
37. Hochschild 1979.
38. On the optimization of life under conditions of neoliberalism, see Rose 2007.
39. Field notes, Thiruvananthapuram, India, November 2006.
40. Field notes, Thiruvananthapuram, India, November 2006.
41. Field notes, Thiruvananthapuram, India, November 2006.
42. Bourdieu 2000:206.
43. Field notes, Thiruvananthapuram, India, July 2006.
44. Dunn 2004; Harvey 1989.
45. Field notes, Thiruvananthapuram, India, May 2006.
46. On the global pursuit of the extracurricular and class formation, see Matza 2012.
47. Field notes, Thiruvananthapuram, India, October 2006.
48. Field notes, Thiruvananthapuram, India, January 2007.
49. Field notes, Thiruvananthapuram, India, March 2006.
50. Urciuoli 2008.
51. Field notes, Thiruvananthapuram, India, November 2005.
52. Jeganathan 2004:69.
53. On the ways parenting advice reproduces similar gendered discourses about the indulgences of mothers in contemporary China, see Kuan 2011.
54. Field notes, Thiruvananthapuram, India, June 2006.

### AFTERWORD

1. Appadurai 1996.
2. Tsing 2005.
3. I borrow this term from Mankekar's (1995) analysis of how representations of "brides who travel" in popular Hindi film work to constitute both national and transnational subjects through discourses of nation, class, sexuality, and gender.
4. For an example, see the optimistic analysis of *Al Jazeera English*'s chief political analyst, Marwan Bishara, of the Arab Spring as a collective movement led by a "miracle generation" that has sought to make itself "visible in public spaces—not through suicide bombings, but rather through the affirmation of life, dignity, and liberty through their protests" (Bishara 2012:65).
5. Hage 2003b.
6. On the ways certain lives appear more grievable than others in the public sphere with reference to the events of September 11, 2001, and the "war on terror," see Butler 2004, 2009.

# References

Agamben, Giorgio. 1998. *Homo Sacer: Sovereign Power and Bare Life.* Stanford, CA: Stanford University Press.

Agarwal, Arun. 1996. "Poststructuralist Approaches to Development: Some Critical Reflections." *Peace and Change* 21(4):464–77.

Ahearn, Laura. 2001. *Invitations to Love: Literacy, Love Letters, and Social Change in Nepal.* Ann Arbor: University of Michigan Press.

Ahmed, Sara. 2004. "Affective Economies." *Social Text* 22(2):117–39.

———. 2007. "The Happiness Turn." *New Formations* 63(1):7–14.

Alexander, William. 1994. "Exceptional Kerala: Efficient Use of Resource and Life Quality in a Non-Affluent Society." *GIAI-Ecological Perspectives for Science and Society* 3(4):211–26.

Allen, Lori. 2002. "There Are Many Reasons Why: Suicide Bombers and Martyrs in Palestine." *Middle East Report* 223:34–37.

al-Maskari, F., S.M. Shah, R. al-Sharhan, E. al-Haj, K. al-Kaabi, D. Khonji, J.D. Schneider, N.J. Nagelkerke, and R.M. Bernsen. 2011. "Prevalence of Depression and Suicidal Behaviors among Male Migrant Workers in the United Arab Emirates." *Journal of Immigrant and Minority Health* 13(6):1027–32.

Anagnost, Ann. 2004. "The Corporeal Politics of Quality *(Suzhi)*." *Public Culture* 16(2):189–208.

———. 2008. "Imagining Global Futures in China: The Child as a Sign of Value." In *Figuring the Future: Globalization and the Temporalities of Children and Youth,* edited by J. Cole and D. Durham, 49–72. Santa Fe, NM: School for Advanced Research Press.

Anagnost, Ann, Andrea Arai, and Hai Ren, eds. 2013. *Global Futures in East Asia: Youth, Nation, and the New Economy in Uncertain Times.* Stanford, CA: Stanford University Press.

Andriolo, Karin. 2006. "The Twice-Killed: Imagining Protest Suicide." *American Anthropologist* 108(1):100–13.

Appadurai, Arjun. 1993. "Number in the Colonial Imagination." In *Orientalism and the Postcolonial Predicament: Perspectives on South Asia,* edited by C. Breckenridge and P. van der Veer, 314–40. Philadelphia: University of Pennsylvania Press.

———. 1996. *Modernity at Large: Cultural Dimensions of Globalization.* Minneapolis: University of Minnesota Press.

Arunima, G. 2003. *There Comes Papa: Colonialism and the Transformation of Matriliny in Kerala, Malabar, c. 1850–1940.* New Delhi: Orient BlackSwan.

Asad, Talal. 2007. *On Suicide Bombing.* New York: Columbia University Press.

Banerjee, Nirmala. 1991. *Indian Women in a Changing Industrial Scenario.* New Delhi: Sage Publications.

Beck, A. T., and R. A. Steer. 1988. *Manual for the Beck Hopelessness Scale.* San Antonio, TX: Psychological Corporation.

Berlant, Lauren. 2007. "Slow Death (Sovereignty, Obesity, Lateral Agency)." *Critical Inquiry* 33(4):754–80.

Bhat, P. N. Mari, and S. Irudaya Rajan. 1990. "Demographic Transition in Kerala Revisited." *Economic and Political Weekly* 25:1957–80.

Biehl, João. 2005. *Vita: Life in a Zone of Social Abandonment.* Berkeley: University of California Press.

Bijoy, C. R., and K. Ravi Raman. 2003. "Muthanga: The Real Story—Adivasi Movement to Recover Land." *Economic and Political Weekly* 38(20): 1975–77, 1979–82.

Billaud, Julie. 2012. "Suicidal Performances: Voicing Discontent in a Girls' Dormitory in Kabul." *Culture, Medicine, and Psychiatry* 36(2):264–85.

Billig, Michael. 1992. "The Marriage Squeeze and the Rise of Groomprice in India's Kerala State." *Journal of Comparative Family Studies* 23(2): 197–216.

Bishara, Marwan. 2012. *The Invisible Arab: The Promise and Peril of the Arab Revolutions.* New York: Nation Books.

Borneman, John. 1997. "Caring and Being Cared for: Displacing Marriage, Kinship, Gender and Sexuality." *International Social Science Journal* 49(154):573–84.

Bose, Sugata. 1997. "Instruments and Idioms of Colonial and National Development: India's Historical Experience in Comparative Perspective." In *International Development and the Social Sciences: Essays on the History and Politics of Knowledge,* edited by F. Cooper and R. Packard, 45–63. Berkeley: University of California Press.

Bourdieu, Pierre. 1984. *Distinction: A Social Critique of the Judgment of Taste.* Cambridge, MA: Harvard University Press.

———. 2000. *Pascalian Meditations.* Stanford, CA: Stanford University Press.

Bourgois, Philippe, and Jeffrey Schonberg. 2009. *Righteous Dopefiend.* Berkeley: University of California Press.

Breckenridge, Carol, ed. 1995. *Consuming Modernity: Public Culture in a South Asian World.* Minneapolis: University of Minnesota Press.

Briggs, Charles. 2005. "Communicability, Racial Discourse, and Disease." *Annual Review of Anthropology* 34:269–91.

———. 2007. "Mediating Infanticide: Mediatizing Relations between Narrative and Violence." *Cultural Anthropology* 22(3):315–56.

Brodwin, Paul. 2013. *Everyday Ethics: Voices from the Front Line of Community Psychiatry.* Berkeley: University of California Press.

Brown, Michael. 2000. *Closet Space: Geographies of Metaphor from the Body to the Globe.* New York: Routledge.

Buchbinder, Mara. 2010. "Giving an Account of One's Pain in the Anthropological Interview." *Culture, Medicine, and Psychiatry* 34(1):108–31.

Buckley, Michelle. 2012. "From Kerala to Dubai and Back Again: Construction Migrants and the Global Economic Crisis." *Geoforum* 43(2):250–59.

Butler, Judith. 2004. *Precarious Life: The Powers of Mourning and Violence.* New York: Verso.

———. 2009. *Frames of War: When Is Life Grievable?* New York: Verso.

Butt, Leslie. 2002. "The Suffering Stranger: Medical Anthropology and International Morality." *Medical Anthropology* 21(1):1–24.

Canetto, Silvia. 1992. "She Died for Love and He for Glory: Gender Myths of Suicidal Behavior." *Journal of Death and Dying* 26(1):1–17.

Canetto, Silvia, and David Lester. 1995. "Women and Suicidal Behavior: Issues and Dilemmas." In *Women and Suicidal Behavior,* edited by S. Canneto and D. Lester, 3–8. New York: Springer.

———. 1998. "Gender, Culture and Suicidal Behavior." *Transcultural Psychiatry* 35(2):163–90.

Carling, Jorgen. 2002. "Migration in the Age of Involuntary Immobility: Theoretical Reflections and Cape Verdean Experiences." *Journal of Ethnic and Migration Studies* 28(1):5–42.

Chakrabarty, Dipesh. 2000. *Provincializing Europe: Postcolonial Thought and Historical Difference.* Princeton, NJ: Princeton University Press.

Chatterjee, Partha. 1989. "Colonialism, Nationalism and Colonized Women: The Contest in India." *American Ethnologist* 16(4):622–33.

Chu, Julie. 2010. *Cosmologies of Credit: Transnational Mobility and the Politics of Destination in China.* Durham, NC: Duke University Press.

Chua, Jocelyn. 2012. "The Register of 'Complaint': Psychiatric Diagnosis and the Discourse of Grievance in the South Indian Mental Health Encounter." *Medical Anthropology Quarterly* 26(2):221–40.

Cohen, Lawrence. 1998. *No Aging in India: Alzheimer's, the Bad Family, and Other Modern Things.* Berkeley: University of California Press.

———. 2001. "The Other Kidney: Biopolitics beyond Recognition." *Body & Society* 7(2–3):9–28.

Cohn, Bernard. 1996. *Colonialism and Its Forms of Knowledge: The British in India.* Princeton, NJ: Princeton University Press.

Cole, Jennifer. 2010. *Sex and Salvation: Imagining the Future in Madagascar.* Chicago: University of Chicago Press.

Cole, Jennifer, and Deborah Durham, eds. 2008. *Figuring the Future: Globalization and the Temporalities of Children and Youth.* Santa Fe, NM: School for Advanced Research Press.

Comaroff, Jean. 2007. "Beyond Bare Life: AIDS, (Bio)Politics, and the Neoliberal Order." *Public Culture* 19(1):197–219.

Counts, Dorothy. 1980. "Fighting Back Is Not the Way: Suicide and the Women of Kaliai." *American Ethnologist* 7(2):332–51.

Crapanzano, Vincent. 1985. *Waiting: The Whites of South Africa.* New York: Random House.

———. 2003. "Reflections on Hope as a Category of Social and Psychological Analysis." *Cultural Anthropology* 18(1):3–32.

Dabbagh, Nadia. 2005. *Suicide in Palestine: Narratives of Despair.* Northampton, MA: Olive Branch Press.

Das, Veena. 1995. *Critical Events: An Anthropological Perspective on Contemporary India.* New Delhi: Oxford University Press.

———. 2000. "The Act of Witnessing: Violence, Poisonous Knowledge, and Subjectivity." In *Violence and Subjectivity,* edited by V. Das, A. Kleinman, M. Ramphele, and P. Reynolds, 205–25. Berkeley: University of California Press.

———. 2007. *Life and Words: Violence and the Descent into the Ordinary.* Berkeley: University of California Press.

Das, Veena, and Renu Addlakha. 2001. "Disability and Domestic Citizenship: Voice, Gender, and the Making of the Subject." *Public Culture* 13(3): 511–31.

Dasgupta, Partha. 1995. "The Population Problem: Theory and Evidence." *Journal of Economic Literature* 33(4):1879–902.

Davis, Elizabeth. 2012. *Bad Souls: Madness and Responsibility in Modern Greece.* Durham, NC: Duke University Press.

de Alwis, Malathi. 2012. "'Girl Still Burning inside My Head': Reflections on Suicide in Sri Lanka." *Contributions to Indian Sociology* 46(1–2):29–51.

Deepa, V. N. 2005. "Queering Kerala: Reflections on Sahayatrika." In *Because I Have a Voice: The Politics of Alternative Sexualities in India,* edited by A. Narrain and G. Bhan, 175–96. New Delhi: Yoda Press.

den Uyl, Marion. 1995. *Invisible Barriers: Gender, Caste, and Kinship in a Southern Indian Village.* Utrecht, the Netherlands: International Books.

———. 2005. "Dowry in India: Respected Tradition and Modern Monstrosity." In *The Gender Question in Globalization: Changing Perspectives and Practices,* edited by T. Davids and F. van Driel, 143–58. Burlington, VT: Ashgate.

Deshpande, Satish. 2006. "Exclusive Inequalities: Merit, Caste and Discrimination in Indian Higher Education Today." *Economic and Political Weekly* 41(24):2438–44.

Devika, J. 2002a. "Domesticating Malayalees: Family Planning, the Nation and Home-Centered Anxieties in Mid-20th-Century Keralam." Working Paper 340. Center for Development Studies, Thiruvananthapuram, India.

———. 2002b. "Family Planning as 'Liberation': The Ambiguities of 'Emancipation from Biology' in Keralam." Working Paper 335. Center for Development Studies, Thiruvananthapuram, India.

———. 2007. *En-Gendering Individuals: The Language of Re-Forming in Early Twentieth Century Keralam.* New Delhi: Orient Longman.

———. 2008. "Rethinking 'Region': Reflections on History-Writing in Kerala. *History and Sociology of South Asia* 2(2):246–64.

———. 2009. "Bodies Gone Awry: The Abjection of Sexuality in Development Discourse in Contemporary Kerala." *Indian Journal of Gender Studies* 16(1):21–46.

———. 2010. "Egalitarian Developmentalism, Communist Mobilization, and the Question of Caste in Kerala State, India." *Journal of Asian Studies* 69(3):799–820.

———. 2013. "Contemporary Dalit Assertions in Kerala: Governmental Categories vs. Identity Politics?" *History and Sociology of South Asia* 7(1):1–17.

Donner, Henrike, ed. 2011. *Being Middle-Class in India: A Way of Life.* New York: Routledge.

Donner, Henrike, and Geert De Neve. 2011. "Introduction." In *Being Middle-Class in India: A Way of Life,* edited by H. Donner, 1–22. New York: Routledge.

Douglas, Jack. 1967. *The Social Meanings of Suicide.* Princeton, NJ: Princeton University Press.

Drèze, Jean, and Amartya Sen. 1997. *Indian Development: Selected Regional Perspectives.* New York: Oxford University Press.

Dunn, Elizabeth. 2004. *Privatizing Poland: Baby Food, Big Business, and the Remaking of the Polish Working Class.* Ithaca, NY: Cornell University Press.

Durkheim, Émile. 1938. *The Rules of Sociological Method.* New York: Free Press.

———. (1897) 1951. *Suicide: A Study in Sociology.* New York: Free Press.

Dwyer, Rachel. 2000. *All You Want Is Money, All You Need Is Love: Sexuality and Romance in Modern India.* New York: Cassell.

Eapen, Mridul. 1992. "Fertility and Female Labour Participation in Kerala." *Economic and Political Weekly* 27(40):2179–88.

———. 2002. "Mental Health of Women in Kerala: The Need for a Gender Perspective." *Samyukta* 2(2):25–38.

———. 2004. "Women and Work Mobility: Some Disquieting Evidences from the Indian Data." Working Paper 358. Center for Development Studies, Thiruvananthapuram, India.

Eapen, Mridul, and Praveena Kodoth. 2003. "Family Structure, Women's Education and Work: Re-Examining the 'High Status' of Women in Kerala." In *Tracking Gender Equity under the Economic Reforms: Continuity and Change in South Asia,* edited by S. Mukhopadhyay and R. Sudarshan, 227–67. New Delhi: Kali for Women.

Ecks, Stefan. 2005. "Pharmaceutical Citizenship: Antidepressant Marketing and the Promise of Demarginalization in India." *Anthropology and Medicine* 12(3):239–54.

Ecks, Stefan, and Soumita Basu. 2009. "The Unlicensed Lives of Antidepressants in India: Generic Drugs, Unqualified Practitioners, and Floating Prescriptions." *Transcultural Psychiatry* 46(1):80–106.

Edelman, Lee. 2004. *No Future: Queer Theory and the Death Drive.* Durham, NC: Duke University Press.

Enns, Diane. 2004. "Bare Life and the Occupied Body." *Theory and Event* 7(3). http://muse.jhu.edu/login?auth=0&type=summary&url=/journals/theory_ and_event/v007/7.3enns.html. Accessed March 13, 2008.

Escobar, Arturo. 1995. *Encountering Development: The Making and Unmaking of the Third World*. Princeton, NJ: Princeton University Press.

———. 2008. *Territories of Difference: Place, Movements, Life, Redes*. Durham, NC: Duke University Press.

Fabian, Johannes. 1983. *Time and the Other: How Anthropology Makes Its Object*. New York: Columbia University Press.

Farmer, Paul. 1992. *AIDS and Accusation: Haiti and the Geography of Blame*. Berkeley: University of California Press.

———. 1996. "On Suffering and Structural Violence: A View from Below." *Daedalus* 125(1):261–83.

———. 2004. "An Anthropology of Structural Violence." *Current Anthropology* 45(3):305–25.

Fassin, Didier. 2000. "Les politiques de l'ethnopsychiatrie: La psyché africaine, des colonies africaines aux banlieues parisiennes." *L'Homme* 153:231–50.

Fassin, Didier, and Richard Rechtman. 2009. *Empire of Trauma: An Inquiry into the Condition of Victimhood*. Princeton: Princeton University Press.

Feldman, Allen. 1991. *Formations of Violence: The Narrative of the Body and Political Terror in Northern Ireland*. Chicago, IL: University of Chicago Press.

Feldman-Savelsberg, Pamela, Flavien Ndonko, and Bergis Schmidt-Ehry. 2000. "Sterilizing Vaccines or the Politics of the Womb: Retrospective Study of a Rumor in Cameroon." *Medical Anthropology Quarterly* 14(2):159–79.

Ferguson, James. 1994. *The Anti-Politics Machine: "Development," Depoliticization, and Bureaucratic Power in Lesotho*. Minneapolis: University of Minnesota Press.

———. 1999. *Expectations of Modernity: Myths and Meanings of Urban Life on the Zambian Copperbelt*. Berkeley: University of California Press.

Fernandes, Leela. 2000. "Nationalizing 'the Global': Media Images, Cultural Politics, and the Middle Class in India." *Media, Culture, and Society* 22:611–28.

Foucault, Michel. 1983. *Discourse and Truth: The Problematization of Parrhesia*. Edited by J. Pearson. Evanston, IL: Northwestern University Press.

———. 1997. "Polemics, Politics, and Problematizations." In *Michel Foucault: Ethics, Subjectivity, and Truth*, edited by P. Rabinow, 111–19. New York: New York Press.

Franke, Richard, and Barbara Chasin. 1994. *Kerala: Radical Reform as Development in an Indian State*. Oakland, CA: Institute for Food and Development Policy.

Fuller, Christopher John. 1976. *The Nayars Today*. Cambridge, UK: Cambridge University Press.

Fuller, Christopher John, and Haripriyan Narasimhan. 2007. "Information Technology Professionals and the New-Rich Middle Class in Chennai (Madras)." *Modern Asian Studies* 41(1):121–50.

Garcia, Angela. 2010. *The Pastoral Clinic: Addiction and Dispossession along the Rio Grande*. Berkeley: University of California Press.

Gardner, Andrew. 2010. *City of Strangers: Gulf Migration and the Indian Community in Bahrain*. Ithaca, NY: Cornell University Press.

George, K.K., and N. Ajith Kumar. 1999. "What Is Wrong with Kerala's Education System?" CSES Working Paper 3. Center for Socio-Economic and Environmental Studies, Kochi, India.

George, T.J.S. 2006. "What It Means to Be Malayali." *New Indian Express*. http://newindianexpress.com/states/kerala/What-it-Means/2006/05/19/article 146587.ece. Accessed September 20, 2006.

Gough, E. Kathleen. 1959. "The Nayars and the Definition of Marriage." *Journal of the Royal Anthropological Institute* 89(1):23–34.

Gulati, Leela. 1993. *In the Absence of their Men: The Impact of Male Migration on Women*. New Delhi: Sage Publications.

Gulati, Leela, and S. Irudaya Rajan. 1991. *Population Aspects of Aging in Kerala: Their Economic and Social Context*. Center for Development Studies, Thiruvananthapuram, India.

Gupta, Akhil. 1998. *Postcolonial Developments: Agriculture in the Making of Modern India*. Durham, NC: Duke University Press.

———. 2001. "Governing Populations: The Integrated Child Development Services Program in India." In *States of Imagination: Ethnographic Explorations of the Postcolonial State*, edited by T. Blom Hansen and F. Stepputat, 65–96. Durham, NC: Duke University Press.

Hacking, Ian. 1990. *The Taming of Chance*. Cambridge, UK: Cambridge University Press.

Hage, Ghassan. 2003a. *Against Paranoid Nationalism*. London: Pluto Press.

———. 2003b. "Comes a Time We Are All Enthusiasm: Understanding Palestinian Suicide Bombers in Times of Exighophobia." *Public Culture* 15(1):65–89.

Hall, Stuart. 1980. "Encoding/Decoding." In *Culture, Media, Language: Working Papers in Cultural Studies, 1972–79*, edited by S. Hall, D. Hobson, A. Lowe, and P. Willis, 128–38. London: Hutchinson.

Halliburton, Murphy. 1998. "Suicide: A Paradox of Development in Kerala." *Economic and Political Weekly* 33(36/37):2341–45.

———. 2005. "'Just Some Spirits': The Erosion of Spirit Possession and the Rise of 'Tension' in South India." *Medical Anthropology* 24(2):111–44.

———. 2009. *Mudpacks and Prozac: Experiencing Ayurvedic, Biomedical, and Religious Healing*. Walnut Creek, CA: Left Coast Press.

Han, Clara. 2012. *Life in Debt: Times of Care and Violence in Neoliberal Chile*. Berkeley: University of California Press.

Hancock, Mary. 2001. "Home Science and the Nationalization of Domesticity in Colonial India." *Modern Asian Studies* 35(4):871–903.

Harvey, David. 1989. *The Condition of Postmodernity: An Enquiry into the Origins of Cultural Change*. Cambridge, MA: Blackwell.

Herzfeld, Michael. 2001. *Anthropology: Theoretical Practice in Culture and Society*. Malden, MA: Blackwell.

*The Hindu.* 2002. "Ending Lives the Easy Way." June 10. www.hindu.com/thehindu/mp/2002/06/10/stories/2002061000890200.htm. Accessed February 16, 2006.

———. 2004a. "Rajani's Family Directs Ire at Politicians." July 24.

———. 2004b. "Student's Suicide: Police File FIR." August 1.

Hippler, Arthur. 1969. "Fusion and Frustration: Dimensions in the Cross-Cultural Ethnopsychology of Suicide." *American Anthropologist* 71(6):1074–87.

Hochschild, Arlie. 1979. "Emotion Work, Feeling Rules, and Social Structure." *American Journal of Sociology* 85(3):551–75.

Isaac, T.M. Thomas, and Richard Franke. 2002. *Local Democracy and Development: The Kerala People's Campaign for Decentralized Planning.* Lanham, MD: Rowman and Littlefield.

Isaac, T.M. Thomas, and P.K. Michael Tharakan. 1995. "Kerala: Towards a New Agenda." *Economic and Political Weekly* 30 (31–32):1993–2004.

Isaac, T.M. Thomas, P.A. Van Stuijvenberg, and K.N. Nair. 1992. *Modernisation and Employment: The Coir Industry in Kerala.* New Delhi: Sage Publications.

Jaworski, Katrina. 2003. "Suicide and Gender: Reading Suicide through Butler's Notion of Gender Performativity." *Journal of Australian Studies* 27(76):137–46.

Jeffrey, Craig. 2010. *Timepass: Youth, Class, and the Politics of Waiting in India.* Stanford, CA: Stanford University Press.

Jeffrey, Craig, Patricia Jeffery, and Roger Jeffery. 2004. "'A Useless Thing!' or 'Nectar of the Gods?': The Cultural Production of Education and Young Men's Struggles for Respect in Liberalizing North India." *Annals of the Association of American Geographers* 94(4):961–81.

———. 2008. *Degrees without Freedom?: Education, Masculinities, and Unemployment in North India.* Stanford, CA: Stanford University Press.

Jeffrey, Craig, and Linda McDowell. 2004. "Youth in a Comparative Perspective: Global Change, Local Lives." *Youth and Society* 36(2):131–42.

Jeffrey, Robin. 1992. *Politics, Women and Well-Being: How Kerala Became "a Model."* Houndsmills, UK: Macmillan Press.

Jeganathan, Pradeep. 2004. "Checkpoint: Anthropology, Identity, and the State." In *Anthropology in the Margins of the State,* edited by V. Das and D. Poole, 67–80. Sante Fe, NM: School of American Research Press.

Kannan, K.P. 2005. "Kerala's Turnaround in Growth: Role of Social Development, Remittances and Reform." *Economic and Political Weekly* 40(6): 548–54.

Katz, Arlene, and Margarita Alegría. 2009. "The Clinical Encounter as Local Moral World: Shifts of Assumptions and Transformation in Relational Context." *Social Science & Medicine* 68(7):1238–46.

Katz, Arlene, and John Shotter. 1996. "Hearing the Patient's 'Voice': Toward a Social Poetics in Diagnostic Interviews." *Social Science and Medicine* 43(6)919–31.

Keane, David, and Nicholas McGeehan. 2008. "Enforcing Migrant Workers' Rights in the United Arab Emirates." *International Journal of Minority and Group Rights* 15(1):81–115.

Kirmayer, Laurence. 2001. "Cultural Variations in the Clinical Presentation of Depression and Anxiety: Implications for Diagnosis and Treatment." *Journal of Clinical Psychiatry* 62:22–30.

Kitanaka, Junko. 2012. *Depression in Japan: Psychiatric Cures for a Society in Distress*. Princeton, NJ: Princeton University Press.

Klaits, Frederick. 2010. *Death in a Church of Life: Moral Passion During Botswana's Time of AIDS*. Berkeley: University of California Press.

Kleinman, Arthur, Veena Das, and Margaret Lock. 1997. "Introduction." In *Social Suffering*, edited by A. Kleinman, V. Das, and M. Lock, ix–xxvii. Berkeley: University of California Press.

Kleinman, Arthur, and Byron Good, eds. 1985. *Culture and Depression: Studies in the Anthropology and Cross-Cultural Psychiatry of Affect and Disorder*. Berkeley: University of California Press.

Kleinman, Arthur, and Joan Kleinman. 1996. "The Appeal of Experience; the Dismay of Images: Cultural Appropriations of Suffering in Our Times." *Daedalus* 125(1):1–23.

Kodoth, Praveena. 2001a. "Courting Legitimacy or Delegitimizing Custom? Sexuality, *Sambandham* and Marriage Reform in Late Nineteenth-Century Malabar." *Modern Asian Studies* 35(2):349–84.

———. 2001b. "Gender, Family and Property Rights: Questions from Kerala's Land Reforms." *Indian Journal of Gender Studies* 8(2):291–306.

———. 2005. "Fostering Insecure Livelihoods: Dowry and Female Seclusion in Left Developmental Contexts in West Bengal and Kerala." *Economic and Political Weekly* 40(25):2543–54.

———. 2008. "Gender, Caste, and Matchmaking in Kerala: A Rationale for Dowry." *Development and Change* 39(2):263–83.

Kodoth, Praveena, and Mridul Eapen. 2005. "Looking beyond Gender Parity: Gender Inequities of Some Dimensions of Well-Being in Kerala." *Economic and Political Weekly* 40(30):3278–86.

Kodoth, Praveena, and V. J. Varghese. 2012. "Protecting Women or Endangering the Emigration Process: Emigrant Women Domestic Workers, Gender, and State Policy." *Economic and Political Weekly* 47(43):56–66.

Kral, Michael, Lori Idlout, J. Bruce Minore, Ronald Dyck, and Laurence Kirmayer. 2011. "*Unikkaartuit*: Meanings of Well-Being, Unhappiness, Health, and Community Change among Inuit in Nunavut, Canada." *American Journal of Community Psychology* 48(3–4):426–38.

Krishnan, T. N. 1976. "Demographic Transition in Kerala: Facts and Factors." *Economic and Political Weekly* 11(31–33):1203–24.

Kuan, Teresa. 2011. "'The Heart Says One Thing but the Hand Does Another': A Story about Emotion-Work, Ambivalence and Popular Advice for Parents." *China Journal* 65:77–100.

Kumar, Krishna. 1988. "Origins of India's 'Textbook Culture.'" *Comparative Education Review* 32(4):452–64.

Kumar, Rachel. 1992. "Women, Work, and Development: Issues in Female Labour Force Participation in Kerala." MPhil thesis, Thiruvananthapuram Center for Development Studies.

Kurien, John. 2000. "The Kerala Model: Its Central Tendency and the 'Outlier.'" In *Kerala—the Development Experience: Reflections on Sustainability and Replicability*, edited by G. Parayil, 178–98. London: Zed Books.

Kurien, Prema. 2002. *Kaleidoscope Ethnicity: International Migration and the Reconstruction of Community Identities in India.* New Brunswick, NJ: Rutgers University Press.

Kwon, Heonik. 2008. *Ghosts of War in Vietnam.* Cambridge: Cambridge University Press.

Lakoff, Andrew. 2005. *Pharmaceutical Reason: Knowledge and Value in Global Psychiatry.* Cambridge: Cambridge University Press.

Lee, Sing, and Arthur Kleinman. 2000. "Suicide as Resistance in Chinese Society." In *Chinese Society: Change, Conflict, and Resistance*, edited by E. Perry and M. Selden, 221–40. New York: Routledge.

Lefebvre, Henri. 1991. *The Production of Space.* Cambridge, MA: Blackwell.

Lester, Rebecca J. 2009. "Brokering Authenticity: Borderline Personality Disorder and the Ethics of Care in an American Eating Disorder Clinic." *Current Anthropology* 50(3):281–302.

Liechty, Mark. 2003. *Suitably Modern: Making Middle-Class Culture in a New Consumer Society.* Princeton, NJ: Princeton University Press.

Lindberg, Anna. 2005. *Modernization and Effeminization in India: Kerala Cashew Workers since 1930.* Copenhagen: NIAS Press.

Linos, Natalia. 2010. "Reclaiming the Social Body through Self-Directed Violence: Seeking Anthropological Understandings of Suicide Attacks." *Anthropology Today* 26(5):8–12.

Livingston, Julie. 2009. "Suicide, Risk, and Investment in the Heart of the African Miracle." *Cultural Anthropology* 24(4):652–80.

———. 2012. *Improvising Medicine: An African Oncology Ward in an Emerging Cancer Epidemic.* Durham, NC: Duke University Press.

Ludden, David. 1992. "India's Development Regime." In *Colonialism and Culture*, edited by N. Dirks, 247–87. Ann Arbor: University of Michigan Press.

Luhrmann Tanya. 2000. *Of Two Minds: The Growing Disorder of American Psychiatry.* New York: Knopf.

Lukose, Ritty. 2005a. "Consuming Globalization: Youth and Gender in Kerala, India." *Journal of Social History* 38(4):915–35.

———. 2005b. "Empty Citizenship: Protesting Politics in the Era of Globalization." *Cultural Anthropology* 20(4):506–33.

———. 2009. *Liberalization's Children: Gender, Youth, and Consumer Citizenship in Globalizing India.* Durham, NC: Duke University Press.

Macdonald, Charles. 2007. *Uncultural Behavior: An Anthropological Investigation of Suicide in the Southern Philippines.* Honolulu: University of Hawai'i Press.

Mains, Daniel. 2007. "Neoliberal Times: Progress, Boredom, and Shame among Young Men in Urban Ethiopia." *American Ethnologist* 34(4):659–73.

———. 2012. *Youth Is Cut: Youth, Unemployment, and the Future in Urban Ethiopia.* Philadelphia: Temple University Press.

Malkki, Liisa. 1996. "Speechless Emissaries: Refugees, Humanitarianism, and Dehistoricization." *Cultural Anthropology* 11(3):377–404.

Mani, Lata. 1998. *Contentious Traditions: The Debate on Sati in Colonial India*. Berkeley: University of California Press.

Mankekar, Purnima. 1995. "Brides Who Travel: Gender, Transnationalism and Nationalism in Hindi Film." *Positions* 7(3):731–61.

———. 1999. *Screening Culture, Viewing Politics: An Ethnography of Television, Womanhood, and Nation in Postcolonial India*. Durham, NC: Duke University Press.

Marecek, Jeanne. 1998. "Culture, Gender, and Suicidal Behavior in Sri Lanka." *Suicide and Life-Threatening Behavior* 28(1): 69–81.

Marecek, Jeanne, and Chandanie Senadheera. 2012. "'I Drank It to Put an End to Me': Narrating Girls' Suicide and Self-Harm in Sri Lanka." *Contributions to Indian Sociology* 46(1–2):53–82.

Marrow, Jocelyn, and Tanya Luhrmann. 2012. "The Zone of Social Abandonment in Cultural Geography: On the Street in the United States, Inside the Family in India." *Culture, Medicine, and Psychiatry* 36(3):493–513.

Martin, Emily. 2007. *Bipolar Expeditions: Mania and Depression in American Culture*. Princeton, NJ: Princeton University Press.

Massey, Doreen. 1994. *Space, Place, and Gender*. Cambridge, UK: Polity Press.

Mathew, E.T. 1997. *Employment and Unemployment in Kerala: Some Neglected Aspects*. New Delhi: Sage Publications.

*Mathrubhumi*. 2006. "Died in Dubai." July 23.

Mattingly, Cheryl. 1994. "The Concept of Therapeutic 'Emplotment.'" *Social Science and Medicine* 38(6):811–22.

Matza, Tomas. 2012. "'Good Individualism'? Psychology, Ethics, and Neoliberalism in Postsocialist Russia." *American Ethnologist* 39(4):804–18.

Mazzarella, William. 2003. *Shoveling Smoke: Advertising and Globalization in Contemporary India*. Durham, NC: Duke University Press.

Mbembe, Achille. 2003. "Necropolitics." *Public Culture* 15(1):11–40.

Melley, Caroline. 2011. "Titanic Tales of Missing Men: Reconfigurations of National Identity and Gendered Presence in Dakar, Senegal." *American Ethnologist* 38(2):361–76.

Mitra, Aparna, and Pooja Singh. 2006. "Human Capital Attainment and Female Labor Force Participation—the Kerala Puzzle." *Journal of Economic Issues* 40(3):779–98.

———. 2007. "Human Capital Attainment and Gender Empowerment: The Kerala Paradox." *Social Science Quarterly* 88(5):1227–42.

Miyazaki, Hirokazu. 2004. *The Method of Hope: Anthropology, Philosophy, and Fijian Knowledge*. Stanford, CA: Stanford University Press.

Mohamed, E., S. Irudaya Rajan, K. Anil Kumar, and P.M. Saidu Mohammed. 2002. "Gender and Mental Health in Kerala." Working Paper. Center for Development Studies, Thiruvananthapuram, India.

Mohanty, Bibhuti. 2005. "'We Are Like the Living Dead': Farmer Suicides in Maharashtra, Western India." *Journal of Peasant Studies* 32(2):243–76.

Mohite, Vijayrao, and Vandana Chavan. 1993. *Law of Cruelty, Abetment of Suicide, and Dowry Deaths*. Mumbai: Bar Council of Maharashtra and Goa.

Mokkil, Navaneetha. 2009. "Shifting Spaces, Frozen Frames: Trajectories of Queer Politics in Contemporary India." *Inter-Asia Cultural Studies* 10(1):12–30.

Mol, Annemarie. 2002. *The Body Multiple: Ontology in Medical Practice.* Durham, NC: Duke University Press.

Mukhopadhyay, Carol, and Susan Seymour, eds. 1994. *Women, Education and Family Structure in India.* Boulder, CO: Westview Press.

Mukhopadhyay, Swapna, ed. 2007. *The Enigma of the Kerala Woman: A Failed Promise of Literacy.* New Delhi: Social Science Press.

Mukhopadhyay, Swapna, Jayanti Basu, and S. Irudaya Rajan. 2007. "Mental Health, Gender Ideology, and Women's Status in Kerala." In *The Enigma of the Kerala Woman: A Failed Promise of Literacy,* edited by S. Mukhopadhyay, 71–101. New Delhi: Social Science Press.

Münster, Daniel. 2012. "Farmers' Suicides and the State in India: Conceptual and Ethnographic Notes from Wayanad, Kerala." *Contributions to Indian Sociology* 46(1–2):181–208.

Murray, Stuart. 2006. "Thanatopolitics: On the Use of Death for Mobilizing Political Life." *Polygraph* 18:191–215.

Nair, P.K. Gopinathan. 1999. "Return of Overseas Contract Workers and Their Rehabilitation and Development in Kerala." *International Migration* 37(1):209–42.

*New York Times.* 2009. "Kerala Travel Guide." April 15. http://travel.nytimes.com/frommers/travel/guides/asia/india/kerala/frm_kerala_3479010001.html. Accessed March 11, 2013.

Ní Laoire, Caitríona. 2001. "A Matter of Life and Death? Men, Masculinities and Staying 'Behind' in Rural Ireland." *Sociologia Ruralis* 41(2):220–36.

Niranjana, Tejaswini. 1999. "'Left to the Imagination': Indian Nationalisms and Female Sexuality in Trinidad." *Public Culture* 11(1):223–43.

Nisbett, Nicholas. 2007. "Friendship, Consumption, Morality: Practising Identity, Negotiating Hierarchy in Middle-Class Bangalore." *Journal of the Royal Anthropological Institute* 13(4):935–50.

Nunley, Michael. 1996. "Why Psychiatrists in India Prescribe So Many Drugs." *Culture, Medicine and Psychiatry* 20(2):165–97.

———. 1998. "The Involvement of Families in Indian Psychiatry." *Culture, Medicine and Psychiatry* 22(3):317–53.

Ochoa, Todd. 2010. *Society of the Dead: Quita Manaquita and Palo Praise in Cuba.* Berkeley: University of California Press.

O'Nell, Theresa. 1996. *Disciplined Hearts: History, Identity, and Depression in an American Indian Community.* Berkeley: University of California Press.

Oomen, M.A. 2007. "Growth and Development: Raising Issues in the Context of Kerala." In *Governance and Development: Lessons and Experiences of Kerala,* edited by R.K. Suresh Kumar and P. Suresh Kumar, 71–92. New Delhi: APH Publishing.

Osella, Caroline, and Filippo Osella. 2006. "Once upon a Time in the West? Stories of Migration and Modernity from Kerala, South India." *Journal of the Royal Anthropological Institute* 12:569–88.

———. 2008. "Nuancing the Migrant Experience: Perspectives from Kerala, South India." In *Transnational South Asians: The Making of Neo-Diaspora,* edited by S. Koshy and R. Radhakrishnan, 146–78. New Delhi: Oxford University Press.

Osella, Filippo, and Caroline Osella. 1999. "From Transience to Immanence: Consumption, Life-Cycle and Social Mobility in Kerala, South India." *Modern Asian Studies* 33(4):989–1020.

———. 2000a. "Migration, Money and Masculinity in Kerala." *Journal of the Royal Anthropological Institute* 6(1):117–33.

———. 2000b. *Social Mobility in Kerala: Modernity and Identity in Conflict.* London: Pluto Press.

———. 2009. "Muslim Entrepreneurs in Public Life between India and the Gulf: Making Good and Doing Good." *Journal of the Royal Anthropological Institute* 15(s1):S202–21.

Ozawa-de Silva, Chikako. 2008. "Too Lonely to Die Alone: Internet Suicide Pacts and Existential Suffering in Japan." *Culture, Medicine, and Psychiatry* 32(4):516–51.

Panda, Pradeep. 2003. "Rights-Based Strategies in the Prevention of Domestic Violence." Working Paper 344. Center for Development Studies, Thiruvananthapuram, India.

Panda, Pradeep, and Bina Agarwal. 2005. "Marital Violence, Human Development and Women's Property Status in India." *World Development* 33(5):823–50.

Pandey, Gyanendra. 1990. *The Construction of Communalism in Colonial North India.* New Delhi: Oxford University Press.

Pandian, Anand. 2009. *Crooked Stalks: Cultivating Virtue in South India.* Durham, NC: Duke University Press.

Pandian, Anand, and Daud Ali, eds. 2010. *Ethical Life in South Asia.* Bloomington, IN: Indiana University Press.

Parajuli, Pramod. 1991. "Power and Knowledge in Development Discourse: New Social Movements and the State in India." *International Social Science Journal* 127: 173–90.

Parayil, Govindan, ed. 2000. *Kerala—the Development Experience: Reflections on Sustainability and Replicability.* London: Zed Books.

Parry, Jonathan. 2005. "Changing Childhoods in Industrial Chhattisgarh." In *Educational Regimes in Contemporary India,* edited by R. Chopra and P. Jeffery, 276–98. New Delhi: Sage Publications.

———. 2012. "Suicide in a Central Indian Steel Town." *Contributions to Indian Sociology* 46(1–2):145–80.

Percot, Marie. 2006. "Indian Nurses in the Gulf: Two Generations of Female Migration." *South Asia Research* 26(1):41–62.

Percot, Marie, and S. Irudaya Rajan. 2007. "Female Emigration from India: Case Study of Nurses." *Economic and Political Weekly* 42(4):318–25.

Pigg, Stacey Leigh. 1992. "Inventing Social Categories through Place: Social Representations and Development in Nepal." *Comparative Studies in Society and History* 34(3):491–513.

Pinto, Sarah. 2011. "Rational Love, Relational Medicine: Psychiatry and the Accumulation of Precarious Kinship." *Culture, Medicine, and Psychiatry* 35:376–95.

———. 2012. "The Limits of Diagnosis: Sex, Law, and Psychiatry in a Case of Contested Marriage." *Ethos* 40(2):119–41.

Prakash, B. A. 1998. "Gulf Migration and its Economic Impact: The Kerala Experience." *Economic and Political Weekly* 33(50):3209–13.

Radhakrishnan, Ratheesh. 2009. "The Gulf in the Imagination: Migration, Malayalam Cinema and Regional Identity." *Contributions to Indian Sociology* 43(2):217–45.

Radhakrishnan, Smitha. 2011. *Appropriately Indian: Gender and Culture in a New Transnational Class.* Durham, NC: Duke University Press.

Rajagopal, Aravind. 1999. "Thinking through Emerging Markets: Brand Logics and the Cultural Forms of Political Society in India." *Social Text* 17(3):131–49.

Rajan, Rajeswari Sunder. 1993. *Real and Imagined Women: Gender, Culture, and Postcolonialism.* New York: Routledge.

———. 2003. *The Scandal of the State: Women, Law, and Citizenship in Postcolonial India.* Durham, NC: Duke University Press.

Raman, K. Ravi. 2002. "Breaking New Ground: Adivasi Land Struggle in Kerala." *Economic and Political Weekly* 37(10):916–19.

Rapp, Rayna. 2000. *Testing Women, Testing the Fetus: The Social Impact of Amniocentesis in America.* New York: Routledge.

Ratcliffe, John. 1978. "Social Justice and the Demographic Transition: Lessons from India's Kerala State." *International Journal of Health Services* 8(1):123–44.

Redfield, Peter. 2013. *Life in Crisis: The Ethical Journey of Doctors without Borders.* Berkeley: University of California Press.

Reichman, Daniel. 2011. "Migration and Paraethnography in Honduras." *American Ethnologist* 38(3):548–58.

Renjini, D. 2000. *Nayar Women Today: Disintegration of Matrilineal System and the Status of Nayar Women in Kerala.* New Delhi: Classical.

Rhodes, Lorna. 1991. *Emptying Beds: The Work of an Emergency Psychiatric Unit.* Berkeley: University of California Press.

Ring, Laura. 2006. *Zenana: Everyday Peace in a Karachi Apartment Building.* Bloomington, IN: Indiana University Press.

Rosaldo, Michelle. 1982. "The Things We Do with Words: Ilongot Speech Acts and Speech Act Theory in Philosophy." *Language in Society* 11(2):203–37.

Rose, Nikolas. 1996. *Inventing Our Selves: Psychology, Power, and Personhood.* Cambridge: Cambridge University Press.

———. 2007. *The Politics of Life Itself: Biomedicine, Power, and Subjectivity in the Twenty-First Century.* Princeton, NJ: Princeton University Press.

Roy, Srirupa. 2007. *Beyond Belief: India and the Politics of Postcolonial Nationalism.* Durham, NC: Duke University Press.

Salim, A. Abdul. 2004. "Opportunities for Higher Education: An Enquiry into Entry Barriers." Discussion Paper 71. Center for Development Studies, Thiruvananthapuram, India.

Sancho, David. 2012. "'The Year That Can Break or Make You': The Politics of Secondary Schooling, Youth and Class in Urban Kerala, South India." PhD thesis, University of Sussex.

Sangari, Kumkum. 2003. "New Patriotisms: Beauty and the Bomb." In *Body. City: Siting Contemporary Culture in India,* edited by I. Chandrasekhar and P. Seel, 199–215. New Delhi: Tulika.

Sangari, Kumkum, and Sudesh Vaid. 1989. "Recasting Women: An Introduction." In *Recasting Women: Essays in Indian Colonial History,* edited by K. Sangari and S. Vaid, 1–26. New Delhi: Kali for Women.

Saradamoni, K. 1999. *Matriliny Transformed: Family, Law, and Ideology in Twentieth Century Travancore.* New Delhi: Sage Publications.

Scheper-Hughes, Nancy. 1992. *Death without Weeping: The Violence of Everyday Life in Brazil.* Berkeley: University of California Press.

———. 1995. "The Primacy of the Ethical: Propositions for a Militant Anthropology." *Current Anthropology* 36(3):409–40.

Schiller, Nina Glick, Linda Basch, and Cristina Blanc-Szanton. 1992. "Towards a Definition of Transnationalism." *Annals of the New York Academy of Sciences* 645(1):ix–xiv.

Scott, James. 1998. *Seeing Like a State: How Certain Schemes to Improve the Human Condition Have Failed.* New Haven, CT: Yale University Press.

Singh, Amita, and Patricia Uberoi. 1994. "Learning to 'Adjust': Conjugal Relations in Indian Popular Fiction." *Indian Journal of Gender Studies* 1(1):93–120.

Sivaramakrishnan, K., and Arun Agarwal. 2003. "Regional Modernities in Stories and Practices of Development." In *Regional Modernities: The Cultural Politics of Development in India,* edited by K. Sivaramakrishnan and A. Agrawal, 1–61. Stanford, CA: Stanford University Press.

Sooryamoorthy, R. 1997. *Consumption to Consumerism: In the Context of Kerala.* New Delhi: Classical Publishing Company.

Spencer, Jonathan. 1990. "Collective Violence and Everyday Practice in Sri Lanka." *Modern Asian Studies* 24(3):603–23.

Spradley, James. 1979. *The Ethnographic Interview.* New York: Holt, Reinhart, and Winston.

———. 1980. *Participant Observation.* New York: Holt, Reinhart, and Winston.

Sreedhar, Krishnaprasad. 1994. *Manashastrante Marganirdeshangal.* Thiruvananthapuram, India: D. C. Books.

Sreekumar, K. K. and Govindan Parayil. 2006. "Interrogating Development: New Social Movements, Democracy, and Indigenous People's Struggles in Kerala. In *Kerala: The Paradoxes of Public Action,* edited by J. Tharamangalam, 215–57. New Delhi: Orient Longman.

Sreekumar, Sharmila. 2007. "The Land of 'Gender Paradox'? Getting Past the Commonsense of Contemporary Kerala." *Inter-Asia Cultural Studies* 8(1):34–54.

———. 2009. *Scripting Lives: Narratives of "Dominant Women" in Kerala.* Hyderabad: Orient Longman.

Staples, James. 2012. "The Suicide Niche: Accounting for Self-Harm in a South Indian Leprosy Colony." *Contributions to Indian Sociology* 46(1–2):117–44.

Staples, James, and Tom Widger. 2012. "Situating Suicide as an Anthropological Problem: Ethnographic Approaches to Understanding Self-Harm and Self-Inflicted Death." *Culture, Medicine, and Psychiatry* 36(2):183–203.

Steur, Luisa. 2009. "Adivasi Mobilisation: 'Identity' versus 'Class' after the Kerala Model of Development?" *Journal of South Asian Development* 4(1):25–44.

Stevenson, Lisa. 2009. "The Suicidal Wound and Fieldwork among Canadian Inuit." In *Being There: The Fieldwork Encounter and the Making of Truth,* edited by J. Borneman and A. Hammoudi, 55–76. Berkeley: University of California Press.

———. 2012. "The Psychic Life of Biopolitics: Survival, Cooperation, and Inuit Community." *American Ethnologist* 39(3):592–613.

Strathern, Andrew. 1975. "Why Is Shame on the Skin?" *Ethnology* 14(4): 347–56.

Tarlo, Emma. 1996. *Clothing Matters: Dress and Identity in India.* Chicago: University of Chicago Press.

Tharamangalam, Joseph. 1998. "The Perils of Social Development without Economic Growth: The Development Debacle of Kerala, India." *Bulletin of Concerned Asian Scholars* 30(1):23–34.

Ticktin, Miriam. 2011. *Casualties of Care: Immigration and the Politics of Humanitarianism in France.* Berkeley: University of California Press.

Tingley, Kim. 2013. "The Suicide Detective." *New York Times.* June 26.

*The Tribune.* 2001. "Dealing with the Death Wish." January 21. www.tribuneindia.com/2001/20010121/spectrum/main4.htm. Accessed July 12, 2004.

Tsing, Anna. 2005. *Friction: An Ethnography of Global Connection.* Princeton, NJ: Princeton University Press.

Urciuoli, Bonnie. 2008. "Skills and Selves in the New Workplace." *American Ethnologist* 35(2):211–28.

Véron, René. 2001. "The 'New' Kerala Model: Lessons for Sustainable Development." *World Development* 29(4):601–17.

Vora, Neha. 2011. "From Golden Frontier to Golden City: Shifting Forms of Belonging, 'Freedom,' and Governance among Indian Businessmen in Dubai." *American Anthropologist* 113(2):306–18.

Waters, Anne. 1999. "Domestic Dangers: Approaches to Women's Suicide in Contemporary Maharashtra, India." *Violence against Women* 5(5):525–47.

Wexler, Lisa. 2006. "Inupiat Youth Suicide and Culture Loss: Changing Community Conversations for Prevention." *Social Science and Medicine* 63(11):2938–48.

Widger, Tom. 2009. "Self-Harm and Self-Inflicted Death amongst Sinhalese Buddhists in Sri Lanka: An Ethnographic Study." PhD thesis, London School of Economics.

———. 2012. "Suffering, Frustration, and Anger: Class, Gender and History in Sri Lankan Suicide Stories." *Culture, Medicine, and Psychiatry* 36(2):225–44.

Wilson, Caroline. 2011. "The Social Transformation of the Medical Professions in Urban Kerala: Doctors, Social Mobility, and the Middle Classes." In *Being Middle-Class in India: A Way of Life,* edited by H. Donner, 139–61. New York: Routledge.

Young, Allan. 1995. *The Harmony of Illusions: Inventing Post-Traumatic Stress Disorder*. Princeton, NJ: Princeton University Press.

Zachariah, K. C., E. T. Mathew, and S. Irudaya Rajan. 2003. *Dynamics of Out-Migration in Kerala: Dimension, Differentials and Consequences*. New Delhi: Orient Longman.

Zachariah, K. C., and S. Irudaya Rajan. 2005. "Unemployment in Kerala at the Turn of the Century: Insights from CDS Gulf Migration Studies." Working Paper 374. Center for Development Studies, Thiruvananthapuram, India.

———. 2007. "Migration, Remittances, and Unemployment: Short-Term Trends and Long-Term Implications." Working Paper 395. Center for Development Studies, Thiruvananthapuram, India.

Zigon, Jarrett. 2009. "Hope Dies Last: Two Aspects of Hope in Contemporary Moscow." *Anthropological Theory* 9(3):253–71.

# Index

adivasi, 35, 66, 68, 197n30
Agarwal, Arun, 50
agency: of dead bodies to "speak," 14, 86;
lateral, 130; suicide as means of
resistance for those with limited, 129
Anand, Rajani S., 10–12, 119n55;
accusations of murder in death of, 12,
199n47; explanations of suicide of,
12–15; reaction to death of, 10
aspiration: broadened horizons of, 3–5,
16–17, 36, 135, 191; of migrants, 60–62,
64, 135–36, 151, 189–90; overambition
as unrealistic, 55–56; parental, 78–80,
93; of the poor, 67–68, 69; scrutinized by
mental health professionals, 55–57,
60–62, 64–65, 67–69, 83; structured by
education and development, 49, 50, 55;
suicide as a pathology of, 5, 15, 17–18,
36–37, 40, 56, 105; suicide stories as
morality tales about, 83–85

Berlant, Lauren, 130
Bhatia, R.L., 29
Bihar, 40, 49, 177, 197n29
Borneman, John, 111
Bourdieu, Pierre, 211n13
Briggs, Charles, 86
Brown, Michael, 146

Chatterjee, Partha, 117
child rearing: experience of crisis in quality,
161–62, 163–65, 166, 170; outsourcing

of, 183–84; to prepare for competition
in global markets, 114, 177–78; pursuit
of extracurricular in, 178, 215n27;
relating consumption to quality of,
161–62, 170; temporality in, 169, 174,
175. *See also* family
classification: postcolonial histories of, 87;
of suicide, 87, 92, 93–94, 209n11; using
preconceived categories can conceal and
obscure, 85–86, 93, 105–6
Cohen, Lawrence, 109, 156
Comaroff, Jean, 19
consumption: as cause of suicide, 37,
169–70; cultural politics of caste and
class in, 38–40; educational-psychology
as new regime of, 172, 176, 177–78;
gender and, 41; as generational problem,
38, 40, 84, 91; linked to visions of
the good life, 3, 16–17, 39, 40; in
nuclear family, 44, 169–70; as parental
investment, 161–62, 170; from pressures
to live up to standards of colleagues, 52;
restrained, 40; as root of problems in
Kerala, 36–41, 85; ways to reduce
children's demands for, 174–75, 181–82

dalit, 10, 11, 12, 14, 35, 68, 203n20
Das, Veena, 23, 24, 84, 104, 198–99n46
de Alwis, Malathi, 129
death: accumulating, 113–14, 123, 129,
131, 211n13; in the Gulf, 158–59,
207n16; histories in the governance of,